THE COMPLETE BOOK OF TRUSTS

Second Edition

D0745121

MAR 1 1 2003

THE COMPLETE BOOK OF TRUSTS

Second Edition

Martin M. Shenkman

John Wiley & Sons, Inc.

New York • Chichester • Weinheim • Brisbane • Singapore • Toronto

DISCLAIMER: This book provides an overview of the topic addressed, with sample forms, checklists, examples, calculations, and other practical information. Reasonable effort has been made to be accurate and complete. However, there can be no assurance that every law reflected is current, that the forms will in fact achieve the desired goal in all circumstances, or that the general situations addressed will apply to your particular situation. Obviously, tax and other laws change frequently and vary from state to state. Trusts are complex transactions and many issues and techniques can be viewed differently by the IRS. Since trusts are formed under the laws of your state, you must expect differences from the general discussions in this book. Therefore, you should carefully review every tax, legal, and other positions with an attorney specializing in estate planning in your state before proceeding with any transaction. Also, be certain your accountant reviews all tax filings, a real estate lawyer reviews all real estate transactions (and other appropriate specialists review any other specific aspects of your trust transaction). If you are making any type of gift to a trust, be certain to have an independent, licensed, and qualified appraiser provide a written valuation report. Thus, if you use common sense and caution, you will get the most benefit from the planning ideas offered.

This text is printed on acid-free paper.

Copyright © 1997 by Martin M. Shenkman
Published by John Wiley & Sons, Inc.

All rights reserved. Published simultaneously in Canada.

Reproduction or translation of any part of this work beyond that permitted by Section 107 or 108 of the 1976 United States Copyright Act without the permission of the copyright owner is unlawful. Requests for permission or further information should be addressed to the Permissions Department, John Wiley & Sons, Inc.

This publication is designed to provide accurate and authoritative information in regard to the subject matter covered. It is sold with the understanding that the publisher is not engaged in rendering legal, accounting, or other professional services. If legal advice or other expert assistance is required, the services of a competent professional person should be sought.

Library of Congress Cataloging-in-Publication Data:

Shenkman, Martin M.
    The complete book of trusts / by Martin M. Shenkman. — 2nd ed.
      p.   cm.
    Includes bibliographical references.
    ISBN 0-471-17044-5 (pbk. : alk. paper)
    1. Trusts and trustees—United States—Popular works. I. Title.
KF730.Z9S53   1997
346.7305'9—dc21   96-53186

Printed in the United States of America

10 9 8 7 6 5 4

PREFACE

YOU CAN BENEFIT FROM USING TRUSTS

Trusts are one of the most powerful and useful estate, tax, investment, and financial planning tools. You don't have to be rich to need or have one. In fact, the less wealthy you are, the less you can afford to risk losing money, so trusts may even be more important for you. But what you do need, in all cases, is to understand what these complex tools can, and cannot, do for you. Within limits, trusts can help you achieve several important goals: management of your assets in the event you are disabled, management of assets for your children or family in the event of your death, avoidance of probate and creditors, minimization or elimination of estate and other transfer taxes, protection of your loved ones, ownership of your insurance policies, and help in controlling your businesses. The first step, however, is to assess your overall financial position, goals, and objectives.

TRUSTS MUST BE PART OF YOUR COMPREHENSIVE PERSONAL PLAN

Only within the context of an overall estate and financial plan can you properly use trusts. My earlier book *The Estate Planning Guide* (New York: John Wiley & Sons, 1991) will provide this background. With your basic plan in place, *The Complete Book of Trusts* will help you select the right plan for your needs and will guide you in working with a lawyer to prepare a trust document based on informed decisions about the assets you should transfer and the legal provisions you should include in your trusts. You will also understand the limitations of your trusts and the tax implications of different trust arrangements.

To properly develop and implement an overall personal plan, you need an estate planning team. You don't need to be superrich, with a family office staffed by professionals, to achieve this; you can get similar results for a nominal cost, with a little creativity and effort. At minimum, an estate planning team should include the following experts:

- Lawyer.
- Broker, money manager, or financial planner.

- Insurance agent, broker or adviser.
- Accountant.
- Pension or retirement consultant.

In many situations, the financial person can also assist you with insurance, or the insurance person can assist you with retirement plans. If you work in a large corporation, the human resources department can often provide professional guidance without any additional cost. The ideal approach is to formulate your plan at a joint meeting with all your advisers. There can be no substitute for a session with all your advisers sitting around a single table to make sure you are taking the optimal planning steps, including trusts. If the cost of such a meeting is prohibitive, try scheduling a conference call with your accountant when you meet with your lawyer. Your insurance or investment professional may not charge for time and may be willing to attend this meeting simply to enhance his or her own networking efforts. Thus, you can closely match the constituency of a personal estate planning team for the incremental cost of a telephone call to your accountant. The value of this "team" approach should not be underestimated. Knowing you have other experts involved helps the professionals coordinate their efforts, which will assure you of a higher level of service and lower costs. It also keeps them on their toes because others are looking over their work. Finally, be sure to direct each professional to forward copies of any important correspondence to the other members of your team.

WORKING WITH PROFESSIONALS

This book will help you work with your lawyer to achieve financial security through the proper use of trusts. These financial tools are complex. It is not only the trust document that must be properly prepared. In some cases, a document from a form book, with the right names inserted, might actually suffice. But this procedure is only a small part of the process. The key is having a highly competent estate planning specialist who can make sure the trust you are using is the correct approach for your goals and circumstances. Reading a book (or two, or three) will not give you the knowledge and judgment that an estate planning specialist has acquired from years of experience formulating hundreds, if not thousands, of estate plans. Similarly, a lawyer in general practice, who has occasionally completed estate plans or trusts in between house closings, personal injury cases, and other legal work, cannot bring to the table the expertise of an estate planning specialist.

How do you find the appropriate specialist? Ask. Obtain references from your insurance agents, financial planner, broker, banker, and other professional sources. Ask the attorney: "What percentage of your practice is estate planning or ancillary work?" (If it is less than 50% to 75%, does that really indicate an estate specialist?) "What types and size estates do you handle?" (Do your circumstances fit the experience level of the attorney?) "Have you published or lectured on estate planning? . . . To whom, when, and on what topics?" Most specialists (in any technical area of law, and in many other professions as well) tend to speak and write to stay abreast of current developments in their field. Also, specialists need the exposure of speaking and writing to generate business since their practice is so limited. Ask to see copies, or where you can obtain copies, of their speeches, articles, and the like. Review them before you make a decision.

Although most consumer books on working with lawyers suggest getting a price quote up front, no lawyer can accurately estimate the cost for preparing a trust without knowing your goals, background information, net worth, tax status, circumstances of your family and loved ones, and so forth. It is impossible to quote the price for creating a revocable living trust without first ascertaining whether you really need one.

NOTE: You've attended a seminar on revocable living trusts and decide this trust would help you avoid probate and publicity. In response to your request for quotes to prepare the trust, one lawyer provides an estimate of $1,000; a second lawyer states a price of $2,500. The third lawyer, an estate specialist, refuses to quote a price, saying that without an initial meeting to obtain more information, he cannot determine what services you will need. Which lawyer should you use?

In considering the first two lawyers, can you tell which will give you a better quality document? Which lawyer will be spending more time customizing the trust form to suit your particular needs? The length of the document, in the age of computers, is no indication of quality. It might just be a long, inferior-quality form. Cost is not necessarily an indication of quality or customized work. If you have real estate to transfer to the trust, has either of the two lawyers included the cost of transferring the real estate? If not, what will be the extra charge? What does the fee include? If you have questions after the work is done, is that included? Will the lawyer help you transfer assets to the trust? Does the quote represent fixed fees or merely an estimate based on certain work? If the work exceeds the estimate (and how can you tell), how will you be charged?

It may very well be that the best choice is the third lawyer, who refused to quote you a fee, as shown in the following example.

EXAMPLE: The experienced estate and trusts lawyer, who would not give you a quote, knows that few consumers/nonestate specialists can determine what type of trust they need. To quote even an estimate for a trust you may not need is not professional or appropriate. As in the following scenario, the living trust may not be the best answer for you. Assume you live in New Jersey and have a rental property in New York. You believe that the living trust will avoid probate and publicity for the New York property. You're right about probate. The publicity is a question. The court may, depending on the circumstances, require that the trust be made public. Also, why are you concerned about publicity? For the vast majority of Americans, this is really not an issue. If you truly have a publicity problem, a host of more sophisticated techniques may be appropriate.

Why was the third lawyer hesitant to quote a fee for a living trust? In the preceding situation, a living trust is not the best answer (the only way an honest estate planner can determine what you need, and hence what it should cost, is first to find out the facts). A living trust will not avoid New York estate tax. A living trust will not facilitate making gifts of interests in that property to reduce your estate tax cost. What will?

A limited liability company may be the best choice. Transferring the New York property to a limited liability company will enable you to (1) avoid probate in New York (just as with the revocable living trust); (2) avoid New York estate tax (which the revocable living trust could not accomplish); (3) protect your personal assets from lawsuits (a tenant or visitor can only sue the limited liability company that owns the property); (4) use the limited liability company to make gifts of noncontrolling interests and claim discounts for lack of marketability and lack of control in valuing the gifts for gift tax purposes. These discounts can range from 20% to 50%+. The gift tax savings can be huge. The benefits of using a limited liability company far outweigh the nominal benefits of using a revocable living trust in this situation. Does this mean you don't need a revocable living trust? Hardly. The answer, like all estate planning answers, depends on your situation. It may be appropriate to have your living trust hold the membership interests in your limited liability company. The key is, don't self-diagnose; seek an expert opinion. If you want the work done right, price is not the only factor.

What is the bottom line? Hire an experienced estate planner, who will not "yes" you, but rather guide you by giving you the pros, cons, and estimated costs of different options. Select a specialist who is published, or who speaks professionally, and thus keeps up with current laws and planning. Select an expert whom other experts recommend. If you have a lot at stake (either financially or personally) in assuring that the right trusts are established for you, consider paying for an initial consultation with several estate planners so that you can make an informed decision after getting a taste of what each can do for you.

INFORMATION AND FORMS ON DISKETTE

If you wish to obtain forms and checklists on computer diskette, call 1-888-LAW-EASY for further information. Visit the LAW EASY web site at www.laweasy.com

A NOTE ABOUT POLITICAL CORRECTNESS

Some effort was made to assure that the examples and text reflect a broad array of people with many different religious, personal, lifestyle, and other preferences. The overarching objective in this book, however, has been to convey complex information in an understandable manner. To achieve this goal, the explanations and examples do not always reflect every situation. Rather, the focus is on simplicity and clarity. In any example that uses the feminine form, masculine could be used instead, and vice versa. In the estate planning examples, either spouse can predecease the other without altering the format. Wherever the term "child" is used, you can substitute "nephew," "friend," or any other appellation. There are only two important situations for which you cannot substitute. When the text or an example refers to "spouse" (or "husband" or "wife"), you cannot readily substitute the term "non-United States citizen spouse" for the term "spouse." Special rules apply in the case of a non-United States citizen spouse. Second, if the person is not legally a spouse, but is a partner, unmarried companion, or a gay or lesbian partner, you cannot substitute that person or the relationship for spouse since the laws are dramatically different. Each of these exceptions—the noncitizen spouse and the nonmarried partner—are addressed in this book. Other than these two exceptions, the text and examples can generally be adapted to fit your circumstances.

TRUST-FINDING TABLE

This book has been organized to help you easily identify the person, asset, or situation for which you want a trust. To make it even easier to find the trust you're interested in, a finding table by trust name has been included.

WHAT'S NEW IN THIS SECOND EDITION

The discussion of trusts has been expanded tremendously from approximately 29 in the first edition to about 50 in this edition. The discussions of many trusts have been completely revised and expanded significantly. Many new laws, planning techniques, and tips have been added.

MARTIN M. SHENKMAN

Teaneck, New Jersey
April 1997

ACKNOWLEDGMENTS

A number of people provided considerable assistance in the preparation of this book: My thanks go to Michael Hamilton of John Wiley & Sons, whose support and encouragement were outstanding, as usual; my associates Abigail Stiefel, Esq., Diane Rivers, Esq., and Michael Mirone for their review and comments on the manuscript; Stephen Leimberg of Leimberg & LeClaire, Inc., P.O. Box 1332, Bryn Mawr, PA 19010 (tel. 610-527-5216) for providing the *Number Cruncher* and *Fin Plan* software and his assistance in discussing the program and planning for charitable giving and other tax calculations throughout the book; Gary R. Greenbaum, CFA, of Greenbaum and Associates, Inc., an investment counsel firm located in Oradell, NJ, for his assistance and materials on investment of trust assets; Gilbert Jacobson of UJA Federation of Bergen and North Hudson for his comments on charitable planning.

M.M.S.

CONTENTS

TRUST-FINDING TABLE

NOTE: The chapters of this book have been organized by topic. Thus, trusts for various types of people or assets can easily be identified. However, you may hear about a trust and wish to investigate its features. In the following table, you can look up the names of many types of trusts and quickly find the chapter(s) where they are discussed. In addition, other names for the trust are provided, and a brief comment describes the special features of the particular trust.

CAUTION: Many estate planners, insurance agents, and financial planners create their own names for trusts to imply they have some unique or proprietary type of planning others don't. These names could not be included. However, when reading the brochures these planners give you, identify the trust by topic (e.g., does the brochure encourage you to buy insurance) and search for that topic in this table, the Contents, or the Index. Also, be suspicious. Calling an insurance trust by a fancy name doesn't make it do anything an insurance trust won't do. But it does make your analysis and comparison in terms of your needs a more difficult and confusing task.

Name of Trust	Other Names	Description/Comment	Chapter
2503(c) Trust		Protects your minor children while qualifying for maximum gift tax benefits from the annual $10,000 exclusion. It can assure that monies left for young children are used for educational and other important purposes.	13
"5 and 5" Trust		Permits a beneficiary, such as your spouse, to demand a distribution, in addition to any other rights to income and principal granted by the trust, the greater of $5,000 or 5% of the trust assets each year, without the entire trust being taxable in his or her estate. This can be added to almost any type of trust. It is most commonly used in a credit shelter or Q-TIP trust.	11, 12, 13
Accumulation Trust	Complex Trust	Can accumulate income if the trustee doesn't believe it is appropriate or advisable to distribute income in any particular year. This can protect assets for a child who is involved in risky or questionable endeavors, or where a lawsuit or divorce is pending. This is contrasted with a trust that is required to distribute all income currently (simple trust).	11, 12, 13

(continued)

Name of Trust	Other Names	Description/Comment	Chapter
Alimony Trust		Used to pay alimony to your ex-spouse. A special tax rule has your spouse, and not you as the person forming the trust, taxed on trust income.	11
Asset Protection Trust (APT)		A trust designed to protect assets. Often established in a foreign country.	15
Bypass Trust		See "Credit Shelter Trust."	
Charitable Lead Annuity Trust		A charitable lead trust where the payment is based on a fixed annuity calculation.	14
Charitable Lead Trust (CLT)		A trust to which you give money or property. One or more charities will receive an annual (or more frequent) annuity payment. Your designated heirs will receive the principal of the trust when it ends. This can help you achieve substantial gift or estate tax benefits on transferring assets to heirs.	14
Charitable Lead Unitrust		A charitable lead trust where the payment is based on a unitrust payment.	14
Charitable Q-TIP Trust		A trust for your spouse's benefit which on your spouse's death is paid to charity.	14
Charitable Remainder Annuity Trust (CRAT)		A charitable remainder trust that makes payments to you based on annuity payment—a fixed percentage of the initial value of the assets contributed. Contrast with CRUT. See also "Charitable Remainder Trust."	14
Charitable Remainder Trust (CRT)		A trust to which you donate appreciated property. The trust can sell the property without paying capital gains tax and invest in a diversified portfolio. You receive annual income and on your death (or the death of you and your spouse), the charity receives the principal of the trust. You obtain a current income tax charitable contribution deduction (based on the present value of the charity's future interest). The gift to the charity won't become effective until your death or some fixed number of years. It is often combined with a life insurance trust.	14
Charitable Remainder Unitrust (CRUT)		A charitable remainder trust that makes payments to you based on a fixed percentage of the value of the assets owned by the trust each year. This is usually used where assets are easily valued, such as publicly traded stocks, not for interests in real estate or closely held business that would require a formal appraisal. Contrast with CRUT. GST consequences of the two types of trusts (CRAT versus CRUT) differ. See also "Charitable Remainder Trust."	14
Children's Trust	Minor's trust	Trust for a child, grandchild, or other minor. Designed to qualify for the $10,000 gift tax annual exclusion and to protect the child from the money.	13
Complex Trust		See "Accumulation Trust."	11, 12, 13
Credit Shelter Trust (CST)	"A" Trust; Bypass Trust; Unified Credit Trust	The very valuable tax-saving trust. It enables both you and your spouse to use your $192,800 unified credit. Proper use of this technique can enable every family with less than $1.2 million in assets to avoid estate taxes entirely.	7

Name of Trust	Other Names	Description/Comment	Chapter
Crummey Trust	Annual Demand Power Trust	A trust with a provision that permits you to make gifts to trusts for children (or others) and qualify for the valuable benefit of having the gift protected by the annual gift tax exclusion. The Crummey power is necessary so that a gift to a trust will be considered a "gift of a present interest."	13, 17
Foreign Situs Trust		A trust formed in a foreign country for legal or tax benefits.	15
Generation-Skipping Transfer Tax Trust (GST Trust)		A trust that very wealthy persons can use to minimize the impact of the extremely costly generation-skipping transfer (GST) tax on gifts or other transfers to their grandchildren or later generations. Frequently, GST trusts are planned to use the $1 million GST tax exemption that each taxpayer has. See also "Grandchildren's Trust."	8, 13
Grandchildren's Trust		A trust a grandparent establishes to provide for the education or other benefits to a grandchild, or to many grandchildren (where a "Pot Trust" is used). This type of trust must be planned to avoid unexpected GST tax consequences.	8, 13
Grantor Retained Annuity Trust (GRAT)		A gift made now, for which grantor keeps receiving income annually based on a fixed annuity payment, for any number of years the grantor chooses. This technique enables wealthy individuals to give away substantial assets at a reduced gift tax cost.	17
Grantor Retained Interest Trust (GRIT)		A trust where grantor retains an interest (e.g., the right to income) for some period of time. After that time, the principal of the trust is transferred to the designated beneficiaries. The time the beneficiaries must wait to receive the actual gift results in a reduction, to reflect the present value of money, in gift tax costs. GRITs are structured as "QPRTs," "PRTs," "GRATs," or "GRUTs." See those entries.	17
Grantor Retained Unitrust (GRUT)		A gift made now, for which grantor keeps receiving income annually based on the fair market value of the property each year, for any number of years the grantor chooses. This technique enables wealthy individuals to give away substantial assets at a reduced gift tax cost. Contrast with GRAT.	17
GST Trust		See "Grandchildren's Trust."	8, 13
Insurance Trust		Protects your family and heirs. You can achieve one of the best tax savings possible by keeping the insurance proceeds out of your taxable estate (and your spouse's taxable estate, if applicable). Protect valuable insurance proceeds from creditors.	16
Inter Vivos Trust	Living Trust	See "Revocable Living Trust," "Inter Vivos Q-TIP Trust"; "Charitable Remainder Trust."	10
Inter Vivos Credit Shelter Trust		Permits you to use pension or IRA assets to fund a credit shelter trust to use your unified credit.	7, 11
Inter Vivos Q-TIP Trust		Permits you to use pension or IRA assets to fund a Q-TIP (marital) trust.	11

(continued)

Name of Trust	Other Names	Description/Comment	Chapter
Irrevocable Trust		A trust that cannot be changed after it is set up. Compare with *revocable* trust, which you can change at any time. An irrevocable trust can offer substantial tax benefits and protection from creditors. See also "Insurance Trust"; "Children's Trust"; "Grandchildren's Trust"; "Inter Vivos Q-TIP Trust."	11–20
Loving Trust		See "Living Trust."	10
Marital Trust		See "Q-TIP Trust."	11
Massachusetts Realty Trust		A special form of trust offering valuable benefits to anyone owning real estate in Massachusetts.	19
Medicaid Trust	Medicaid Avoidance Trust; Nursing Home Trust	Keeps your assets or your special child's assets safe from nursing home/Medicaid claims so that Medicaid will pay for your nursing home care rather than your heirs. This trust is intended to give you access to, and benefit from, the trust assets that the law will permit without making those assets subject to the risks of being attached to pay medical bills. Subject to "look-back" and other limitations.	13, 15
Multiple Children's Trust		Sets up a separate trust for each child so that each child receives exactly the amount you intend (whether equal or not). This keeps each child's assets safe from the demand, needs, and creditors of your other children. This is contrasted with the use of a single trust for many children, called a "Single Children's Trust" or "Pot Trust."	13
Personal Residence Trust (PRT)		A trust used to remove your home or vacation home from your estate at a reduced gift tax cost. See also "Qualified Personal Residence Trust."	19
Pooled Income Trust		A trust to which you contribute property. In exchange, you gain the right to participate in an investment pool managed by the charity for the term of the trust (or your life). This provides valuable tax benefits and professional management of your money and diversification of your assets. See also "Charitable Remainder Trust."	14
Pot Trust	Single Children's Trust	A single trust set up for all of your children or other beneficiaries so that all of your assets are available to distribute to the child or beneficiary based on the need of each child. This can be used to minimize trustee fees and administrative costs compared with setting up a separate trust for each beneficiary.	13
Probate Avoidance Trust		A trust designed to avoid probate. A revocable living trust is but one. When title to assets are transferred to a trust, those assets will usually pass to the beneficiaries of the trust without the requirement for probate. See also "Revocable Living Trust."	10
Q-DOT		See "Qualified Domestic Trust."	11
Qualified Domestic Trust (Q-DOT)		Obtains maximum gift or estate tax savings by qualifying a gift or bequest to your spouse for the unlimited gift or estate tax marital deduction where your spouse is not a citizen of the United States.	11

Name of Trust	Other Names	Description/Comment	Chapter
Qualified Personal Residence Trust (QPRT)		A trust used to remove the value of your home or vacation home from your estate at a discounted gift tax cost.	19
Qualified Subchapter S Trust (QSST)		A special trust to hold stock in an S corporation, the most popular legal form for small businesses, without jeopardizing the valuable S corporation tax benefits.	18
Q-TIP Trust		See "Qualified Terminable Interest Property Trust."	11
Qualified Terminable Interest Property Trust (Q-TIP)	Marital Trust; "B" Trust	A trust that qualifies for the unlimited estate tax marital deduction (no tax on bequests or gifts to your spouse), but preserves your right to name the ultimate beneficiaries of your assets. It is commonly used for second marriages so that your current spouse can be protected, but your children from your first marriage can be assured of an inheritance.	11
Rabbi Trust		A trust designed to provide some security for compensation benefits.	20
Revocable Trust		Any trust that can be changed, as contrasted with *ir*revocable trusts that you cannot change once signed and set up. Most common is the "Living Trust." Assets given to a revocable trust may not be removed from your estate for tax purposes nor may they be protected from the reach of your creditors. See also "Living Trust."	10
Right of Election Trust		Provides your spouse with the least amount of assets permitted by law, and retains (if state law permits) the maximum control over where those assets will ultimately be distributed. Used where the marriage is unstable, divorce possible or imminent, and you desire to limit your spouse's rights to your estate to the minimum the law requires your spouse to get.	11
Single Children's Trust		A trust that holds assets for all of your children. See also "Pot Trust."	13
Special Needs Trust		Protects and provides for a child or other heir with special needs without losing the valuable state or other benefits to which the beneficiary may otherwise be entitled. It often limits the distributions to items not provided by state programs.	13, 15
Spendthrift Trust		A provision added to many irrevocable trusts to help protect trust assets from the reach of the beneficiary's creditors. Almost any type of trust could be a spendthrift trust. It is commonly used when a trust is set up for a child where divorce or future lawsuits are a worry.	11, 12, 13
Spray Trust		See "Sprinkle Trust."	1
Sprinkle Trust	Spray Trust	A trust where flexibility is given to the trustee to distribute income and assets to the persons most in need (e.g., your spouse, or one of your children). This enables you to defer the decision as to which child or other beneficiary needs the most money or assistance until the time for the payments occurs. This can be done in many different types of trusts.	13

(continued)

Name of Trust	Other Names	Description/Comment	Chapter
Unitrust		A type of grantor retained trust or charitable remainder or charitable lead trust where payments are based on a percentage of the value of the assets in trust each year. See also "Charitable Lead Trust"; "Grantor Retained Unitrust."	4, 18
Voting Trust		A trust that provides control of stock in a closely held or family business to assure management and operations as you determine best.	18
Zero Inclusion	GST Trust	Trust for grandchildren are planned to be fully exempt from GST tax. This means the trust will have a zero inclusion rate.	8

Part One

UNDERSTANDING THE BUILDING BLOCKS OF A TYPICAL TRUST

1 WHAT IS A TRUST?

From among the dozens of types of trusts, almost certainly there are some that could benefit you, depending on your personal goals and life circumstances. For you to identify and then implement appropriate trusts, however, general background information will be useful. A basic understanding of trusts will help you select and implement the right ones for you, while minimizing your costs. Also, a good overview will help you weed out the puffing and sales pitches you encounter from the useful information you really need.

OVERVIEW

Trusts are a highly useful and flexible financial planning tool. Trusts can help you accomplish many tax, estate, asset protection, legal, and other goals, including the following:

- Provide for you, and your loved ones, in the event of sickness and disability.
- Bridge the gap between life and death by continuing after your death to care for your family.
- Assure management expertise and continuity for your business or investments in the event of your illness or disability.
- Achieve significant tax savings.
- Protect assets from creditors, malpractice claimants, and divorce actions.
- Manage business or other assets.
- Protect children or other heirs while managing assets for their benefit.
- Minimize or avoid probate.

In accomplishing these important goals, trusts can often remain confidential thus protecting your privacy.

Trusts are not only tools for the wealthy. When properly used, trusts can benefit everyone. There are many misunderstandings about trusts because much of the information for consumers is inaccurate or incomplete, or is self-serving (i.e., from sources selling a product, such as a computer program or an investment). The following sections will address these misunderstandings and clarify the true advantages and benefits that trusts can offer you.

WHAT IS A TRUST?

A trust, like a corporation, limited liability company, or limited partnership, is a creature or fiction of your state's laws. You establish a trust by following the procedures outlined in the laws (statutes) of your state.

The simplest way to explain a trust is with an illustration.

EXAMPLE: Greta Grandmother has her lawyer prepare a trust and obtains a tax identification number from the IRS for this legal contract, which is about 22 pages long. Greta then transfers $10,000 to an account opened by her daughter, Debby, as trustee, using the trust's name and tax identification number. Debby is required to invest the $10,000 in a certificate of deposit and use all the interest each year to pay for dancing and music lessons for Debby's two daughters (Greta's grandchildren). When the youngest child reaches age 21, Debby is instructed to divide the money in the trust equally and distribute it to her daughters.

This simple example highlights the important time periods in a trust's existence. First the trust is formed by having a legal document prepared and signed. This document is a contract between the grantor, who sets up the trust, and the trustee, who administers the trust. Assets are then transferred to the trust to complete its establishment. Next, the trust is administered for its duration, which is its most important time frame, since this is when the trust fulfills the primary purpose for which it was formed. Finally, when the trust has fulfilled those purposes, the money and assets it holds are distributed, and the trust is terminated.

TRUSTS SEPARATE LEGAL AND BENEFICIAL OWNERSHIP OF AN ASSET

A basic principle of trusts is that they separate the legal ownership of an asset from the benefit of that asset.

EXAMPLE: If you own a brokerage account, you can spend the money in your account as you wish. You could, for example, use the money to pay for a vacation for your niece, Jane. You own the account, you are in charge of it, and you or anyone you choose, can benefit from the account. In the case of paying for the child's vacation, your niece benefits. This contrasts with a trust. In a trust, the trustee owns the assets, but cannot benefit from the trust assets (unless, as in a revocable living trust, the trustee is also a beneficiary). Assume that your local bank, Bigbank, is the trustee of the trust for your niece. What is the difference between the two situations? The first scenario allows more flexibility. You would retain control over the brokerage account. If you wished to benefit from the funds, you could do so. If you wished to benefit your niece, you could do so. In a common type of trust, such as a trust for a minor niece, you would give as a gift assets (e.g., part or all of the particular brokerage account) to Bigbank, as trustee of Jane's trust. Bigbank would then own the assets and use them to benefit Jane.

The person holding the legal title, the trustee, has a fiduciary duty to the persons entitled to the benefits of the trust property. A fiduciary duty is a responsibility of care. The trustee is charged with exercising certain care in carrying out the requirements and intent of the trust document governing the relationship of the trustee to the property and to the beneficiary. This duty of care is imposed on the trustee by the provisions of the trust document. In addition, state law, and the court cases of your state, also create certain obligations and duties on the trustee.

Many of the advantages of a trust arrangement come from the separation of ownership and benefit. Where the IRS respects this separation, the tax savings may be considerable. This generally holds true for irrevocable trusts. These are trusts that cannot be changed once they are formed.

EXAMPLE (Continued): As is apparent from the example, you had a price to pay in setting up a trust with Bigbank as trustee for your niece, Jane. You no longer control the assets—Bigbank does, subject to the requirements of state law and all the detailed instructions you included in the trust document. But the benefits of using the trust instead of retaining the brokerage account in your name are also very valuable. Giving the brokerage account to the trust should remove it from your taxable estate (more on this later). Thus, you could save substantial estate taxes. If you are sued in future years, the assets transferred to the trust for Jane should not be reached by your creditors.

Where the persons to benefit cannot, or should not, be in control of the assets, a trust provides an ideal vehicle for management. Trusts can permit a bank or financially astute family member to manage money for the benefit of a special child, a child who is a minor or otherwise not mature enough to handle large assets, or an incapacitated family member who cannot manage the funds for his or her own benefit.

EXAMPLE (Continued): Your niece, Jane, may not have been of sufficient age to handle her own assets, she may suffer from a disability (e.g., be a special child), or you may be concerned about the stability and influence of her husband or partner. A trust addresses any of these concerns by assuring that Bigbank manages and protects those assets from creditors or other claimants.

Where the separation of the ownership and benefit is recognized by the courts, assets can be used for the benefit of the beneficiaries but may escape the creditors of the beneficiaries (asset protection trusts).

FIVE KEY ELEMENTS OF EVERY TRUST

In a trust, (1) a *grantor* transfers (2) *trust property* to (3) a *trustee* to hold for the benefit of (4) the *beneficiary* in accordance with the purpose or (5) *intent* of the trust.

Every trust requires these five elements.

Grantor

The person who transfers the trust property to the trust is the grantor, also commonly called the trustor, settlor, or donor. The grantor must generally be the owner of the property transferred to the trust. This, however, is not always a requirement. Many trusts, including several illustrated in this book, permit the trustee to accept contributions from people other than the grantor (e.g., Aunt Nellie may wish to make a gift to the trust your mom established for your son's education to help celebrate your son's graduation from high school).

The grantor must also have the proper legal capacity to sign the trust agreement, and to transfer assets to the trust. This means that the grantor must be of sound mind and have the intent to form a trust. This intent of the grantor to form a trust must be manifested, generally in the form of a written and signed trust agreement.

CAUTION: The level of competence you must have to sign a trust is greater than the level required by the courts to sign a will. As a result, an older person, or someone who is ill, may have the competence to sign a will but not to sign a revocable living trust. This technical legal decision should only be made under the guidance of your attorney, and in consultation with the attending physician of the person involved. This is also a reason why living revocable trusts are not always the best answer.

Trust Property

This is the principal or subject matter of the trust. It is also called the *trust res*. Property is usually transferred to the trust. This is called a "funded" trust. An insurance trust is an example of a trust which is almost always funded immediately, with the insurance policy and money to pay annual premiums. In other cases, you may establish a trust to receive property at some future date, but none presently. This is called an "unfunded" or "standby" trust. When you set up a standby trust, you form the trust now, but the intended assets may not be transferred to it until some future date, such as your death. A trust formed under your will does not need to be funded now. It will instead be funded when your executor transfers assets from your estate to the trust following your death.

CAUTION: If you believe an unfunded trust is appropriate, review this with an estate planner in your state. It may be advisable to transfer some nominal asset, say $100, to fund the trust so that it exists. Apart from legal requirements, it is often useful to fund a trust to assure everything will be running smoothly when you need it. For example, you may wish to establish a revocable living trust to manage assets in the event of your disability. If you decide to sign the trust, but not fund it now, your agent will have to address all the administrative matters (e.g., obtaining a tax identification number, opening accounts) if you become disabled. Funding the trust today, even if it is not presently needed, may save time and difficulties when the trust is needed.

Assets can be transferred to a trust during life, after death through your will, by gift, or by the exercise of a power of appointment.

EXAMPLE: Your mother, through her will, bequeaths assets to a trust for your benefit. On your death, the assets in this trust are to be distributed to your children in any proportions you designate in your will. This is done because your mother has decided she wants your children to receive the assets on your death rather than someone else. However, she may not know the relative economic needs of the children when her will is written. Therefore, she gives you the power to determine what portion of the assets go to each child. This is called a power of appointment.

The property of a trust can be cash, a life insurance policy, stock in a corporation (special rules affect the types of trusts that can hold stock in an S corporation), or any other asset that serves your purposes and that can be owned in a trust. In most trusts, a formal legal description of the trust property is attached as a schedule. Merely listing the asset in a schedule attached to a trust is not enough to transfer ownership of that asset. For real estate, a deed must be filed transferring ownership (title) of the property. For personal property, a bill of sale may be required (see Chapter 3).

Trustee

The trustee is the person responsible for managing and administering your trust. The trustee should make a declaration, often by signing the trust agreement, that he or she accepts the trust property as trustee. The trustee may be you, a trusted friend, a family member, a bank trust department, or any combination of these and other persons.

CAUTION: Selection of a trustee is one of the most important, and often one of the most difficult, decisions in setting up a trust. With the passage of variations of the Prudent Investor Act in many states (and the likelihood of additional states passing it) using an institution such as a bank at least for a co-trustee is becoming more important. This act requires that trust assets be reasonably diversified to minimize risk and invested according to an appropriate plan that considers the purpose of the trust, tax issues, investment planning, and so forth. Most individuals such as friends and family members who would serve as trustees may not have the investment acumen to handle this. Even if they do, they may not wish the liability exposure if investments are not handled properly. The solution will increasingly be to name an institution or other professional trustee to serve as co-trustee with a friend or family member. Where the friend or family member (or more than one) serve without an institution, reliance on a plan by a qualified financial professional will be essential.

An important legal requirement to serve as trustee is that the trustee have the legal capacity to accept title (ownership) of the trust property. For example, a minor or incompetent person cannot be a trustee. The grantor will generally specify the trustee, and successor trustees in the event the first-named trustee is no longer willing or able to serve in that role. Where the grantor fails to do this, a court may have to name a trustee. It is always advisable to name several successors. Where the trust could be in existence for many years, even more persons, especially those young enough to serve into future years, should be named.

The trustee will generally hold legal title to the assets in the trust, but not beneficial title. "Legal title" means the trust assets are owned in the name of the trustee. The trustee generally has specific duties and responsibilities for the trust property, or has certain powers concerning the disposition of the trust property. "Beneficial title" to the trust property is held by the beneficiaries of the trust.

EXAMPLE: Tom Taxpayer establishes a trust for the benefit of his children. Tina Taxpayer is the named trustee. The stock that Tom transfers is owned by Tina, as trustee of the trust. Thus, Tina holds legal title to the stock "in trust" for the beneficiaries. Beneficial title, however, is held by the children who, as the named beneficiaries, have the sole right to benefit from the dividends and principal value of the stock.

NOTE: The same person should not be the only trustee and the only beneficiary because there would be no split of legal and beneficial title, which is essential for a trust. In such circumstances, the legal and beneficial interests may merge, or become one, under state law. This could result in the termination of the trust. While most states permit the same person to be trustee and primary beneficiary, others do not. If you are setting up a revocable living trust, discuss this issue with your estate attorney before deciding to serve as the sole trustee and beneficiary of your own trust.

Beneficiary

The beneficiary is the person, or persons, designated to receive the benefits and advantages of the property transferred to the trust. For example, you set up a trust by transferring stock to a trustee. The dividends are to be used to pay for educational expenses of your children, who are the beneficiaries of this trust. The persons who are beneficiaries should be described in clear and certain terms. For example, if you name "my descendants" as beneficiaries, there must be a stated time for identifying those descendants. Otherwise, it is impossible to know when to make the decision. What about children or grandchildren born after you set up the trust? Are they to be included or not? Beneficiaries can be charities as well (Chapter 14).

Intent of Trust

Every trust has a purpose, or intent, that motivates the grantor to set it up in the first place. Apart from the obvious requirement that the intent must be legal, there are few restrictions on the grantor's intent. The purpose can be:

- Benefiting a particular beneficiary (yourself, your spouse or partner, your child, a cousin, your favorite charity, or some combination of these).
- Providing for the management of certain assets (real estate, mutual funds, stock in a closely held corporation).
- Achieving certain tax benefits (charitable remainder trust to minimize capital gains and estate taxes, or a marital trust to qualify for the gift or estate tax unlimited marital deduction).

All these intents may be combined and will be spelled out in detail in the trust document. Where the trust document is silent, state laws and court cases may fill in some of the blanks.

COMPARING TRUSTS WITH OTHER LEGAL ARRANGEMENTS

You can enhance your understanding of trusts by comparing them with similar legal arrangements.

Power of Attorney

A common legal arrangement is an agency relationship. The most frequently used is a power of attorney. A power of attorney is a legal document through which you authorize another person to handle your financial matters. Powers of attorney, however, automatically terminate when you, the grantor, become disabled. The solution is to use what is called a durable power of attorney. Where state law permits, and the appropriate language is included in the power of attorney, it will remain effective if you become disabled. No power of attorney, however, will remain effective after your death. A trust can remain valid after your death. Therefore, where you wish to provide for the management of your assets after death, a trust, and not a power of attorney, is the appropriate vehicle.

Even during your life, there are several advantages in using a trust compared with a power of attorney. A trustee has legal ownership of the trust's assets, whereas in a power of attorney relationship, a person is designated as your agent. The trustee's relationship to the assets is clearer, and the trustee's powers over the assets are likely to be greater. For example, in a trust (such as a revocable living trust), you can include details as to how you should be cared for, the type of nursing home you should be in (or that you should be in your home as long as feasible), and so forth. This level of detail is rarely included in a power of attorney. Frequently, a bank or institution is named as a co-trustee (but banks or institutions will generally not serve as agents under a power of attorney). Using an institutional co-trustee can help assure that your assets are used fully for your care. This situation can compare quite favorably with having only a family member as agent under a power of attorney to provide for your care if you are disabled. What if the family member serving as this agent decided to conserve your assets instead of spending them on your care, in order to inherit them as a beneficiary of your estate after your death? Thus, where you wish to plan for potential future disability, a trust arrangement is often preferable to merely using a durable power of attorney. The costs of the trust approach, however, make the durable power of attorney the more practical solution in many situations with limited assets.

Custodial Accounts/UGMA/UTMA

Another common arrangement is a transfer under your state's uniform gifts to minors act (UGMA) or under your state's uniform transfers to minors act (UTMA) (see Chapter 13). In the most common type of UGMA transfer, you open a bank account as custodian of your child under your state's uniform gift or transfers to minors act. There are important differences between such an account and a trust. If you are the custodian, set up the account, and die before the child who is beneficiary, the entire amount in the account can be taxed in your estate. This is not true for a trust. The beneficiary (your child in the preceding example) owns the property, not the custodian (you, in the preceding example). When the beneficiary attains the age specified in your state's UGMA or UTMA law, he or she will receive control of the assets. This is typically an age from 18 to 21. In some instances, you can specify a slightly older age. Trusts offer much greater flexibility since you can tailor the trust document to address any concerns you may have, in particular, holding assets until the child attains an older age and is more mature. Trusts, however, require legal fees to set up and may require annual tax returns. Assets can be placed in a uniform gifts or transfers to minors act account at no cost.

PRIVACY AND ANONYMITY OF TRUSTS

Unlike wills and many other documents, trusts do not always have to be filed in the public record, thus offering the possibility of anonymity and privacy. This is often touted as an important advantage, particularly where most assets are placed in trust to avoid the probate process. Privacy, however, can be breached where the court orders that the trust be made part of the public probate record, or where the parties sue each other, forcing the trust into the court records.

NOTE: If your will stipulates the transfer, or pouring, of assets into a trust (a *pour-over* will), some probate courts (also called *surrogate's* courts) may require inclusion of the trust in their file. Also, if there is a will contest (someone sues to receive more of your assets following your death, by claiming that your will was defective or that you were not competent when you signed it), the court may require entering the trust in the public record.

The privacy aspects of trusts can also be breached by the legal steps necessary to transfer assets into the trust. Where real estate is transferred, a deed must be filed, and deeds are recorded in the public record. So even if the trust document itself remains private, the transfer of real estate to the trust will be public knowledge. In some counties, the county clerk (where deeds are filed) may require that the trust, or a summary of the trust (called a "memorandum of trust") be recorded. Since recording makes the document part of the public record, anyone can look up the trust (or the summary, if only it is required) in the county records. Transferring certain other property to the trust could trigger a public filing requirement under the provisions of the Uniform Commercial Code. Thus, the privacy factor, while available in many situations, is not as foolproof as many people like to believe. The real issue is, do you need to be concerned?

NOTE: The typical will, or the comparable provisions of a typical living trust addressing distribution of your assets, may provide for the distribution of property to your spouse, and on your spouse's death, equally to your children. In most cases, neither a will or living trust includes any personal information, or financial details, so why be so concerned about disclosure?

DIFFERENT TYPES OF TRUSTS

Trusts can be as varied as the people who set them up. The following sections describe factors used to categorize trusts. This information will help you better understand the uses of trusts, and how to pick the right one(s) for you.

When the Trust Is Formed

- *During Your Life.* You can set up a trust during your lifetime (inter vivos or living trust). Common living trusts include a revocable living trust (sometimes called a loving trust) (Chapter 10), a charitable remainder trust (Chapter 14), an insurance trust (Chapter 16), a children's trust (Chapter 13), or a charitable lead trust (Chapter 14).

- *At Your Death.* Alternatively, a trust can become effective only on your death (testamentary trust). Testamentary trusts are frequently contained in wills. Common testamentary trusts include trusts for a spouse (Chapter 11) and for minor children (Chapter 13), and a charitable lead trust (Chapter 14). The charitable lead and children's trusts, like many others, can be formed either while you are alive, or following your death under your will. The choice as to when will depend on the facts and circumstances.

- *Upon Starting a New Business or Purchasing an Investment.* Some trusts are formed when you are considering making an investment or setting up a new business. For example, if you wish to purchase a rental property and your overall estate and financial plan includes transferring assets to your children or other heirs, perhaps you should form a trust for them before purchasing the investment. You can then have your children's trusts purchase some or all of the investment.

EXAMPLE: Paul Parent found a rental property with excellent prospects and cash flow. Paul gifts $20,000 of cash that he and his wife Pauline would have used to purchase the rental property to the trustee of the trusts he establishes for his two children, with Pauline as co-trustee. The trustees then use this money to purchase some portion, or all, of the rental property. As a result, the trust will receive rental income that can be accumulated or paid out to or for the benefit of the children. The appreciation in the value of the rental property—to the extent owned by the trust—is owned by the trust, and not by Paul or Pauline's estates. Forming a trust to own a portion of the rental property can protect the property from creditors, yet still permit Pauline to have some control over the property and the income it generates.

Type of Beneficiary

Trusts can be established to benefit any type of person or cause. You can set up a trust to benefit yourself: A revocable living trust is an excellent tool for planning for your own disability and can also help avoid probate. Several types of trusts can be set up for a spouse and for children. A special trust can be used to make gifts to children under the age of 21 and still qualify for favorable tax benefits. Where a special child is involved, a trust can protect the child while preventing the loss of governmental benefits. A charitable trust is another possibility.

Purpose of the Trust

Trusts can be classified by the purposes for which formed. Often, tax benefits are a primary purpose (e.g., contributions under charitable trusts can provide significant tax advantages) (Chapter 14). Marital trusts are designed to qualify transfers of assets in the trust for the gift or estate tax unlimited marital deduction. This could include a "qualified terminable interest property" (Q-TIP or "B" trust) or "qualified domestic trust" (Q-DOT) (see Chapter 11). Perhaps the most common tax-oriented trust is the credit shelter trust (also called "bypass trust" or "A" trust). This is used to take advantage of the unified credit available to every taxpayer (see Chapter 11).

Trusts can be designed to avoid creditors and claimants, and to protect assets from Medicaid claims (Chapter 15). Wealthy taxpayers can use foreign situs asset protection trusts to shelter assets in an overseas haven.

Powers of Trustees

Trusts can be classified by the scope of powers given to the trustees. In some trusts, the trustees can be required to pay the income to a single beneficiary. Other trusts may grant trustees flexibility to accumulate the income and only pay it when they deem it appropriate ("accumulation trust"). In some cases, the grantor may wish to give the trustee broader powers to address future uncertainty. In these trusts, the trustee may be permitted to distribute the income and principal among various beneficiaries (called a "sprinkle trust").

"Spendthrift" trusts contain restrictions that prevent the beneficiaries from assigning their interests in advance (they cannot purchase something and assign future distributions to the seller to pay for the item).

Trustees can be given the power to buy, rent, or mortgage real estate, operate a business, or almost any other type of management control. Alternatively, the powers of the trustees over the assets can be more limited (Chapter 6).

Since there are many kinds of trusts with widely varied powers, these powers—while essential—are not a practical category for organizing discussions of trusts.

Grantor's Control

Another method of categorizing trusts is by the degree of control retained by the person setting up the trust (the grantor). If the grantor has the total right to terminate or change the trust, it is called revocable. Living trusts are perhaps the most common revocable trust (see Chapter 10).

If the grantor relinquishes the right to change or terminate the trust, it is said to be irrevocable. Where tax considerations are important, the trust is likely to be irrevocable.

The distinction between revocable and irrevocable is not complete. The grantor may be permitted very limited rights under even an irrevocable trust, such as the right to replace an institutional trustee with another institution.

Assets Held

The types of assets transferred to a trust can be used to characterize different trusts. Trusts that hold insurance are commonly used to protect the insurance proceeds from estate tax (Chapter 16). Special trusts to hold stock of S corporations or real estate, are frequently used (Chapters 18 and 19). A voting trust can be used to hold stock of a closely held corporation (Chapter 18).

Powers of the Beneficiaries

Although the beneficiaries are generally passive and the trustees make most decisions, several powers can be afforded to the beneficiaries. For example, the beneficiary may be given the right to require the distribution of certain amounts of principal each year from the trust, although this often is limited to what is called a "five-and-five power" (Chapter 5). A beneficiary may have the power of appointment and be allowed to designate where the assets of the trust will eventually be distributed (Chapter 5). A beneficiary may be given a limited right to replace one trustee with an independent replacement trustee (e.g., a bank or institutional trustee).

Since almost any type of trust can give the beneficiaries any of these powers, the beneficiaries' rights, while important, are not a practical category for organizing later discussions of trusts.

CHOOSING A TRUST MUST BE PART OF YOUR OVERALL PLAN

Although this is a book about trusts and how they can help your financial and estate planning, you cannot decide in a vacuum what trust or trusts are necessary to meet your goals. You should coordinate your selection and use of any trust with each of the following considerations.

Your Financial Plan

Any sound decision must include a thorough review of your present and anticipated future financial position. You must evaluate your own health, educational, and other needs, as well as the needs of your family, your loved ones, and others for whom you feel responsible.

Your Will

The use of any trusts must be coordinated with your will. In fact, many trusts appropriate for you may be included in your will. If you intend to distribute assets to a designated trust through a pour-over will, that trust must be coordinated with your will. The trust, for example, should have provisions permitting the trustees to accept, or reject, assets from your executor under your will. The trust should also be executed prior to the will.

(If the trust does not exist when you sign your will, what would your will pour into?)

Your Power of Attorney

The use of powers of attorney should be coordinated with your trust planning. A power of attorney is a legal arrangement that permits others to take financial actions on your behalf, in many cases when you are disabled. If you establish a trust, particularly a revocable living trust or another type of trust that may not be funded completely, your agent under your power of attorney should be given the specific authority to transfer assets to your trust. No matter what type of trust you set up, you almost always should still have a durable power of attorney.

Insurance Planning

Because a common use of trusts is to own insurance policies, evaluation of your insurance needs and coverage is critical for enabling coordination with your selection of trust. The need to hold insurance policies is only the most obvious factor to coordinate; your level of insurance coverage can affect your use and selection of other trusts as well.

EXAMPLE: Frank Father established an insurance trust that purchases a $2 million insurance policy on his life. Since his wife will receive the benefit of the $2 million of insurance on his death, he decided that only his children should be made beneficiaries of the credit shelter trust under his will (see Chapter 11).

NOTE: Gene Generous formed an insurance trust to benefit his primary beneficiaries, his three nephews. Because of the large amount of insurance coverage in this trust, Gene has decided not to form education trusts for the nephews while he is alive or under his will. Prior to opting for the insurance coverage, he had debated forming an education trust for each of the three nephews with annual gifts of $10,000.

Business Interests

Before deciding to use a trust as part of a plan to own or transfer ownership of business interests, you should consider the future growth of the business; the concerns of any other partners, members, or shareholders; and any restrictions in the partnership, operating, or shareholders' agreement that might prevent the contemplated transfer to the trust.

The key to effective planning for any trust is to coordinate the process with your overall financial and estate plan. Review your plan with all your advisers—your accountant, attorney, and insurance and investment specialists. Any attempt to plan in isolation is dangerous.

SELECTING THE RIGHT TRUST FOR YOU

The myriad of trusts and trust provisions make professional advice essential in selecting an optimal arrangement for any individual. This book, however, can provide substantial help by introducing you to many of the available trust formats. As mentioned earlier, selection of the most appropriate trusts for you must begin with a thorough and objective analysis of your personal, financial, estate planning, business, and other goals. Your financial and tax status must also be reviewed. The current and projected financial and management needs of you and your family must be anticipated. Based on this information, a comprehensive estate and financial plan can be devised. Within this context, the trusts appropriate for you can be identified and then implemented.

EXAMPLE: To protect his family, Gary Grantor has a $1 million term life insurance policy. If either Gary or his wife Gail owned this policy, it would create a tax cost on the death of the second partner. Life insurance is not tax free. The solution—have a life insurance trust own the policy (Chapter 16).

Because Gail and Gary have young children, they have provided trusts for them in their wills. These trusts name a succession of close and trusted friends to handle the children's financial affairs if both Gail and Gary die while their children are still minors. These trusts are coordinated with the planning for Gail's children from her prior marriage.

If Gail and Gary were concerned about planning for disability and avoiding the expenses and delays of probate, they could each transfer their assets to a revocable living trust. If this approach were to be used, the credit shelter and Q-TIP trust could be included in each of their living trusts.

Gary and Gail's net worth is approximately $1.4 million. As a result, their estate planner recommends that they use credit shelter trusts so that each of their estates can benefit from the once-in-a-lifetime $600,000 exclusion (the unified gift and estate tax credit of $192,800 exempts $600,000 of assets from taxation) (see Chapter 11). Each of their wills thus incorporates a credit shelter trust. In Gail's will, following Gary's later death, the assets of hers remaining in the credit shelter trust will be distributed (in part) to her children from her prior marriage.

Because this is the second marriage for Gail, she wishes to set up a trust for any assets she owns above the $600,000 amount. A marital (Q-TIP or "B") trust is used. This trust will qualify for the estate tax marital deduction so that there will not be any estate tax on Gail's death (Chapters 7 and 11). Following Gail's death, Gary will be entitled to all the income from this trust. Following his death, the assets from Gail's Q-TIP trust will be distributed to Gail's children from her first marriage. With this arrangement, no federal estate tax will be due on Gail's death. This is because the first $600,000 of her estate will avoid tax as a result of her unified credit. Amounts above $600,000 are included in a Q-TIP trust, which will be exempted from tax on Gail's death by the unlimited estate tax marital deduction (but the Q-TIP assets remaining will be taxed in Gary's estate when he dies).

CONCLUSION

Trusts are a valuable and flexible tool that can provide substantial benefits for meeting estate, financial, personal, and business goals.

2 THE TRUST DOCUMENT: BASIC BUILDING BLOCKS

Many trusts are made up of several similar components. Understanding these basic building blocks will help you work with trusts and assure that any you ultimately use will be best tailored to your needs. Where you are named a beneficiary or trustee of someone else's trust, understanding the basics will make it much easier for you to read and understand your rights and responsibilities as a trustee. Finally, the format used here to explain these building blocks is the same order of discussion that will be used in Part Two of this book to explain, in detail, the provisions of many trusts.

NOTE: Several primarily tax-oriented trusts form an exception to this common "building block" approach. Although similar concepts are found in these trusts, they are often modeled after IRS forms. Although estate planners may make changes to the sample IRS forms, they are likely to follow the IRS recommendations quite closely.

> **SCHEMATIC OF BASIC TRUST BUILDING BLOCKS**
>
> INTRODUCTORY PARAGRAPHS
> TRANSFERRING ASSETS TO YOUR TRUST
> GRANTOR'S POWERS AND RIGHTS UNDER THE TRUST
> BENEFICIARIES' DESIGNATIONS AND RIGHTS
> TRUSTEES—THEIR RIGHTS, OBLIGATIONS, AND POWERS
> DISTRIBUTION OF INCOME AND PRINCIPAL
> OPERATIVE PROVISIONS OF YOUR TRUST
> TERMINATION OF YOUR TRUST
> MISCELLANEOUS TRUST PROVISIONS
> SIGNATURE LINES AND EXHIBITS

BUILDING BLOCK 1: INTRODUCTORY PARAGRAPHS

Trusts set up during your lifetime are called living trusts (in legal jargon, *inter vivos* trusts). There are many different types of trusts which can actually be set up during your lifetime, including the revocable living trust. Parts Two, Three, and Four of this book will explain many types of trusts that you can set up during your lifetime.

A living trust, as contrasted with a trust formed at your death (called a testamentary trust), will typically begin with several introductory paragraphs. Trusts in your will do not need similar introductory provisions since the provisions of the will, the event of your death, and state laws substitute for much of this information.

EXAMPLE: If you establish an inter vivos trust today for your child, or one under your will, the key provisions of both will be similar. Both trusts may give the trustee discretion to distribute income and principal to the child when the trustee deems it to be appropriate. At specified ages, predetermined portions of the trust principal may be required to be distributed to the child (e.g., 1/3 each at ages 25, 30, and 35). However, many of the administrative and boilerplate (standard or commonly used) provisions in the will are likely to appear in a different format than in the inter vivos trust. In your will, these provisions are likely to be written more generically, and ordered differently, so that they apply to both your executor (the person who administers your estate and distributes your assets to your trustee) and your trustee (the person who then administers the trusts formed under your will). In an inter vivos trust, the provisions will be written solely in the context of applying to the trustee.

SAMPLE INTRODUCTORY TRUST CLAUSES

NOTE: The Lawyer preparing the trust document will often sign his or her name on the top. In some states, this is required for the trust to be recorded. Even if you do not intend to record the trust, you may wish to have this included in case the trust has to be recorded at some future date in a state with such a requirement.

PREPARED BY:

_____

Martin M. Shenkman, Esq.

*YOUR NAME *TRUST-TYPE Trust

NOTE: Insert the tax identification number received from the IRS for the trust. This can be obtained by completing the Form SS-4.

Trust EIN:

DECLARATION OF TRUST

THIS TRUST AGREEMENT dated as of *MONTH *DAY, *YEAR, between, *GRANTORNAME, who resides at *GRANTOR-ADDRESS (the "Grantor") and *CO-TRUSTEE1-NAME, who resides at *CO-TRUSTEE-1ADDRESS and *CO-TRUSTEE2-NAME, who resides at *CO-TRUSTEE-2ADDRESS, and any successor Trustee appointed as provided in this Trust Agreement (the "Trustee").

RECITALS

WHEREAS, the Grantor desires to create a trust, and transfer the assets listed below to the trust, on the terms which are detailed below, and the Trustee has consented to accept and perform said trust in accordance with such terms.

NOTE: The following paragraph is used where you are amending a prior trust, such as a revocable living trust.

WHEREAS, the Grantor executed the *GRANTORNAME Revocable Living Trust on *ORIGINALTRUST-DATE and under Article III.A. Grantor reserved the right to amend, modify or revoke said trust. The Grantor is hereby exercising such power and restating and amending hereby such trust in its entirety.

NOW, THEREFORE, in consideration of the mutual covenants and promises of the parties hereto, and other good and valuable consideration, receipt and adequacy of which is hereby acknowledged, this Trust shall be effective as of the date and the terms following:

NOTE: The actual trust provision would follow here.

Selecting a Name for Your Trust

One of the first steps is to select a name for your inter vivos trust. You may want to avoid the use of a family name that will immediately convey to third parties that your family has a trust. For most people, however, this is not a concern, and your surname is a convenient identifier for banks, accountants, attorneys, and others handling your trust and related matters.

Also, consider using a name that is sufficiently descriptive of the trust and its functions to enable you, your family, and professional advisers to easily identify the trust. This becomes particularly important where you set up several trusts. Since you cannot know when you establish your first trust what additional trusts you may form in the future, plan ahead.

EXAMPLE: Tom Taxpayer sets up a Grantor Retained Annuity Trust (GRAT) in 1998 (Chapter 17). The trust is called the "Tom Taxpayer 1998 Trust." If this were Tom's only trust, the name used might be reasonable. In 1999, however, Tom sets up a second GRAT and calls it the "Tom Taxpayer 1999 Trust." In 1999, Tom sets up an irrevocable life insurance trust (Chapter 16). The trust is called the "Tom Taxpayer 1999 Trust." Administration will become exceedingly confusing because the names are so similar. Tom could consider the following names instead: "Tom Taxpayer 1999 GRAT," "Tom Taxpayer 1999 GRAT," and "Tom Taxpayer Irrevocable 1999 Life Insurance Trust." These names are clearer and more descriptive.

The Date of the Trust

The first introductory paragraph of your trust lists the date the trust is established, the name of the grantor establishing it (if it is your trust, this will generally be you), and the initial trustee (or trustees, if there is more than one). This paragraph demonstrates three of the five essential elements of a trust discussed in Chapter 1—a grantor, a trustee, and the intent of the grantor to form a trust.

The date of your trust is particularly important. Where you wish to use your annual $10,000 per person gift tax exclusion, the trust must be established prior to year-end. Every taxpayer is entitled to give away up to $10,000 to any other person during each tax year without incurring a gift tax. When properly planned (this often requires the use of what are called "Crummey powers," discussed in Chapter 7), you can make such gifts without using any of the lifetime unified credit against the gift and estate tax, which can exempt $600,000 of assets. This $10,000 gift can be given to an unlimited number of people each year. If the gift is to your minor child, grandchild, or any other minor, you may wish to make the gift into a trust to provide some control over the child's use of the money (see Chapter 13). When setting up this type of trust, it is best to allow enough time before the end of the year to open a bank account and make an initial deposit. This will help demonstrate to the IRS that the trust was in fact properly formed prior to year-end.

NOTE: You may need a tax identification number from the IRS prior to opening the bank account. To expedite matters, you can obtain this number over the telephone (with confirmation via facsimile). The form you should complete for sending via facsimile is IRS Form SS-4. Each district of the IRS has its own facsimile number for sending such forms. Call the main IRS office serving your area for additional information, the main IRS form number 1-800-TAX-FORM, or write the IRS forms center for Form SS-4 and instructions.

If you use a will with a pour-over provision (i.e., a direction that assets from your estate be poured into, or transferred to, your trust), the trust should not have a date after the date of your will. A pour-over will transfers assets to your trust, and then the trust document specifies which beneficiary is to receive which assets (see Chapter 10).

If one or more of your trusts is established under the provisions of your will, the preceding sections concerning date or effective date will not appear. The trust will simply become effective on your death.

Who Is the Grantor?

Who should be the grantor of the trust? Generally, there is little issue since the grantor is usually the person setting up the trust and contributing most of its assets. Careful consideration must be given to this question, however, because it can have important implications, depending on the specific circumstances:

- The grantor of most trusts (GRATs, living trusts, etc. are exceptions) usually cannot also serve as a trustee or successor trustee.
- The grantor is often assumed to be the person transferring assets to the trust.

- The grantor of most trusts (GRATs, living trusts, etc. are exceptions) usually cannot be a beneficiary of the trust.
- The powers and rights that the grantor reserves in the trust (and the trust assets, called the "trust estate") are often severely restricted. In most irrevocable trusts, one of the few powers that the grantor can retain, without causing the trust assets to be taxable in the grantor's estate, is a limited power to replace an independent trustee with another independent trustee.
- If the grantor is subject to a lawsuit or other claim, the grantor's creditors or claimants may attack the trust by claiming that the transfer of assets by the grantor to the trust was a fraudulent conveyance (done with the intent, or within a statutory time frame, to defraud the creditors of the assets transferred).

The introductory descriptive paragraph of a typical trust also demonstrates the point noted in Chapter 1—a trust is a contract between the grantor and trustees.

Who Should Be Listed as Initial Trustees of Your Trust?

The introductory paragraph will name the initial trustee (or initial cotrustees) for your trust; successor, or alternate, trustees will be named in later provisions. In choosing the initial trustees, you should carefully consider the purpose of the trust, the duration of the trust, the different phases of the trust, and the persons named as successor trustees.

Purpose of the Trust

If the trust is an irrevocable life insurance trust, designed to remove insurance proceeds from your estate, there is likely to be very little activity in the trust prior to the death of the insured. The only functions may be to receive an annual gift, issue a Crummey power notice (see Chapter 9), and write a single check to pay the insurance premium. For these purposes, someone who is readily available, and who is agreeable to performing these administrative functions, could be a good choice as an initial trustee.

If you are establishing a trust for your child, or another minor, you will probably make annual or more frequent gifts to the trust. Depending on the facts, such a trust might grow quite quickly in size. Investment acumen might be a key criterion for the trustee of such a trust.

If the trust is a voting trust for a business interest, your partners in the business may insist that you, or you and they jointly, serve as trustees. The provisions of any existing business agreement you are party to may govern who can serve as trustee.

If the trust is a revocable living trust (sometimes called a loving trust), you may be both the grantor and the trustee (Chapters 4 and 9). However, it is generally preferable that you be a co-trustee and not the sole trustee of any trust for which you are a beneficiary.

Duration of Trust

The likely duration of the trust is an important factor in determining who should be a trustee and how many successor trustees to name. If your youngest child is age 19, and you wish to establish a trust until he reaches age 25, you might be comfortable naming one of your parents as a co-trustee. If your child was just born, however, and the trust you wish to fund will remain in existence until your newborn child reaches age 35, your parents may not be an ideal choice. Younger trustees, or perhaps a bank or institutional trustee, would be appropriate to consider.

Different Phases of Your Trust

In some instances, it may be appropriate to name different trustees for different phases of your trust. If you establish a revocable living trust, you and a close friend or family member may be the initial trustees. It may not be wise to be the sole initial trustee—legal issues of merger could affect your trust, and in the event of disability, there is no other currently serving trustee to take over quickly. If you become disabled, your spouse or partner may be your successor. After the death of you and your spouse, the trust may continue for the benefit of your minor children. To provide for this contingency, you may name two co-trustees: one with investment acumen to manage the children's investments and the other a guardian or close family member who knows the children on a personal level.

For many types of trust, you should consider the different stages of the trust when designating trustees. Although it is always simpler to work from the same list and simplicity is an important goal, make sure that the result is appropriate. If not, set up your trust with trustees selected to fit each phase.

Persons Named as Successor Trustees

The more secure the successor trustees you have (e.g., because of selecting a large number of trusted family members or friends, or using an institution), the more flexibility you have. For example, if you want to name your father as a co-trustee of your child's trust, is it appropriate considering your parent's age? If he is 65 and your child is 5, it would appear not. However, if you have a comfortable and secure list of successor trustees, perhaps you can name your parent with the understanding that when he is no longer able to serve, the next successor trustee listed in your trust document will take his place.

BUILDING BLOCK 2: TRANSFERRING ASSETS TO YOUR TRUST

As explained in Chapter 1, identification and transfer of property to the trust is one of the five essential elements of a trust. The provisions identifying the assets that are transferred to your trust on formation, however, may not meet this requirement. Merely identifying the assets to be transferred is only one step toward accomplishing the goal of funding your trust. The legal ownership (called title) of the assets must be transferred to your trustees to hold in their capacity as trustees. This can require the deed of real estate, the change in the ownership, registration, or title of a brokerage account, and so forth.

Finally, you do not want to arbitrarily transfer assets to your trust. To meet your goals, you must carefully consider what assets to transfer to your trusts. This decision requires evaluation of income, gift, and estate tax issues, asset protection concerns, economics (e.g., which asset is most likely to appreciate), and personal preferences. These matters are addressed in detail in Chapter 3.

Do not assume that only the person named as the grantor can transfer assets to the trust. If you set up a trust for your children, as grantor, your parents, for example, can also contribute assets to the trust. Many trusts include a provision permitting other persons to contribute or transfer property to the trust, if the assets are acceptable to the trustee. It is often advisable to give the trustee discretion to reject assets that may have adverse tax or legal consequences. For example, a rental property that someone sought to transfer to the trust might not be practical to manage, or worse, might have a leaky oil tank or other hazardous waste.

Sample provisions for adding assets to a trust are discussed in Chapter 3.

BUILDING BLOCK 3: GRANTOR'S POWERS AND RIGHTS UNDER THE TRUST

The grantor (also called a settlor or trustor) is the person setting up a trust. In most revocable living trusts, the grantor will retain substantial rights and powers over the trust and the property transferred to the trust. In other inter vivos (set up during the grantor's lifetime) trusts, the grantor may have few, or no, rights or powers over the trust. The nature and extent of these powers will depend on the objectives of the trust and the type of trust involved. For example, where the trust is formed to remove assets from your estate, you will retain no significant powers over the trust. Similarly, if you establish a foreign situs asset protection trust to protect assets from creditors, you will limit, although not always as severely as for a tax-motivated trust, your rights as grantor to the trust assets and to trust decision making.

On the other hand, if you set up a revocable living trust (i.e., a trust you can change at any time) for purposes of administering assets in the event of your later disability, and to avoid probate, you will probably retain total control over the assets and trust.

Where a trust is formed under a will, the grantor obviously cannot retain any rights or powers.

These matters are discussed in detail in Chapter 4.

BUILDING BLOCK 4: BENEFICIARIES' DESIGNATIONS AND RIGHTS

Beneficiaries are the fifth and final essential trust element. Every trust must carefully identify the persons who are to benefit from the trust assets during each phase of the trust.

CAUTION: The beneficiaries of a trust must almost always be people. Only a few states permit pets to be named beneficiaries of a trust. At least one of the state statutes permitting pets to be beneficiaries of a trust gives the court considerable latitude to review the trust if the assets transferred to the trust are excessive.

The provisions that affect a beneficiary can be quite simple.

EXAMPLE: I, Gary Grantor, hereby transfer $10,000 to Terri Trustee to hold in trust for the benefit of Mary Minor, as beneficiary. The Trustee shall pay the income from this money to or for the benefit of the beneficiary until the beneficiary reaches age 25. At such time, any assets remaining in this trust shall be distributed outright (i.e., without further trust) to John Smith.

CAUTION: The preceding listing of beneficiaries has an important gap as a result of poor drafting. What happens if Mary Minor dies before reaching age 25? Can John Smith receive the assets immediately? The trust is not clear. This example illustrates how important it is for every trust to clearly delineate who should be beneficiaries, when, and what they can receive.

In many trusts, however, the provisions concerning beneficiaries are far more detailed and complex. You may name alternate beneficiaries. If the primary beneficiary, Mary Minor in the preceding example, were to die, other persons could be named beneficiaries before John Smith is to receive the remainder.

Some trusts may give the beneficiary the right to demand that certain payments be made to them, or for their benefit. This is discussed in detail in Chapter 5.

BUILDING BLOCK 5: TRUSTEES—THEIR RIGHTS, OBLIGATIONS, AND POWERS

This is one of the longest portions of a trust document. These provisions specify who will serve as trustees, and the various rights, administrative obligations, and powers of the trustees. Although you named the initial trustee in the introductory paragraphs of your trust, you should always name alternate ("successor") trustees if the initial trustee cannot continue to serve. This is vitally important. If the listing of trustees you provide is exhausted, a court will have to step in to appoint a successor.

Numerous details—how the trustee should serve, what rights the trustee has, what powers and authority the trustee can exercise over the trust property, how the trustee should manage the trust—must all be provided for. These provisions are the "guts" of your trust; they are what make it work. Although most of these provisions are often skimmed quickly as boilerplate provisions that don't warrant attention, this can be a serious mistake. If you are named as a trustee, you must read these provisions with great care. These matters are discussed in detail in Chapter 6.

BUILDING BLOCK 6: DISTRIBUTION OF INCOME AND PRINCIPAL

The distribution provisions of your trust are vital for the carrying out of your wishes. In prior building blocks, the beneficiaries were clearly identified, the trustees who manage the trust were named, and the powers and rights of the trustees were specified. But how should the trustees use their powers to distribute trust assets to your beneficiaries? That determination is the objective of the distribution provisions of the trust.

Distribution provisions are not as simple as many people think. In prior years, many trusts provided that income would be paid out annually or more frequently. Principal (the actual assets of the trust) may have been held for the remainder beneficiaries (the beneficiaries who receive their interests after the initial phase of the trust). However, modern investment theory has resulted in trusts generally investing for total return (i.e., current income and appreciation or capital gains). Thus, for a trust merely to state that income should be distributed currently may not be workable.

Similarly, every trust contains rules stipulating when principal of the trust can be distributed.

EXAMPLE: You transfer $25,000 to a trust. This amount is the principal of the trust. The trustee invests this amount in common stocks. The trust earns $2,300 of common stock dividends. This is income of the trust. The difference between income and principal is not always so clear. The payment of a stock dividend or a cash payment for fractional shares in a stock split will probably be characterized as principal. However, the trust can provide detailed rules for making these decisions.

The provisions of your trust stating how and when income and principal should be distributed are extremely important.

EXAMPLE: You are divorced and married for the second time. You establish a trust for the benefit of your second spouse during her lifetime. On the death of your second spouse, the assets will be divided among your children from your first

marriage. You name a close family friend as trustee. Any receipts that are characterized as income will be distributed to your second spouse. Any receipts that are
characterized as principal will be allocated to your children from a prior marriage. The distinction is obviously important. Further, the clearer your trust is
about the rules of allocating receipts between income and principal, the less likely
your trustee will be embroiled in difficult problems.

Further questions and issues must be addressed. When should principal
be invaded? Should the trustee use the trust assets to pay for college education? If so, what about postgraduate studies? Should restrictions be
placed on the distribution provisions to protect the trust assets from the
beneficiary's creditors? The list goes on.

BUILDING BLOCK 7: OPERATIVE PROVISIONS OF YOUR TRUST

The provisions that govern how income and principal can be distributed
are closely related to the particular type of trust. Your trust may require
special provisions to address the unique characteristics of the beneficiary,
the special nature of the assets, or other special circumstances. These provisions give the trust its unique classification or characteristics for tax
purposes.

Insurance Trust

An insurance trust can take many forms depending on the purpose for
which it is established, the persons to benefit, and the rules for distributing those benefits. These decisions, however, are similar to those made for
many types of trusts. To facilitate a trust holding insurance as an asset,
however, several important provisions concerning the trustees' power to
deal with insurance companies and related matters should be added (see
Chapter 16).

Qualified S Corporation Trust (QSST)

An S corporation is a corporation that is, for federal (and some state) income tax purposes, treated like a partnership. It generally avoids the corporate level tax; income, gains, losses, and so forth pass through to the
shareholders and are reported on their personal tax returns. Where a trust
owns stock in an S corporation, stringent requirements must be met to
prevent the corporation from losing its favored tax status as an S corporation. Generally, all income must be distributed currently to a single beneficiary for a trust to be a shareholder in an S corporation. Thus, the
provisions of your trust governing when income and principal can be distributed must meet these requirements (Chapter 18).

Charitable Lead or Remainder Trust

These trusts are formed to achieve specific tax advantage. The provisions of the trust governing the distribution of income and principal must conform strictly to applicable IRS requirements or the intended tax benefits will be lost. The documents governing these trusts are generally modeled very closely after suggested IRS forms (see Chapter 14).

Marital Deduction Trust

The estate tax can apply at rates of 55 percent, and even higher. There are several important exclusions from this tax. Every taxpayer is permitted to give away (during your lifetime or following your death under your will) up to $600,000 with no federal estate tax cost. Another exception permits every taxpayer to give away an unlimited amount to his or her spouse, where the spouse is a United States citizen. If you wish to protect the assets put aside for your spouse while still qualifying for the marital deduction, you can place those assets in a trust. To qualify for the marital deduction, however, the trust must meet the requirements of a Qualified Terminable Interest Property Trust (called a Q-TIP trust). One of the basic requirements is that all the income from that trust must be distributed, at least annually, to your spouse. The income and principal payment provisions of your trust must conform specifically to these requirements of the tax law for your estate to qualify for this deduction (Chapters 7 and 11).

The preceding provisions demonstrate how the income and distribution provisions of your trust may have to address the specific character and nature of the assets transferred to your trust, the purpose of your trust, tax planning, and other factors. These matters are addressed in detail in later chapters which discuss specific types of trusts (Chapters 10–20).

BUILDING BLOCK 8: TERMINATION OF YOUR TRUST

No trust can go on forever. The distribution provisions are a major determinant of when a trust must end. If your trust provides that all assets must be distributed on the child-beneficiary attaining age 35, then the trust will end shortly thereafter because it will have fulfilled its purpose and will no longer have any assets. Perhaps the only steps to be performed after the final payment to the beneficiary pursuant to the terms of the trust will be an accounting to the beneficiaries (preparation of an analysis of all financial transactions demonstrating that the final payment was correct) and a final income tax return.

A trust may end, however, at an earlier date than when the final (residual or contingent) beneficiary reaches a particular milestone. Illegality, impossibility, or decisions by the trustee (e.g., you give the trustee the power to terminate the trust if it should become so small as not to be economical to manage) could all end a trust at an early date. How and when a trust should terminate is discussed in the chapters addressing specific trusts (see Chapters 10–20).

BUILDING BLOCK 9: MISCELLANEOUS TRUST PROVISIONS

Several important provisions are included in most trusts: definitions of key terms in the document (if not defined in earlier provisions of the trust), specification of which state law should govern, the situs of the trust (the state or country in which the trust should be deemed located), and several technical legal provisions governing how your trust document should be interpreted in the event there are ever questions as to what should be done.

BUILDING BLOCK 10: SIGNATURE AND EXHIBITS

Where your trust (or trusts) is created under your will, the final paragraphs, signature lines, and other formalities, are governed by the state laws applicable to wills. Where you set up a trust during your life, the following final provisions are common.

SAMPLE TRUST PROVISIONS

IN WITNESS WHEREOF, the undersigned Grantor and Trustee have executed this Trust as of the date first-above written.

NOTE: The signature lines will have to be adjusted to reflect the nature of the trust and the persons named. For a life insurance trust designed to hold second-to-die insurance (pays on death of the last of husband and wife) both spouses could be grantors (and neither should be trustee). In many trusts, two persons will serve as co-trustees. In some situations, you may prefer one trustee alone. In a revocable living trust, there is usually only one grantor, except some advisers in community property states may have a single trust. Also, in a revocable living trust you may have the grantor as a co-trustee. This may also be true of certain other types of "grantor" trusts (a tax designation discussed in Chapters 4, 17, 18, and 19), such as QPRTs (Chapter 19). It is preferable to have a witness (a person who is not a trustee, beneficiary, or the grantor) for each signature.

CAUTION: Get your trust signed quickly. Even if the grantor signs the trust, the law may not view the trust as effective until the trustee signs. If there are more than one grantor, or more than one trustee, have everyone sign to avoid any legal question as to the validity of the trust.

WITNESS:

_____   _____ (L.S.)
                                     *YOURNAME, Grantor

_____   _____ (L.S.)
                                     *SPOUSENAME, Co-Grantor

_____   _____ (L.S.)
                                         *AGENT1-NAME, Co-Trustee

_____   _____ (L.S.)
                                         *AGENT2-NAME, Co-Trustee

                                         Bigbank, as Co-Trustee

_____   By: _____ (L.S.)
                                            *VP-NAME, Vice President

NOTE: Each signature should be notarized. Sometimes this is not done because of time constraints or other problems. Some people can be so private about their trust that they are uncomfortable having even a witness or notary sign. If feasible, however, have every trust both witnessed and notarized.

NOTE: Notary forms omitted.

NOTE: A schedule is always attached to every trust stating the assets transferred to the trust. In many situations, this may only list an initial deposit of $100 to start the trust, with the primary assets being transferred at a later date. Be cautious: Merely listing an asset on schedule is often insufficient—you may have to take additional steps to properly transfer ownership to the trust (see Chapter 3).

Schedule A
Property Transferred to Trust

1. Cash in the amount of $100.00.

2. Real estate located at 123 Main Street, Any Town, USA, as provided in a deed dated January 12, 1996, copy attached hereto.

NOTE: To transfer insurance, you must work with your insurance agent to complete the insurance company forms naming the trust as owner. In most insurance trusts, you will irrevocably name the trust as the sole owner and beneficiary of the policy. Wherever possible, try to have the trust purchase the policy initially; you should avoid purchasing the policy and then transferring it.

3. Life insurance policy insuring the life of *CLIENT NAME, with the *NAME OF INSURANCE COMPANY. Policy Number: *POLICY NUMBER issued *DATE POLICY ISSUED.

NOTE: In some trusts, it can be helpful to have a chart of the power holders for purposes of the Crummey power (see Chapter 7).

CONCLUSION

This chapter has summarized the key components of a typical trust. The chapters that follow will expand on this summary in great detail to provide you with tools for understanding and working with trusts. Keeping this summary in mind when you review any trust will help you see the relevance of any particular part of the document to the trust's overall purpose.

3 TRANSFERRING ASSETS TO YOUR TRUST

IMPORTANCE OF TRUST ASSETS

As discussed in Chapter 1, the assets transferred to your trust (the trust property, or "res") are one of the five key elements to any trust. The selection of the property to transfer to your trust can be quite important. Certain types of property, such as insurance and stock in an S corporation, require special trust provisions to deal with them. Special expertise on the part of the trustee may be required for other assets. For example, stock in a closely held business may imply a need for a trustee with relevant business experience. A large securities portfolio could indicate a need for a trustee with investment expertise. This is especially true if you reside in a state that has adopted a revised version of the Prudent Investor Act. The Prudent Investor Act and its predecessor, the Prudent Man Rule which is still law in many states, set standards for the types of investments a trustee can use.

The nature and quantity of the assets transferred is also critical. If you hope to avoid probate, you should transfer to your trust every asset of yours that would otherwise require probate.

CAUTION: This is not nearly as easy as many seminars and "how-to" books imply. A pension, other retirement asset, or insurance policy made payable to your estate could then require your will be probated. A lottery winning, business asset your partners will not permit you to transfer, and so forth could all prevent you from achieving a no-probate goal (see Chapter 9).

This chapter will consider some of these and other questions, and will also discuss the methods to transfer various types of assets to your trust.

TRANSFER OF ASSETS TO YOUR TRUST

A trust can either be funded or unfunded. A funded trust is one to which you transfer assets. For example, if you wish to set up a trust for the benefit of your children, you will probably transfer assets to the trust each year. An unfunded trust is one that has no assets at present. However, you may transfer a nominal amount of cash, perhaps $100, to such a trust to activate it and open a bank account. Unfunded trusts have many uses. For example, if you want the assets in your estate to be poured over into a trust, you could establish a trust that has no assets, but that will later receive the assets from your estate.

How you fund your trust may in part be determined by the nature of the trust you are setting up. If the trust is being set up to manage your assets, it must be funded to meet its objective. If you wish to use a trust to avoid probate, then the trust must be funded to accomplish its objective, since only assets transferred to the trust will avoid probate. In these instances, you should try to transfer all your assets that could be subject to probate to the trust. As a safety precaution, you should also have a pour-over will and a durable power of attorney that specifically authorizes your agent to transfer assets to your trust. The benefits of avoiding probate, however, are not what many people believe. These matters are discussed at length in Chapter 7.

Where you have assets in different states, it can be advantageous to avoid probate in several states (called ancillary probate). This can be accomplished only if the assets in states other than where you live (in legal terms, where you're domiciled) are transferred to your trust.

To establish a funded trust, the trust property must be designated and then transferred to the trust. Several portions of a typical trust address this issue, beginning with the introductory provisions.

Another portion of your trust that is likely to address the transfer of assets is an attached schedule. This technique is often used simply for administrative or drafting convenience. The assets to be transferred are listed in detail on the attached schedule. This schedule, however, merely identifies these assets. As will be discussed, important, and often formal, legal steps must be taken to actually transfer many such assets.

Where real estate is to be transferred to the trust, you may attach a copy of the deed to the trust agreement because the deed will contain a full legal description of the property, thus properly identifying it as the asset transferred.

WHAT TYPES OF ASSET SHOULD BE TRANSFERRED TO YOUR TRUST?

Almost any type of asset can be held in trust. The assets can be tangible (equipment, buildings), intangible (stocks, bonds, patents), real (buildings, land), or personal (equipment, paintings). The decision as to which specific assets to transfer to what type of trust, however, can be much more complex.

Deciding what assets you should transfer to your trust, or trusts (you may need more than one, many people do), must start with an assessment of your overall financial and estate planning goals, the nature and value of your assets and the likely appreciation of those assets, and your current and future cash needs.

EXAMPLE: You are a retired widower and concerned about managing your money and financial affairs. Your estate consists of a condominium worth $375,000 and marketable securities worth $500,000, for a total estate of $875,000. It may be appropriate to transfer all your assets into a revocable living trust. You will continue to manage your assets while you are able. When this is no longer possible, a mechanism is in place for your chosen trustees to immediately assume management responsibility. Your estate could avoid probate (if that was a concern), possibly saving your heirs expenses and delays. In this scenario, all assets could be transferred to your trust. The problem with this plan is that it is not complete. You have not addressed a potentially substantial estate tax cost. You probably will not wish to gift or encumber your securities since you are living off the income. Perhaps a Qualified Personal Residence Trust (QPRT) to remove the value of your home from your estate at a substantially discounted rate could be used (see Chapter 19).

EXAMPLE: Tom and Tina Taxpayer are a couple in their 40s and have an estate valued at approximately $1.8 million. This consists of $800,000 of rental real estate; $250,000 equity in their home; and $750,000 in certificates of deposit, bonds, and stocks. The Taxpayers' estate is in excess of the amount that can be shielded by the $600,000 unified credit that each of them is entitled to. The Taxpayers wish to begin a gift program whereby they will give gifts to trusts for their children to reduce their combined estate to approximately the $1.2 million level where no federal estate tax will be due. The investment real estate is perhaps the preferable asset to use for the gift: The parents may still exercise significant control over the asset; the real estate may be the asset most likely to appreciate and thus the gift will remove the most future appreciation from their estate; and the real estate is likely to be the least liquid of their assets. An alternative may be to transfer the real estate to a limited liability company (LLC) and make gifts of membership interests in the LLC to the trusts established for their children. This can limit liability, assure a greater measure of control (with either Tom or Tina serving as manager of the LLC), and most importantly, qualify gifts to the trusts for discounts for lack of marketability and lack of control.

EXAMPLE: The Youngcouples are in their early 30s and have a combined estate worth approximately $150,000. However, the husband, the sole breadwinner, has a $1 million term insurance policy on his life. If the husband establishes an irrevocable life insurance trust, and transfers the life insurance, and all incidents of ownership in the insurance, to the trust, the couple will have effectively eliminated any potential estate tax (assuming the husband survives for three years after the transfer). The trust will provide for the management of the substantial insurance proceeds in the event of the husband's untimely death. A spendthrift provision in the trust offers a measure of protection for the insurance proceeds from the wife's and children's creditors.

The type of trust can also affect your selection. Because you can change a revocable trust at any time, you can be less concerned about which assets you transfer. If your objective is to provide for your own needs in the event of disability, then it may be advisable to fund the trust with some amount of liquid assets to facilitate immediate continuation of income if necessary. Remaining assets can be transferred by someone named as your agent (attorney-in-fact) under a durable power of attorney.

Where you are a resident of one state, and have a real property in another state (perhaps a vacation home), this property can be ideal to transfer to a trust. This may enable your estate to avoid a second (ancillary) probate proceeding in the second state.

CAUTION: Having real estate owned by a trust may not always enable you to avoid estate or inheritance tax in the state where the property is located. Check with a local tax adviser.

Always investigate the costs, and possible legal restrictions, on transferring assets to a trust. Real estate transfers may require transfer taxes, recording fees, mortgage or deed taxes, a new title insurance policy, and so forth.

Business and investment interests may have restrictions on transfer. For example, investment limited partnership interests may only be transferable with the consent of a general partner, which may be withheld for any reason. Stock interests may be restricted from transfer. Interests in a professional corporation (e.g., medical or law practice) may be prohibited from transfer by law. Don't despair, however, there may be more creative ways to address the issue. For example, while the interests in a professional practice may not be transferable, it may be possible to transfer the building in which the practice is located, the equipment, and perhaps other assets to a trust.

EXAMPLE: Terri Taxpayer is a doctor and quite concerned about the risk of expensive and unwarranted medical malpractice claims. She makes a gift of all her equipment and the building in which she operates her practice to an irrevocable trust for the benefit of her children. She then leases the equipment back from the trust at the current fair rental rate established by an independent appraisal. If the transfer is made sufficiently in advance of any claim, and the lease is on terms an unrelated party would accept, it may be possible that the assets held in the trust for her children will escape unscathed. Further, this plan may be advantageous from an estate-planning perspective by removing assets from Dr. Taxpayer's estate.

Whenever an irrevocable trust is involved, exercise caution since the transfer cannot be changed once it is signed. Before transferring assets to an irrevocable trust for the benefit of someone else (e.g., a child, grandchild, or other heir), be certain that, even in the worst case financial scenario, you will not need the assets in the future.

For certain tax-oriented trusts (grantor retained annuity trust, charitable remainder trust, etc.), it may be preferable to transfer income-producing assets in order to make the required annual payments. In these instances, careful selection of assets, based on your specific situation, is vital. Raw land may be inappropriate, whereas leased property may be ideal. However, if the raw land can be sold by a charitable remainder trust and the proceeds reinvested in a diversified income-producing portfolio, it may be an excellent asset to transfer. On the other hand, nonincome-producing assets can work well in these types of trusts where it is feasible to pay principal to the beneficiaries where current income is inadequate.

Finally, it is important to consider when your trust will be funded. Where the trust is established under your will, no steps are required (other than signing the will) before your death. Instead, the trust is formed following your death under the terms of your will. For such testamentary trusts, your executor may decide what assets to transfer to the trust after your death. It is generally advisable not to specify in your will which assets are to be transferred to which trusts, unless special circumstances necessitate it. Some testamentary trusts are funded by your will specifying a dollar amount (Chapters 7 and 11).

HOW TO TRANSFER ASSETS TO YOUR TRUST

Once you have decided which assets to transfer, you and your attorney must carry out the necessary legal steps and documentation based on the current ownership arrangements for each of the assets involved. The following discussion highlights some of the considerations. Since custom, practice, and law can vary from state to state, it is important to consult with an attorney in your area.

Real Estate

Real estate can be transferred to your trust by properly completing a quit claim or gift deed from the current owners to the trust. It is important to review your prior deed to verify the present owners and how their names appear. If you are not the sole owner, you will have to obtain the consent and signature of the other owners. Also, where there will be owners other than your trust, you should carefully consider how this will affect the management or use of the property.

EXAMPLE: You own 25 percent of a rental property. Three friends each own the remaining 25 percent interests. You gift this property interest to a trust for your partner. This trust will now own 25 percent of the property while your three friends will continue to own the remaining interests. There should be a partnership agreement between the four owners (i.e., the three friends and the trust) governing the ownership, use, financing, sale, and other aspects of the property.

There are several important ancillary considerations when transferring real estate:

- You may require a new title insurance policy in the name of the trust to retain coverage. Title insurance protects you against claims that you do not own the property (e.g., someone sues claiming he purchased a portion or all of the property in the past, or a utility company claims it has an easement (right of way) over your property). Whenever there is a transfer of title, the title company may require that the new owner purchase a new policy. You should be certain this matter has been properly resolved with the title company in advance and the costs considered.

- The liability and fire insurance policies must be properly amended to reflect the names of the new owner, your trust.
- Mortgage recording fees and taxes, real estate transfer taxes, and recording fees for the deed should all be considered. In some situations, the costs will be so significant that your planning may change.

CAUTION: Inquire whether the transfer of real estate to your trust may trigger a property tax reassessment. If your property is presently undervalued, this could result in a substantial increase in taxes.

- If there is also a mortgage on the property, you should have your lawyer review the mortgage and note that were signed. They will very likely require that the mortgage be repaid unless the lender consents otherwise. This may not be a simple matter to resolve. Many mortgages are sold, and often resold, in the secondary markets. Just identifying whom you should ask the question may take some legwork.
- You should also review any potential tax consequences with your accountant prior to the transfer.
- If you are using the property personally, you must sign a lease with the trust to retain the legal right to use the premises. You must pay a fair market rental for this use. Where the trust is a revocable living trust for your own benefit, a lease won't be necessary since for tax purposes you will continue to be treated as the owner of the property.
- The transfer of real estate to certain types of trusts may trigger environmental inspection and/or reporting rules.

Bank Accounts

You should simply contact your bank. They will provide you with the necessary forms, including signature cards. The bank will also probably ask to see the trust agreement. You will need to complete Form SS-4 to obtain a federal tax identification number for the trust to open a trust bank account (see Chapter 2). You will have to order new checks with the name of the trust. Also, it will be the trustee who will have to sign checks after the transfer of the account to the trust is complete. Ask the bank for details as to any formalities that they may require.

Securities

If you directly own stocks or bonds in your own name, you will have to contact the transfer agent for the security and obtain the necessary transfer forms, such as a stock power. Complete the forms and return them with the stock or bond certificates. The transfer agent will reissue the stock or bond certificates in the name of the trust.

CAUTION: Never send any original stock or bond certificate through regular mail. Always use certified mail, return receipt requested, so that you will have proper records in the event the securities do not arrive. Also, make photocopies of all documents before sending them.

For some transfers, you may be requested to provide a guarantee or verification of signature. This can be troublesome, particularly for the infirm seeking to establish a trust to manage their assets since this will require a separate trip to the bank.

NOTE: If you have a considerable number of securities, open a brokerage account and transfer the securities to the account. Once the securities are in an account in your name, it will be relatively easy for your broker to change the name of the entire account to the name of your trust. The broker, however, will likely require the documents previously noted for the transfer of bank accounts.

Partnership Interests

Partnership interests are transferred by signing an assignment of partnership interest form. A sample is reproduced in the For Your Notebook section at the end of this chapter. You must carefully review the partnership agreement prior to making any transfer. The agreement may prohibit any type of transfer, or may require the approval of some or all of the other partners. If the partnership is a limited partnership, you will probably have to receive the permission of the general partner. In some states, certificates of limited partnership must be filed at the state or county level. The partners, or the partnership agreement, may require that you pay the legal and filing fees to complete the necessary filings.

CAUTION: Carefully ascertain whether your attempted transfer of a partnership interest could trigger mandatory buyout provisions in the agreement. This is critical because some buyout agreements could require you to sell the partnership interest to the other partners. Other agreements simply prohibit any transfer. Verify with your tax adviser that your transfer, when aggregated with other recent transfers, will not cause a technical termination of the partnership agreement for federal income tax purposes. If it could, rethink the transfer to avoid adverse tax consequences.

Business Interests

The transfer of stock is accomplished by signing a stock power authorizing the transfer of the particular stock on the corporation's books. You will have to surrender your stock certificates. These will be canceled and retained by the corporation. The corporation will then issue new stock certificates in the name of your trust. The changes will be noted in the corporation's stock transfer ledger. In most closely held corporations, you will also have minutes of the board of directors, or a unanimous consent of all shareholders and directors, signed authorizing the transaction. The trustee will probably have to sign a copy of the corporation's shareholders' agreement, agreeing to be bound by its terms. The corporation may require a legal opinion that the trustee has the authority to invest in the stock.

Many of the considerations affecting the transfer of stock are similar to those affecting the transfer of partnership interests.

If the corporation is an S corporation, your trust must meet the strict requirements of a qualified subchapter S corporation trust (QSST) in order not to jeopardize the tax status of the corporation (see Chapter 18).

Furniture, Art, Jewelry, and Other Personal Property

A signed bill of sale demonstrates ownership of personal assets. If the transfer is a gift, a gift declaration is often signed as well. This is a statement, usually signed by the donor, witnessed and notarized, indicating that the transfer of the asset is a gift (rather than a sale or other type of transaction). This is particularly important where you wish to prove to the IRS that certain assets were transferred to the trust at a certain time and as a gift.

The preceding steps should be taken in addition to the listing of the assets of the trust in a schedule attached to your trust agreement. Some illustrative forms are provided in the For Your Notebook section following this chapter. Also, ask your accountant about any sales or personal property tax issue.

CONCLUSION

Selecting the right assets and then properly transferring them is critical if your trust is to accomplish the desired goals. Proper formalities must be observed to make the transfers effective. Most of these transfers will require the assistance of a professional (broker, accountant, real estate attorney, corporate attorney, or estate planner).

For Your Notebook:

NOTE: If you assign property of any nature to your trust for no consideration (i.e., as a gift), you should demonstrate your intent by preparing and signing a declaration of gift form similar to the following one. Consult with your tax adviser concerning any requirements to file a federal or state gift tax return. The IRS tax form is Form 709, which can be obtained from any IRS office or forms distribution center.

DECLARATION OF GIFT

SAMPLE ONLY — CONSULT A TAX AND ESTATE PLANNING ATTORNEY BEFORE USING ANY BILL OF SALE FORM

I, Sandy Taxpayer, hereby state and declare that:

1. I am a resident of the State of New Jersey, residing at 111 West State Street, Sometown, New Jersey.

2. I, Sandy Taxpayer, have this day executed a Bill of Sale to transfer 200 Shares of XYZ Corporation, Inc. common stock to John Taxpayer, Trustee of the Sandy Taxpayer Irrevocable Children's Trust, dated December 13, 1996, c/o John Taxpayer, 123 Main Street, Anytown, New York, valued at $9,850.00, by way of gift and without any consideration.

3. I declare under the penalties of perjury that the foregoing is true and correct and further declare that this Declaration of Gift is being executed this 27th day of December, 1996.

_____

Sandy Taxpayer, Donor

State of New Jersey   )
                             :   ss:
County of ABC   )

On this 27th day of December, 1996, before me personally came, Ms. Sandy Taxpayer, to me known and known to me to be the 111 West State Street, Sometown, New Jersey, individual described in and who executed the foregoing instrument, and she duly acknowledged to me that she understood the meaning of the instrument and that she executed the same.

_____

Notary Public

For Your Notebook:

NOTE: Where personal property (as opposed to real estate) is to be assigned to your trust, you should prepare and sign a bill of sale form similar to the following one. Legal publishers make standard forms available in office supply stores in most states. If the transfer is a gift, consider completing a declaration of gift form as well.

BILL OF SALE

SAMPLE ONLY — CONSULT A TAX AND ESTATE PLANNING ATTORNEY BEFORE USING ANY BILL OF SALE FORM

KNOW ALL MEN BY THESE PRESENTS, that MS. SANDY TAXPAYER, an individual who resides at 111 West State Street, City of Sometown, County of ABC, State of New Jersey (the "Donor") for and in consideration of the sum of $1.00 and as a gift to John Taxpayer, Trustee of the Sandy Taxpayer Irrevocable Children's Trust, dated December 13, 1992, c/o John Taxpayer, 123 Main Street, Anytown, New York (the "Donee"), has granted, transferred, and conveyed and by these presents does grant, transfer, and convey unto the said Donee, and said Donee's successors and assigns property as hereinafter described:

ALL THE RIGHT TITLE AND INTEREST in the following asset ("Asset"): 200 Shares of XYZ Corporation, Inc. common stock including all Donor's right, title, and interests in the Asset.

Donor hereby represents and warrants that she has good and marketable title to the Asset named hereinabove, subject to no liens, mortgages, security interests, encumbrances, or charges of any nature. This Bill of Sale has been executed to complete the gift contemplated herein. Nothing herein contained shall be deemed or construed to confer upon any person or entity other than Donee any rights or remedies by reason of this instrument.

TO HAVE AND TO HOLD the same unto the said Donee and the Donee's successors and assigns forever; and the Donor covenants and agrees to and with the said Donee to warrant and defend the said described Asset against all and every person or persons whomsoever.

IN WITNESS WHEREOF, the Donor has set her hand and seal to be hereto affixed this 27th day of December, 1996.

Sworn, Signed, Sealed, and Delivered
Sandy Taxpayer

_____

in the Presence of:

_____

Witness

For Your Notebook:

NOTE: Where an interest in a partnership is to be assigned to your trust, you should prepare and sign an assignment of partnership interest form similar to the following one. If the transfer is a gift, consider completing a declaration of gift form as well. Your attorney may also need to amend the certificate of partnership filed with the state. The trustee may also have to sign a partnership agreement indicating that the trust agrees to its terms.

ASSIGNMENT OF PARTNERSHIP INTEREST

SAMPLE ONLY — CONSULT A TAX AND ESTATE PLANNING ATTORNEY BEFORE USING ANY ASSIGNMENT FORM

I Sandy Taxpayer, who reside at 111 West State Street, Sometown, New Jersey, hereby assign by gift to John Taxpayer, Trustee of the Sandy Taxpayer Irrevocable Children's Trust, dated December 13, 1996, c/o John Taxpayer, 123 Main Street, Anytown, New York (the "Donee" or "Assignee"), a percentage interest in ABC Property Associates. The percentage interest hereby assigned is Twenty-Two percent (22%) of the total interests in the partnership. The value of this partnership interest is $2,785.00.

ASSIGNOR/DONOR:

_____ Date: December 21, 1996
Sandy Taxpayer

STATE OF NEW JERSEY   )
                                          : ss:
COUNTY OF ABC   )

On this 21st of December, 1996, before me personally came, Sandy Taxpayer, to me known and known to me to be the individual described in and who executed the foregoing instrument, and she duly acknowledged to me that she understood the meaning of the instrument and that she executed the same.

_____
Notary Public

[ATTACH APPRAISAL OF PARTNERSHIP INTEREST MADE NEAR DATE OF GIFT]

For Your Notebook:

NOTE: Where the asset involved is transferred over a period of more than one year, a schedule detailing the changing percentage of ownership should be attached. If a partial interest in a family partnership is to be transferred, this schedule could be attached to the partnership agreement for the family partnership, and to the gift declaration forms. Each year in which new transfers are made, a new schedule of ownership should be prepared until the intended percentages of ownership are achieved. A major reason for partial transfers over several years is to make gifts within the available $10,000 per person annual exclusions from the gift tax (Chapter 7).

SCHEDULE OF OWNERSHIP OF THE ASSET

SAMPLE ONLY — CONSULT AN ATTORNEY CONCERNING THIS FORM AND THE APPLICABLE PARTNERSHIP OR OTHER AGREEMENT

The following parties hereby own the following ownership interests in the Asset described in the Bill of Sale to which this Schedule is attached:

1. Sandy Taxpayer	78%
2. Sandy Taxpayer Irrevocable Children's Trust, dated December 13, 1992	22%
Total	100%

STATE OF NEW JERSEY   )
                                          :   ss:
COUNTY OF ABC   )

On this 21st day of December, 1996, before me personally came, Ms. Sandy Taxpayer, to me known and known to me to be the individual described in and who executed this schedule of partnership interests, and she duly acknowledged to me that she understood the meaning of the instrument and that she executed the same.

_____
Notary Public

4 GRANTOR'S RIGHTS AND POWERS

GRANTOR'S POWERS DETERMINE TYPE OF TRUST

When setting up a trust it is important to carefully review any right or power the grantor—the person(s) setting up the trust—will have under the trust agreement because these rights can dramatically affect tax consequences. The powers that the grantor should, or should not retain, will vary depending on the type of trust involved. Your power to revoke or modify your trust can only apply to living trusts (inter vivos trusts). Obviously, you cannot have any control over trusts established under your will (testamentary trusts) since these trusts are not formed until after your death. You always have the right to change your will, however, as long as you have sufficient awareness and ability (in legal terminology, *capacity*) to do so. Thus, even testamentary trusts can be changed prior to your death.

Your rights, as grantor, have significant legal, tax, and personal ramifications. The grantor may reserve the right to modify or revoke a trust, in whole or in part. The extent of these rights can affect both income taxes and the transfer taxes (gift, estate, and generation-skipping transfer). They could also be vital in determining the ability of creditors to reach the trust assets. In the following sections, the other powers that you can retain and still meet your goals are reviewed.

INCOME TAX CONSEQUENCES OF GRANTOR TRUST STATUS

When a trust is taxed as a grantor trust for income tax purposes, the income, gain, and losses of the trust are reported on the grantor's personal income tax return. Where the powers you as grantor retain over your trust are sufficient, the income earned by the trust will be taxed on your personal tax return, and not on a separate tax return filed by the trust (see Chapter 9). This type of trust is called a grantor trust.

Grantor trust status for income tax purposes is not always negative. For example, there generally will not be any income tax consequences to transactions between the grantor and the trust. Thus, if you transfer appreciated property (worth more than you paid at purchase) to a grantor trust, there will be no income tax cost to doing so.

The income tax consequences of grantor trust status can be independent of the estate tax consequences of the grantor's powers.

The option you prefer (grantor trust taxable to you, or non-grantor trust that files its own income tax return) will depend on the circumstances. You may even wish to intentionally structure a trust to be a grantor trust for income tax purposes, but not for gift and estate tax purposes. Consider the following:

- If a trust has significant tax deductions that you could claim on your personal tax return, you would want the trust to be a grantor's trust. A charitable lead trust can be structured to be a grantor trust to permit an income tax deduction on formation. This trust may then invest in tax-exempt bonds to avoid adverse income taxes in future years.

- If you set up a revocable living trust, it will have to be a grantor trust because you will probably wish to retain complete power over the assets. Thus, you will report all of the income from the trust on your personal tax return, which can significantly simplify the tax-reporting requirements (see Chapter 9).

- If you set up a Qualified Personal Residence Trust (QPRT, see Chapter 19), make certain it is a grantor trust so that if the trust sells the house you can qualify for the tax-deferred rollover provisions or the special exclusion of $125,000 for taxpayers over age 55 (Congress is considering adding greater capital gain exclusions for sales of residences).

NOTE: Tax results should not be the sole factor in determining the powers you, as grantor, retain over a trust you form. Be careful to consider your personal, financial, and other goals in the process. For example, if you are concerned about malpractice suits, you may prefer to severely restrict any rights you have to a particular trust to make it less likely for a claimant to be able to attack the trust. Under U.S. law, you generally cannot be a beneficiary of a trust that you establish (i.e., you are the grantor and fund the trust) and have the trust assets protected from creditors. The trust will be deemed a self-funded trust and courts will likely pierce it to satisfy claims. To accomplish the goal of protection, trusts may have to be established under foreign jurisdictions with more favorable laws.

ESTATE AND GIFT TAX CONSEQUENCES OF A GRANTOR TRUST

If your powers and rights in your trust exceed certain permissible limits, the assets of the trust will also be included in your estate for tax purposes. While the goal of the grantor in retaining sufficient powers is to have the trust treated as a grantor trust for income tax purposes, the grantor may not wish the trust treated as a grantor trust for estate tax purposes. Thus, the powers retained must not be so substantial so as to prevent the transfer of the assets to the trust from being deemed incomplete, and hence included in the grantor's estate. The option you prefer (grantor trust taxable to you, or nongrantor trust that files its own income tax return) will depend on the circumstances. Consider the following:

- You set up a foreign situs asset protection trust to protect assets. To avoid the 35 percent excise transfer on certain overseas transfers, you may wish to structure the trust so that the transfer of assets is not a completed gift. If this is done, the assets of the trust could be included in your estate (see Chapter 15).
- If you set up an insurance trust, or a trust for a child or grandchild, you will invariably wish those assets to be excluded from your estate. Therefore, you should be certain that your lawyer carefully drafts the trust to avoid tainting it with powers that would cause its inclusion in your estate.

WHAT MAKES A TRUST A GRANTOR TRUST?

If you, as the grantor, retain impermissible or excessive controls over the trust, the trust will be treated as a grantor trust for tax purposes. A trust can be classified as a grantor trust with respect to the principal portion of the trust or the income portion of the trust. The following are some of the factors that could cause a trust to be treated as grantor trust.

Grantor Trust Status Based on Reversionary Interest Greater than 5 Percent

If the grantor retains a reversionary interest in the corpus (principal) of the trust in excess of 5 percent, the trust will be characterized as a grantor trust with respect to the principal of the trust.

PLANNING CONSIDERATION: If the grantor does not meet this test and you wish to have the trust classified as a grantor trust, consider lengthening the trust term until the test is met.

Grantor Trust Status Based on Grantor's Right to Substitute Property

A common technique for qualifying a trust as a grantor trust with respect to its principal is to have the trust agreement give the grantor the right to substitute property of an equivalent value for the trust corpus (i.e., the securities held by a grantor retained annuity trust).

The grantor's retaining of the right to substitute property should result in the entire trust (i.e., the income and corpus components) being taxed to the grantor under the grantor trust rules. However, this power should not be sufficient to taint the transfer of assets to the trust as an incomplete gift for gift and estate tax purposes (i.e., the assets can still be removed from your estate).

For this power to be sufficient, however, it must be exercised by the grantor in "a nonfiduciary capacity" and without the consent of any fiduciary of the trust.

This power can also be given to a person other than the grantor, such as grantor's spouse, if the power is held in a nonfiduciary capacity. If the person holding the power is also a trustee of the trust, the presumption is that the power is held in a fiduciary capacity (i.e., that the power will not taint the trust as a grantor trust). If a nontrustee holds the power, then the determination whether the power is held in a nonfiduciary capacity depends on the terms of the trust agreement, and the facts and circumstances at the execution and later administration of the trust. The IRS has indicated that this determination will be based, in part, on an examination of the federal income tax return of the parties. Where there are minor beneficiaries, it may be inappropriate for any third party to take action that is not in the best interest of the minor beneficiaries without a court order approving it. This could affect the issue as to whether the grantor has acted in a capacity as other than a fiduciary. The IRS has indicated that it will not permit the use of this power to substitute property to make a QPRT taxable as a grantor trust. Therefore a 5 percent reversion could be used to achieve this result.

Grantor Trust Status Based on Grantor's Right to Appoint Trust Corpus

If the grantor retains a general power of appointment over the corpus of the trust, inclusive of capital gains, exercisable under grantor's will, the trust will be characterized as a grantor trust with respect to the trust principal.

GRANTOR'S RIGHT TO REVOKE OR MODIFY THE TRUST

Your right to modify, change, or revoke your trust will determine whether your trust is revocable or irrevocable. Revocability has profound tax and legal implications. Even if income or gift and estate taxes are not of primary concern, the legal repercussions are important. If your goal is to remove trust assets from the reach of creditors, or Medicaid and health care providers, your right to modify or revoke the trust will almost certainly defeat your efforts (see Chapters 15 and 16).

When establishing a revocable living trust to provide protection in the event of disability, or to avoid probate, it is almost always preferable for such a trust to be revocable (see Chapter 9).

The following sample trust provisions illustrate the type of clauses you can add to your trust.

SAMPLE TRUST PROVISIONS

Irrevocable Trust

> **NOTE:** The following type of provision is included in most insurance, children, grandchildren, GST, QSST, and other types of trusts. It is not included in a revocable living trust.

The Grantor has been advised with respect to the difference between revocable and irrevocable trusts and hereby declares that any trust formed under this Trust Agreement, and the Trust Estate created hereby, are to be irrevocable. The Grantor has no power to alter, amend, revoke, or terminate any Trust provision or interest whether under this Trust Agreement, or any rule of law. Grantor shall not have any reversionary interest in this Trust or the Trust Estate.

Not a Grantor Trust

> **NOTE:** The following paragraph is included in many irrevocable trusts. It is not included in a grantor retained annuity trust (GRAT), grantor retained uni-trust (GRUT), or qualified personal residence trust (QPRT). It is generally inappropriate for an irrevocable life insurance trust.

Notwithstanding anything in this Trust to the contrary, this Trust shall not be interpreted in a manner that would make this Trust a Grantor trust. The Grantor shall not be permitted to reacquire the property set forth in Schedule A attached hereto, or any other property transferred to this Trust after the execution of this Trust. This restriction shall apply notwithstanding the Grantor's offer to pay fair market value and full and adequate consideration for such property, or to offer replacement property therefore.

Revocable Trust

> **NOTE:** The following paragraph is included in a revocable living trust.

The Grantor has been advised with respect to the difference between revocable and irrevocable trusts and hereby declares that any trust formed under this Trust Agreement, and the Trust Estate created hereby, are to be revocable, so that Grantor, during Grantor's life, may change, amend, or modify, in any manner and to any extent, the provisions of this Trust Agreement. The Grantor has retained every right and power to alter, amend, revoke, or terminate any Trust provision or interest, whether under this Trust Agreement, or any rule of law. Grantor may revoke this Trust, or amend any provision of this Trust, by giving Notice to the Trustee. Such revocation or amendment shall be effective Five (5) business days after such Notice is properly dispatched to the Trustee.

Make sure to have a specific provision in you revocable living trust stating that it is revocable. Under the laws of many states, if your trust doesn't specify that it is revocable, then it will, by law, be treated as irrevocable. The preceding recommended provision includes a procedure for the grantor to amend or revoke the trust. A provision included in the miscellaneous provision of the trust will define the specific procedures required to give notice. The purpose is to give the trustees reasonable notice, and a sufficient time, so that they do not unknowingly contradict the grantor's actions.

What can you do if you created an irrevocable trust and circumstances change so dramatically that you really have to change the trust? It may be possible, if every person with any interest in the trust (grantor, trustees, current beneficiaries, remainder beneficiaries, and perhaps even certain contingent beneficiaries) agrees to your proposal. This, however, is not a simple matter to achieve, and it may take an expensive court proceeding to do so, especially if minor children are beneficiaries. Never rely on this approach at the outset as an affirmative planning tool. If you are not certain that the trust should be irrevocable, consider alternatives to an irrevocable trust.

TIP: In some instances, a family limited partnership (FLP) or a limited liability company (LLC) can accomplish similar objectives to a trust without having to be irrevocable. The agreement governing the FLP or LLC can be changed by the partners or members, respectively, so long as the terms of the agreement are met (e.g., a requirement that at least two thirds of the partners or members approve a particular change). Using these entities, the parent or donor can retain substantial control as the general partner in the FLP, or as the manager in an LLC.

Before agreeing to make your trust irrevocable, consider the following:

• Are you confident in the ability of the trustees and the successor trustees named in the trust agreement to carry out their duties in a professional manner? This problem can sometimes be remedied through rethinking the trustees. For example, perhaps you can name an institution and an individual as co-trustees.

• Have the needs of the beneficiaries been adequately provided for? If the trust is not permitted to pay more than income to the current beneficiary, what will happen if that beneficiary suffers an unforeseen calamity, such as disability? Where a trust is irrevocable, and adequate safeguards and discretion have not been built in, tremendous hardship can result. This is why it is so important to ask many "what-if" questions when planning a trust, and to make the distribution provisions as flexible as appropriate to address future uncertainties.

• Can you and those for whom you are responsible afford to live comfortably and handle any emergencies that may arise for the remainder of your lives if you make gifts to irrevocable trusts for children or other heirs?

CAUTION: Too often parents, aunts, uncles, and other seniors are pushed hard by future heirs to establish trusts for the heirs' benefits to remove assets from the seniors' taxable estates, save taxes, and perhaps protect against possible future costs of a long-term illness. Once the assets are transferred to a trust, the senior has no further control. Don't set up such a trust unless you are truly comfortable doing so, and under even the worst case scenario, you will be left with sufficient resources to support your lifestyle. No senior can relish the thought of having to ask a child, niece, nephew, or other heir for money. Don't!

- Will marriage, divorce, or other major family events require changing the trust to conduct basic business matters or provide for basic living needs? But then again, properly set up irrevocable trusts are one of the best techniques to protect assets from the claims of a divorced spouse.

EXAMPLE: An obstetrician, concerned about malpractice risks, transfers every asset he owns, except his practice, to an irrevocable trust for his wife who is a homemaker and thus does not face any particular risk of creditors or other claimants. He even transfers all of the equipment and the office building used by his practice to a trust for his children. He then enters into a lease agreement to rent the equipment from the trust. The trustee of both trusts is an independent trust company, Bigbank. The trusts, in addition to being irrevocable, do not provide any right to the trustee to distribute any income, or principal to the obstetrician. Trust distributions can only be made to the wife, and after the wife's death to the children (and only for expenses that are not the obligation of the obstetrician under local law) under her trust. Distributions can only be made to the children under their trust.

The wife and the obstetrician husband divorce. He has virtually no assets as a result of the trust arrangements. To terminate the trust will require the consent of an independent trust company (which may view the premature termination as violating its fiduciary obligations to the minor children), the wife (who, unless forced to do so by the courts is unlikely to be interested in providing assets to her ex-husband), and the children. How can the minor children consent to termination of the trust? A court proceeding may be required with the court appointing a guardian to act on behalf of the interests of the children. What about the interests of any unborn child? How can they be protected? Even if termination of this trust is possible, which it probably will not be, it will be an expensive and time-consuming task.

When determining whether your trust is revocable or irrevocable, remember that on your death the trust becomes irrevocable. Further, if you are disabled, you may no longer have the legal capacity to revoke your trust, and at that point, it will become irrevocable. It is important to have a provision in your trust defining when you should be considered disabled. Finally, every trust you establish may have several trusts incorporated in its trust agreement. For example, if you establish a revocable living trust to manage your affairs in the event of disability, and to avoid probate, that trust may include a credit shelter trust, a Q-TIP trust, and so forth. These trusts, included in your revocable living trust agreement will become effectively irrevocable on your death. So even though the main trust is revocable, it still can include trusts that are more commonly considered irrevocable.

SHOULD THE GRANTOR SERVE AS A TRUSTEE OR CO-TRUSTEE?

Where your trust is revocable, there is no particular disadvantage from a tax perspective for you to serve as a trustee; a revocable trust will probably have no tax advantages in any event. For many tax-oriented trusts intentionally structured as grantor trusts (e.g., QPRT, GRAT, etc.), you may wish to serve as a trustee or co-trustee.

Serving as trustee gives you a measure of control over trust affairs and the trust assets. If you are disabled, you will not be able to serve as a trustee and your successor trustees will take over management. If one goal of setting up your trust is to provide for current management assistance, you may wish to have another person serve as sole trustee, or at least as co-trustee, to obtain this assistance.

Where your trust is irrevocable and not one of the tax-oriented grantor trusts noted earlier—and particularly where a goal of establishing your trust is to move assets beyond the reach of creditors or malpractice claimants—you should generally not serve as trustee or even as co-trustee. Where, for tax or legal purposes, it is inappropriate for you to serve as trustee, your spouse should probably also not serve as trustee. This is because your spouse is not considered an adverse party. Thus, any adverse tax consequences that would occur if you were a trustee could also occur if your spouse held that position. There are, however, exceptions. It may be possible for you, or your spouse, to serve as trustee where the powers and rights as trustee are carefully restricted. For example, your rights to appoint trust income or principal may be limited to appointing income or principal to persons other than yourself.

Where legal considerations, rather than tax considerations are paramount, the conclusions can differ. Depending on the laws of your state, and the goals of your trust, it may be possible to have your spouse serve as trustee of your trust and still achieve certain of your goals. Review the decision with your attorney, however, before making any final decision since the risks can be substantial.

CAN THE GRANTOR CHANGE OR APPOINT A TRUSTEE?

Where your trust is revocable, you will probably serve as trustee. Reserving the right to change or remove trustees is not a problem with a revocable trust since the trust is revocable by you in any event. Since most revocable trusts are not formed primarily for tax benefits, reserving this right should not create any problem.

Irrevocable trusts present a more complex situation. If you have no power or right in your trust other than to change trustees at your discretion, you may defeat the objectives of setting up your trust. An unrestricted right to remove existing trustees at your sole discretion can be interpreted as giving you complete control over the trust since you could dismiss any trustee who doesn't perform exactly as you wish. For tax purposes, your right to remove trustees without restriction will be treated as if you have retained the rights of a trustee yourself. This could defeat any tax objectives you had for the trust. It would probably also make it much easier for creditors to reach trust assets. If, however, your right to replace a trustee is properly restricted, you can have a limited right to do so without losing the hoped-for benefits.

In some trusts, an institutional fiduciary is named as sole trustee, or perhaps as a co-trustee with a family member or friend. Often, an institutional fiduciary might be appropriate (due to a lack of qualified friends or relatives, the long duration of the trust, etc.) but is not named because of a perceived fear that institutional fiduciaries will provide poor or insensitive service. An alternative approach to address these concerns is to vest in the grantor a limited right to remove and replace the institutional fiduciary. If the IRS deems the power to remove is too broad, however, the corpus of the trust could be included in the estate of the grantor.

The grantor's reserved power to replace a corporate trustee can be limited to naming a successor corporate trustee. As long as the corporate trustee is independent from the grantor, this power will not taint the tax benefits of the trust and will not cause the trust corpus to be included in the grantor's estate. To be independent of the grantor, any successor trustee must be an entity other than the grantor or any firm or corporation in which the grantor has an interest, and it should, in all events, be an independent corporate trust company. To be conservative for tax purposes, the grantor may decide to have such a power only where the trust permits distributions in accordance with an ascertainable standard, or the grantor should only be permitted to remove the trustee for cause.

SAMPLE TRUST PROVISION: It shall be permissible for Grantor, not more frequently than once in any twenty-four (24) month period, to remove any institutional Trustee if one should then be serving, any Trustee then serving, for an Independent Trustee which is also an institution, bank, or other professional fiduciary.

CONCLUSION

The trust you intend to establish should meet your nontax needs and goals as well as the tax issues identified by your estate planner. Where your trust is revocable, you have more freedom to retain whatever rights you wish without affecting the tax results. Where tax issues are important, you will generally be best served by severely limiting any rights you retain over your trust. Where protection of assets is important, you will face rapidly changing laws and complex regulations that govern the rights you can retain. Be certain to review these with your attorney before completing your trust.

5 BENEFICIARY DESIGNATIONS AND RIGHTS

Beneficiaries, the persons or organizations to receive the income and principal of the trust, are one of the five essential elements to a trust (see Chapter 1). You need to resolve several issues concerning beneficiaries to achieve your goals in establishing a trust. Beneficiaries must be clearly designated, and you must determine how and when they should receive distributions. Contingent beneficiaries should be named in the event the primary beneficiaries are not alive when distributions are to be made, or do not wish to accept the benefits the trust bestows on them. When done properly, this can provide important planning flexibility to the beneficiaries.

EXAMPLE: You leave $50,000 to your aunt, Kate Smith. If Aunt Kate dies, this $50,000 would be distributed as part of your "residuary estate" under your will, or under a comparable provision under your trust, perhaps called "Alternative Distribution." These are backstop provisions that address where assets should be distributed if all prior provisions in the document lapse as a result of the death of the beneficiaries (or their unwillingness to accept the distributions). Perhaps if Aunt Kate died, you would prefer that her husband or surviving children receive the money. This can be accomplished with the following more detailed provision: "$50,000 to my aunt, Kate Smith, who resides at 555 Main Avenue, City Name, State Name. If she shall not survive Grantor's death, to her surviving spouse. If she has no surviving spouse, then to her children in equal shares. If any child is not then living, or disclaims such bequest, to the then living issue of such child, per stirpes. If there be no living issue, then this legacy shall lapse." The preceding provision adds planning flexibility. If Aunt Kate and her husband do not need the money, they can file a disclaimer (renunciation) in the appropriate court. This will have the legal effect as if they had died before you, so that they can cause the $50,000 to be distributed to their children. If a child is, for example, concerned about being sued, he too can file a disclaimer, causing the assets to pass to his children. See the discussion of GST tax in Chapter 7.

Finally, certain powers and rights can be given to the beneficiaries depending on your objectives and the nature of the trust.

NAMING BENEFICIARIES OF YOUR TRUST

It is often obvious who should be the primary beneficiaries of your trust. Even so, the decision is more complex than most people realize, and can trigger tax or other issues that are easily overlooked.

Revocable Living Trust

If you are setting up a revocable living trust to provide for the management of your assets if you become disabled, you will be the primary beneficiary. You may, however, permit other persons to be beneficiaries as well (spouse, children, etc.). Because such distributions will likely constitute gifts for gift tax purposes, a gift tax may be due if the distributions are to people other than your spouse and exceed $10,000.

You will also name beneficiaries to receive the trust assets after your death: your family, loved ones, friends, a favorite charity, or anyone else you select. Quite likely, it may be a combination of trusts that you name as beneficiaries. This could include a credit shelter trust to sprinkle income among your spouse and children while taking advantage of the unified credit available to your estate, a marital or Q-TIP trust for your surviving spouse that will take advantage of the unlimited marital deduction, and trusts for children or other heirs to protect their inheritances until they reach more appropriate ages for distribution. Thus, you, your spouse, and your children could all be beneficiaries. The issues that affect the determination of beneficiaries of these other trusts will then also affect your revocable living trust.

Trust for Spouse

When setting up a trust for your spouse, or other partner, as described in Chapters 11 and 12, your spouse or other partner will be the primary beneficiary. If the trust is a credit shelter trust to take advantage of the unified credit available to your estate, you may wish to name children or other heirs as beneficiaries along with your spouse. This can provide greater flexibility without sacrificing any tax benefit. However, if the trust is intended to benefit your spouse and take advantage of the unlimited marital deduction, you cannot name anyone other than your spouse to receive income or you will jeopardize the important tax benefits (see Chapter 11).

If the person is not a spouse, but rather a partner, the marital deduction will not be available. You must then carefully plan with your tax adviser to address this.

How do you specify who your spouse will be? In most cases, you will name your spouse ". . . to my wife, Jane Doe . . ." in the trust. However, with the divorce rate exceeding 50 percent, perhaps you would rather use what is called a floating spouse clause. This approach to preparing a trust has whichever person you are married to at the relevant time (e.g., your spouse at the time of your death) defined as your spouse.

In a credit shelter trust (but not a Q-TIP or Q-DOT trust, which are intended to qualify for the unlimited marital deduction), you could provide that in the event of divorce your ex-spouse would cease being a beneficiary (or trustee).

The preceding planning allows you to establish an irrevocable trust while preserving some flexibility if divorce or remarriage occurs.

For most marital trusts mentioned previously, the trust will terminate only on the death of your spouse or partner. Thus, you must carefully designate who the successor or contingent beneficiaries will be.

Trust for Children or Other Heirs

In any trusts for your descendants (issue), your children or grandchildren will be beneficiaries. You must carefully delineate who is to be considered a child. Is a person who is adopted a child for purposes of making distributions from the trust? What about a child born after the trust is established? What happens if a child dies before all distributions are made from the trust? Who should receive the deceased child's share? His or her own children? Your other children (i.e., the siblings of the deceased child)?

EXAMPLE: You name your children as beneficiaries of a trust, but something totally unexpected happens years later: You have another child. Is that child to be a beneficiary? It depends on the language used in the trust. If the trust says ". . . my children Dick Doe and Jane Doe, only," a future child may not be covered. To plan for this contingency, the trust might state, ". . . my children, Dick, Jane, and Tom, and any later-born children."

What if you adopt a child after setting up a trust for your natural children? Is the adopted child to be included? An appropriate provision might be "My children Dick, Jane, and Tom, and any later-born or adopted children."

Trust for Charity

When you are forming a charitable trust, as described in Chapter 14, qualifying charities will be among your beneficiaries. Often, when naming charitable beneficiaries, there is a presumption that the charity qualifies for an unlimited gift or estate tax charitable contribution deduction. For some inter vivos trusts, the income tax charitable contribution deduction, where you are seeking a current income tax deduction such as a charitable remainder trust, is similarly important. If this deduction is essential for your planning, verify when establishing the trust that the charity is qualified. Call the charity and confirm the name and principal business address (these can sometimes differ from the common public names) and request a copy of the letter the charity received from the IRS approving tax-exempt status. Save this with your permanent trust papers.

EXAMPLE: You name a charity as a beneficiary, "The sum of $70,000 to the ABC charity located at 123 Main Street, City Name, State Name, for its general purposes," but the charity ceases to operate. Now ABC is defunct. Instead you could stipulate: "The sum of $70,000 to the ABC charity located at 123 Main Street, City Name, State Name, for its general purposes, or to its successor. In the event that such charity no longer exists, or no longer qualifies for the gift and estate tax unlimited charitable contribution deduction, to the DEF charity located at 456 State Street, City Name, State Name, for its general purposes, or to its successor. In the event that charity no longer exists to a charitable organization named at the discretion of my trustee which has a similar purpose and which does qualify for the gift and estate tax unlimited charitable contribution deduction."

A legal doctrine called *cy press* can act to preserve an intended charitable bequest. But it is always preferable to name alternatives. The following clause may also help avoid an unintended problem, or lapse, in a hoped-for charitable gift.

SAMPLE TRUST/WILL PROVISION: Where one of the above organizations is subject of a mere change in name, or merger into a successor charitable organization serving substantially the same purposes, such organization shall be considered to exist and the gift and bequest above shall not lapse.

When discussing with your attorney the provisions of your trust that relate to charitable gifts, be certain to address the tax qualification issue as well as the naming of successors. Also, determine which assets should be used to fund the charitable bequests. There can be advantages to using Individual Retirement Account (IRA) or other pension plan assets to fund your charitable gifts.

CAUTION: Where charitable trusts are being formed under your will, have your estate planner carefully review the tax allocation clause of your will. This clause governs which bequests and assets bear the federal and state estate and inheritance tax. Because charitable contributions are deductible, you will generally not wish them to bear any tax cost. If they do, you will reduce the amount of charitable deduction by the tax paid, hence increasing the tax cost. The result is a circular calculation and often not the economic result you want. If your plan is best served by a charity bearing a portion of the tax, consider adding the following statement to the tax allocation clause of your will "I require this allocation with full knowledge that this allocation will reduce the bequest to my children and any institution which does not qualify for a charitable deduction."

SAMPLE WILL PROVISION: Any organization which receives a bequest under my residuary estate, and which organization does not qualify for the unlimited estate tax charitable contribution deduction, shall pay from such bequest (and I direct and authorize my Executor to withhold such amount from the distribution pursuant to such bequest) its allocable share of estate and other tax. Such tax shall be calculated on a marginal basis, and not on an average basis.

For those of us fortunate enough to have an estate tax problem, and an estate of such size that distributions must be carefully planned, bequests to charities offer one last opportunity to contribute something back to society and to make a final positive and helpful statement. Charitable bequests under a will or as part of a trust also can send an important message to your heirs. Don't overlook these vital nontax aspects of charitable giving.

SAMPLE TRUST PROVISION: When my child, Joan Smith, attains the age of 35 years, the Trustee shall distribute 95 percent of the trust estate to my child, outright and free of further trust, and the remaining 5 percent of the trust estate to XYZ Charity, for its general purposes, in honor of Joan Smith. It is my hope and desire that the charitable portion of this distribution set an example for Joan and encourage her further and continued charitable involvement in the years to come.

HOW SHOULD ASSETS BE DIVIDED AMONG BENEFICIARIES?

If you set up a trust for a single child, the division of assets at the primary level of the trust (i.e., when the child who is the primary beneficiary is alive) is quite simple. Assets will be distributed to that child. In many cases, however, the distribution mechanism must be more complex to accomplish your goals. For example, if the child is no longer alive or reaches a specified age and his or her interests in the trust terminate, alternate beneficiaries will have to receive the trust assets. How should assets be distributed to a list of alternate or successor beneficiaries? If these provisions are not carefully drafted, tremendous complications could ensue as a court may have to be involved to sort out who gets what.

Apart from the common mistake of not listing enough beneficiaries and clarifying when successors should receive the bequests, another common problem is phrasing the distributions in a manner that cannot work if circumstances change.

EXAMPLE: You contemplate funding a trust with $1 million. After your death, $100,000 will be distributed to each of your four nieces and nephews, and the remainder to your partner, your primary heir. Your anticipation is that your partner would receive $600,000. First, this distribution scheme does not contemplate the effects of estate tax. If a $150,000 tax is paid out of the trust, your partner will not receive what you anticipated. Second, what happens if your estate declines? If, say, it drops to $500,000 and your partner was your primary concern, he or she will end up with little. Not your goal.

When preparing distribution provisions always ask "what if" questions. What if the size of the estate or trust increases significantly? What if it decreases? How will expenses and taxes affect the distributions? One alternative is to set limits on dollar bequests so that they do not consume your primary bequests.

SAMPLE TRUST PROVISION: One Hundred Thousand Dollars ($100,000) to *PECUNIARY RECIPIENT-1 [e.g., name of niece, or other beneficiary], or such beneficiary's issue, per stirpes, if such beneficiary is deceased. However, in no event shall this bequest exceed *PERCENTAGE-1 LIMIT of the trust estate at the date of my death.

Another common problem is drafting your trust to make distributions by percentages. Say you have four cousins you are leaving the trust assets to following your death. If your trust says "Distribute 25 percent to Jane Doe, 25 percent to Tim Smith, 25 percent to Joe Perez, and 25 percent to Susan Chen," what happens if Tim Smith is not alive? Have you only distributed 75 percent of your trust? What happens with the remaining 25 percent? A better approach is to divide the trust estate into shares and subshares. If one or more of the bequests lapses (e.g., by the beneficiary dying or disclaiming), there is no issue as to the distribution of the assets. The math works.

SAMPLE TRUST PROVISION: Upon my death, the Trustee shall divide the trust estate into the equal number of shares required by this provision, and distribute such shares outright, free of trust to the persons named below. Should any such bequest lapse, then the remaining persons listed shall continue to share in the trust estate in the proportions set forth. The number of shares into which the trust estate shall be divided shall be the number of shares for those beneficiaries listed below, which bequests have not lapsed by the death, disclaimer or other failure of such beneficiaries named. The following beneficiaries shall take under this provision:

(1) Three and one-half (3.5) shares shall be paid to my son John Smith.

(2) Three (3) shares shall be paid to my daughter Jane Doe.

(3) One (1) share shall be allocated to my grandchildren, (the "Grandchildren's Share") to be disposed of by the provision entitled "Grandchildren Pot Trust," below.

(4) One (1) share to be divided into the number of equal subshares into which such amount shall be divided shall be the number of shares for those charitable beneficiaries listed below. The following beneficiaries shall take under this provision:

i) One (1) subshare to UJA of Bergen County and North Hudson, New Jersey, doing business at 111 Kinderkamack Road, River Edge, New Jersey.

ii) One (1) subshare to the Jewish National Fund, (Keren Kayemeth Leisrael), Inc., a not-for-profit corporation.

A little extra care and planning in designing the appropriate distribution scheme for your trust can assure that your distributions are made the way you want, to the people or causes you want, and with the least expense and time delays. The bit of extra time and legal fees to have the provisions completed properly and thoroughly at the outset, and to run through various hypothetical "what if" scenarios, can be of tremendous benefit to your intended heirs.

HOW SHOULD THE BENEFICIARIES RECEIVE THEIR DISTRIBUTIONS?

It is not enough to merely make sure the right people or organizations receive the distributions from your trust. They must receive them at the right time. This is one of the most complicated and often ignored aspects of trust preparation. It is ignored because it cannot be done in isolation. You must review your entire estate plan, including all trusts, will distribution provisions, gift planning, and the like to properly address how distributions should be made. The most difficult aspect, however, is that you must ask the tough questions. "How will the distribution of money affect my child [nephew/heir]?" "Am I giving too much too fast so that I will impair the heir's motivation to become a productive individual?" "Am I being so controlling that my child or other heir will never develop the maturity necessary to best handle the money involved?" "Am I being so stingy that my child will resent me forever?" These are not easy questions. Most estate planners do not address these personal imperatives. The answers can hurt! But if you do not carefully address these issues, all the best tax and legal planning will be for naught.

EXAMPLE: A child has received such large gifts from his grandparents, and such significant distributions from the trust his parents have set up, he has never bothered completing college, obtaining a job, doing volunteer charitable work, or making any productive contribution to society. What difference does it make how much tax has been saved? Lack of forethought has perhaps destroyed the child whose welfare was the very goal of the family. Perhaps it would have been better had the grandparents made their gifts in trust and had distributions withheld. Perhaps for this particular child (but not necessarily for his siblings), certain distributions should have been made contingent on completion of a semester of college courses with a specified minimum grade-point average.

EXAMPLE: A wealthy family establishes a Qualified Personal Residence Trust (QPRT) for their house for a 12-year period. They also established a 15-year Grantor Retained Annuity Trust three years ago. The insurance trust and trusts for their child under their will provide that all assets be distributed to the child at age 25, which they believe to be an age of sufficient maturity to handle assets. This plan could result in every trust and thus all of the child's inheritances, being received in a single year. Is this prudent? What if the child is sued, divorces, or has an emotional breakdown? Would it not be more prudent to coordinate each trust, and the will, at the planning stage, to spread out the distributions? This would allow the child to acclimate to handling ever larger sums of money, rather than an avalanche all at one time. If there is a suit, divorce, or other difficulty, the assets then remaining in trust will still be protected.

Should a minor (whether your child, grandchild, a niece or nephew, or other heir) receive a distribution of a substantial sum of money on your death? Probably not. How should "minor" be defined? Just because someone is 18 and can vote, does not mean the person has the maturity and knowledge to manage tens or hundreds of thousands of dollars. This is why most trusts provide that children (or adults) under a certain age will receive their distributions through a trust. The income and principal should be distributed in a calculated manner that assures proper care of the beneficiary, while giving the beneficiary reasonable opportunity to acclimate to handling the responsibilities of money.

Any beneficiary who is disabled and unable to handle their financial affairs should have their share distributed into a further trust for their benefit. These important issues are explored in Chapter 13.

Income tax considerations also affect the distribution provisions. Because trust income can be taxed at the marginal tax rates quite quickly, many trusts provide for the distribution of income to the beneficiaries (see Chapter 7).

TAX CONSEQUENCES OF BENEFICIARY'S POWERS OVER THE TRUST

Many trusts are set up for tax benefits. For example, the credit shelter trust (also called a bypass trust) discussed in Chapter 11 is designed to keep a portion of your estate out of the taxable estate of your surviving spouse. The objective is to use up as much as possible of your unified credit (which exempts $600,000 of assets from estate tax) and give your surviving spouse substantial interest in the trust as a beneficiary, but without having the assets (corpus) of the trust included in your surviving spouse's estate. How much control can you give your surviving spouse, as a beneficiary of the credit shelter trust, without having the IRS consider the control sufficient to tax the trust assets in her estate? A similar question affects the beneficiaries of many different types of trusts.

If a beneficiary is to be the trustee of a trust, several precautions should be considered. (Because this issue is so technical, be certain to review it with an estate tax specialist.) If a beneficiary is made trustee, the right to be trustee should not apply to making decisions concerning the distribution of income or property to himself or herself. This can be accomplished by having the beneficiary serve as a co-trustee with an independent trustee (e.g., a bank trust department). The bank will then be given the sole authority concerning decisions to make distributions to the co-trustee who is also a beneficiary. The co-trustee who is a beneficiary will be prohibited from making these decisions. Another option to discuss with your estate planner is limiting the distributions to maintaining the standard of living of the beneficiary (an "ascertainable standard"). Some attorneys prefer both restrictions. Thus, only the independent trustee can make distributions, and only to maintain the standard of living of the beneficiary.

BENEFICIARY DESIGNATIONS AND RIGHTS

As noted, an additional precaution is that the right to make distributions to her can be limited to an ascertainable standard, so as to maintain her health, education, and welfare in accordance with her accustomed standard of living. Although this right can be given to a beneficiary also serving as a trustee without tax problems, and should be sufficient to assure that the beneficiary's standard of living is maintained, some estate planners prefer a more restrictive approach.

TAX PLANNING FOR THE POWERS GIVEN TO BENEFICIARIES

Beneficiary Crummey Power Withdrawal Right

When setting up a trust that may receive later contributions (gifts) of property or cash, and where tax considerations will be important, it is critical to structure the trust so that such gifts will qualify for the annual $10,000 gift tax exclusion. Any contributions that do not qualify will use up a portion of your once-in-a-lifetime unified credit ($600,000 exclusion), and once that is used up, the gifts will trigger a gift tax cost. These concepts are explained in Chapter 7.

One solution to this potential dilemma is to include in your trust an annual demand power (called a *Crummey power* after the court case where it was recognized). This power permits your beneficiaries a limited right to withdraw an amount each year equal to the amount of gift made to the trust. When properly handled, this can enable gifts to the trust to qualify for the annual gift tax exclusion.

In this approach, following the donor's gift to the trust, the trustee must give written notice to the beneficiary of the amount the beneficiary can withdraw from the trust. If the beneficiary does not exercise this right within the prescribed time period, say 30 to 60 days, the money or property then remains part of the trust to be distributed as provided under the general trust terms.

Beneficiaries' Power of Appointment to Avoid Generation-Skipping Transfer Tax

When planning for a large estate where transfers to grandchildren are involved, the generation-skipping transfer (GST) tax can be a major concern (see Chapter 8). When assets are transferred to certain types of trusts for which the only beneficiaries are grandchildren (in tax jargon, "skip persons"), a substantial GST tax could be incurred. This tax can be planned for in several ways. First, if the trust is properly structured (see Chapters 7 and 13), annual exclusion gifts of $10,000 to a trust for a single grandchild may remain exempt. In other instances, it can be beneficial to allocate some portion of your $1 million GST exclusion to the trust so that all assets in the trust will remain GST exempt (see Chapter 7).

Another approach to avoid the GST tax relates to the powers the beneficiaries are given under the trust. In this arrangement, you give your children (who are not skip persons for GST tax purposes) the right to appoint the principal of the trust under their wills. Although the children may or may not be actual beneficiaries, this right can be an important planning step for the grandchildren who are beneficiaries. This right (called a general power of appointment) causes the assets of the trust to be included in your children's estate for estate tax purposes (i.e., their estate tax). This will prevent the transfer from being subject to the GST tax. While this GST savings will be at the cost of having the assets taxed in your children's estate, it can be less costly overall.

SAMPLE TRUST PROVISION: (The following illustrates a power of appointment.)

Upon the death of such Child, the Trustee shall transfer the principal of the trust to such persons other than Child, or his or her estate, but including his or her creditors and the creditors of his or her estate, to such extent, in such amounts or proportions, and in such lawful interests or estates, whether absolute or in trust, as such Child may by his or her last will and testament appoint by a specific reference to this power.

Beneficiaries' Limited Right to Replace a Trustee

Another power that a beneficiary can be given under a trust is a limited right to replace a corporate trustee with a successor corporate trustee. The beneficiary's unrestricted right to remove the corporate trustee without notice and replace it with another independent corporate trustee should not cause the trust corpus to be included in the beneficiary's estate. It is important that the institutional trustee be completely independent from the beneficiary having this power.

CAUTION: If you are setting up a trust for children or other beneficiaries, do you really want them to have an unrestricted right to change trustees? Will this cause the beneficiaries to go "trustee shopping" to find the trustee most likely to give them what they want? Will this undermine the trustees' ability to carry out your wishes and instructions as indicated in the trust agreement (and perhaps in your meetings with the trust company and in side letters further detailing your wishes)?

Although perhaps no longer necessary from a tax perspective, some parents and other grantors prefer to restrict when a beneficiary can change trustees. One approach is to only permit the beneficiary to change the trustee for a valid reason, as specified in a clause of the trust. Many of these reasons were listed in a prior IRS private letter ruling and may still serve as a useful starting point.

SAMPLE TRUST CLAUSE

By a unanimous vote of all current income beneficiaries, or by the written Notice of Grantor (where the successor institutional Trustee is independent of Grantor), it shall be permissible to remove an institutional Trustee, if one should then be serving, for "cause," as defined by the following thirteen factors:

1. The legal incapacity of a trustee.

2. The willful or negligent mismanagement of the trust's assets.

3. The abuse or abandonment of, or inattention to, the trust.

4. A federal or state charge involving the commission of a felony or serious misdemeanor.

5. An act of stealing, dishonesty, fraud, embezzlement, moral turpitude, or moral degeneration.

6. The use of narcotics or excessive use of alcohol.

7. The poor health such that the trustee is physically, mentally, or emotionally unable to devote sufficient time to administer the trust.

8. The failure by the trustee to comply with a written fee agreement or other written agreement in the operation of the Trust.

9. The failure of a corporate trustee to appoint a senior officer with at least five (5) years of experience in the administration of trusts to handle the trust account.

10. Changes by a corporate trustee in the account officer responsible for handling the trust account more frequently than every five (5) years (unless such change is made at the request of or with the acquiescence of the other trustee).

11. The relocation by a trustee away from the location where the trust operates so as to interfere with the administration of the trust.

12. A demand from the trustee for unreasonable compensation for such trustee's services.

13. Any other reason for which a court of competent jurisdiction in the State, would remove a trustee.

Without some reasonable assurance of an opportunity to manage the trust for a time period that becomes economically feasible, an institutional trustee may be reluctant to accept the trust's business. There are substantial up-front costs for an institution to accept a trust. Many institutions will want to have trust officers personally meet all current beneficiaries and spend considerable time getting to know them and understanding their needs. The trust agreement will have to be reviewed carefully to understand the limitations and requirements the new institutional trustee will face. Finally, the financial accounts will have to be transferred in from the current trustee to the new institution. This all takes time and expense. If the institution is not assured of the business from the trust for a reasonable period, it may be reluctant to make this investment. Thus, to best protect the beneficiaries of the trust, consider some limitations on a power to remove the trustee.

Another approach (which could be combined with the restriction on the beneficiaries of having to show cause to change a trustee) is to limit the number of times a beneficiary can change a trustee. For example, "Removal and replacement of an institutional Trustee shall only be permitted once in any Twenty-Four (24) month period by the current income beneficiaries."

Beneficiaries' Right to Withdraw $5,000 or 5 Percent of Principal

A final area of power or rights of the beneficiaries that you must consider is whether to give a beneficiary the absolute call or right to demand, without limitation, some amount of money from a trust.

You may be concerned that if a person you named as beneficiary needs additional money, the trustee may not provide it. Therefore, you want the beneficiary to have the right to demand distribution of some amount of money each year. You could set any limit you felt would meet the beneficiary's needs without excessively depleting the trust if tax considerations were not a concern. To avoid adverse tax consequences, however, you will need to limit the beneficiaries' rights. You can achieve this objective by giving a beneficiary what is called a "five-and-five power." This permits the beneficiary to demand a distribution in any year of the greater of $5,000 or 5 percent of the trust assets in that year. If the beneficiary's power is limited to this statutory formula, the power will not alone cause all of the assets of the trust to be included in the beneficiary's taxable estate. If the power is anything greater, even $6,000 or 6 percent, as an example, the entire trust will be taxable in the beneficiary's estate.

The following provision could be added to a credit shelter trust to give your surviving spouse greater comfort in having the assets on your death held in trust rather than given outright to him or her. This could encourage him or her to agree to the use of a credit shelter trust to save estate taxes. Any power greater than this would defeat the entire goal of the credit shelter trust since it would cause the trust assets to be taxed in the surviving spouse's estate.

SAMPLE TRUST PROVISION: Grantor's spouse shall have the right to request of the Trustee of this Credit Shelter Trust to pay over to such surviving spouse, upon written request, out of the principal of this Credit Shelter Trust, in each successive calendar year commencing with the calendar year in which Grantor's death occurs, a sum not exceeding the greater of Five Thousand Dollars ($5,000) or Five Percent (5%) of the assets of the principal of this Credit Shelter Trust valued as of the date of the receipt of such request, provided, however, that only one such request may be made in any one calendar year, and such right to withdraw sums of principal shall not be cumulative from year to year.

CAUTION: Where the beneficiary has a five-and-five power, his or her estate could be taxed on the amount of principal he or she could have demanded to be distributed in the year of death, even if the demand for the money is not made. Thus, for some trusts, if the power is not really necessary, it should not automatically be included.

CONCLUSION

Naming the beneficiaries of your trust is usually presumed to be a straightforward task although that is not always the case. Be careful to properly identify your beneficiaries, naming successor, alternate, or contingent beneficiaries. Further, you should pay close attention to how and when each beneficiary can or must receive distributions from the trust. Finally, you must discuss with your estate planner the appropriate powers and rights for beneficiaries to have over the trust. Be certain to review the tax implications of each of these matters to avoid costly and unintended surprises.

6 TRUSTEE RIGHTS, POWERS, AND OBLIGATIONS

WHO SHOULD BE THE TRUSTEES OF YOUR TRUST?

This is the single most important question in this book. The success of your entire trust depends on your making a wise decision. Who should be your trustee and your successor trustees?

Trustees are the persons, or institutions (such as a bank or trust company), who manage your trust. The trustees, under the provisions of your state's laws governing trusts (the differences between states can be important, so always consult with an attorney experienced with your state's regulations) and within the framework you provide in your trust document, are charged with carrying out the intent of your trust.

Your selection of the trustees and successor trustees (those who take over when prior trustees are no longer able or willing to serve) is one of the most important, difficult, and sensitive issues in setting up a trust.

You must consider numerous factors when selecting a trustee. Because many of them differ from people's usual assumptions, it is important to review them. In addition to general characteristics, some special considerations can vary depending on the trust you are setting up. These will be discussed later.

The first step should be to make a list of everyone who could reasonably be a trustee. Prepare this list as quickly as possible, without making judgments or canceling off any potential candidates. Try to come up with at least 10 names. If feasible, have your partner or spouse come up with his or her own list, independently. Try to make the list long. The next several sections of this chapter will help you narrow and rank the list. For many people, the toughest part is coming up with that initial list of names. Try not to be too selective at this stage. The problems some of your candidates may have often can be addressed by having them serve as co-trustees, or by ranking them after better candidates. Even a reluctant, though reasonable, choice, may be better than no choice once your first several preferences are not able to serve.

TIP: If you only name one trustee and one successor and neither can serve (e.g., one moves away and the other is sick or dies), what happens? A court proceeding may have to be initiated by the beneficiaries (or their guardians if they are minors) to have a court select a trustee. Not only is this process expensive and time-consuming, the records of the trial may be public information. Most importantly, can a judge who does not know you or the beneficiaries possibly select a trustee who will be more to your liking than you could have selected? Keep this in mind. It will help you lengthen your trustee list.

GENERAL FACTORS TO CONSIDER WHEN SELECTING A TRUSTEE

The following basic checklist of factors for selecting a trustee will help you evaluate each person in your "possible trustee" list. If the decision is tough, set up a chart of the candidates and weigh or rank them by factors to come up with your listing. Next, you will have to analyze your list to be certain the persons are all appropriate for the trusts you have planned. This will be discussed later in this chapter. For now, consider these factors:

- *Trustees for Both Spouses.* Spouses and partners should carefully consider any differences between the persons they would wish to select as trustees in their respective documents. If there is one economic unit (e.g., assets are used for both) or the beneficiaries are similar or identical, consider naming the same fiduciaries. This means using the same trustees under your respective trusts, the same executors under your wills, and the same agents under your durable powers of attorney. Differences in trustees could make administration more complex where estates and various trusts become involved. While there is nothing inappropriate about naming different fiduciaries, be certain that the benefits from doing so are worthwhile.

- *Selection Based on Skills.* Trustees should be selected because of their skills, not because of any perceived debt or your concern about insulting someone left out. The job is far too important to base decisions on such considerations. If you feel someone will be hurt by not being selected, consider writing some explanation or apology in your letter of last instruction (a personal letter you should write to your executor and guardians stating personal preferences, concerns, and the like).

- *Ability to Manage Assets.* If there is an interest in a business or other difficult-to-manage asset, consider the specific skills necessary. Alternatively, make sure your trust gives the trustees the power to hire an appropriate adviser or management company. You may wish to write a separate letter of instruction concerning your business interests. Also, the correct documents to address many of these concerns are the partnership or other agreements controlling the business, not your trust. In fact, your partners may insist on some input in choosing a trustee of a trust holding business interests.

- *Pleasant Temperament in Dealing with All of the Beneficiaries.* The trustee does not need to be the best "buddy" of any beneficiary; in fact, it is preferable that he or she not be. A relationship that is too close may make it difficult for a trustee to say no, even when the beneficiary makes a request that you would have frowned on. On the opposite extreme, if the trustee and beneficiary cannot communicate or have an antagonistic relationship, the trust operations will never be as smooth and helpful as you might wish.

- *No Conflict of Interest.* Your longtime business partner may be your most trusted friend and the most financially astute individual you know, but if her decisions about the business could adversely affect your family's interests, she may not be the best choice. An alternative may be to name her co-trustee and prohibit her from making any decisions concerning the voting of the stock in the company. Also, consider whether a buyout agreement to dispose of the stock may not be the best option. This could leave your trust with cash instead of business interests and eliminate the problem entirely.

- *Business and Investment Acumen.* Many trusts, even for people who do not consider themselves particularly well off, can have substantial assets. If an insurance policy is paid to the trust, this alone could be a significant sum. Can the persons you select be trusted to handle this much money properly? If they do not have the necessary investment skills, will they consult proper advisers and use them effectively? You can address these concerns to some extent by including your brokers and investment advisers in your estate planning team. This will set a precedent that your trustees can follow when they are appointed. You should not dismiss a trusted, honest friend or family member who understands your goals and objectives, but does not have investment acumen. The ideal situation may be to combine such a person's talents with an institutional trustee (or one of your longtime and trusted advisers) to provide accounting, investment, and other professional advice.

- *Judgment to Determine the Needs of Your Beneficiaries.* The most financially astute person may not exhibit the sensitivity you want toward your beneficiaries. Again, the solution to this dilemma is to name co-trustees. One trustee can be someone, or a company, with substantial investment or trust management expertise. The co-trustee can be someone who exhibits the personal sensitivity and skills you desire. Together, they can likely do a better job than either would alone. This approach is frequently used with an institutional trustee, such as a bank's trust department, which serves as a co-trustee with a family member. Or, you might select friends or family members to serve jointly where their skills and personal characteristics complement each other.

- *Beneficiaries as Trustees.* Naming a person who is a beneficiary as trustee can create several legal and tax problems. Legally, if the same person is the only trustee and the only beneficiary, there is no trust (the legal doctrine of "merger"). If you have several beneficiaries and only one of them is a trustee, the other nontrustee beneficiaries could be put at a disadvantage. This becomes more problematic as the discretionary authority given to your trustee is increased. Tax problems can also affect a trustee-beneficiary. Where a person as trustee can distribute all of the trust assets to him- or herself as a beneficiary, the entire amount of the trust could be included in the person's estate for tax purposes.

NOTE: One approach to addressing this problem is to have two co-trustees. In addition, the provisions of the trust defining the trustees' powers can prohibit any trustee who is also a beneficiary from participating in any decision to distribute money to him- or herself.

- *The Term of the Trust.* Where you are setting up a trust for young children, or grandchildren, which may be in existence for a long time, you should consider this factor in selecting trustees. Naming more successor trustees than you would for a shorter trust will increase the likelihood of one or more trustees being able and willing to serve as the minors age. You may wish to name an institution, such as a bank trust department as a trustee. Institutional trustees do not get old, cannot die (they may, however, merge or be taken over by another institutional trustee), and they usually do not resign. If you prefer not to name an institution initially, you may wish to name one as a final successor trustee in the event that the individuals named cannot serve. Another alternative is to give the trustee the right to name a successor trustee, which may include an institution. Thus, if your last named trustee realizes that there is a possibility of the trust agreement not designating a trustee, he or she can then appoint a successor.

- *Discretion in Selecting Trustees.* Be sensitive in stating your selection of trustees. For example, assume that you have three children (or siblings, or friends, etc.) and you feel comfortable with one or two of them as trustees, but not all. How will the persons not selected as trustee react? Will you create difficult friction and other problems between the one or two serving as trustee and those who are not? Often, a nonbinding comment explaining the appointment to the trust, or a side letter, can defuse the potential problem.

SAMPLE COMMENT: I select my youngest son John as Trustee. I have selected John prior to his older siblings as first choice for Trustee, not out of any lack of love or concern for my other children, but in recognition of his background as an accountant, which makes him best suited for this role.

In many situations, a personal note may suffice. In some cases, the friction may be caused by desire to earn trustee fees. This may be resolved by providing that no trustee shall earn a fee. Alternatively, you could make larger gifts to the persons not serving as trustee to maintain equality.

This list is far from exhaustive. Every family or individual's circumstances will raise additional general issues. Discuss them with the people who will be affected to the extent that you feel comfortable, and then with your estate planner. In addition, circumstances specific to each trust should also be considered.

SELECTING A TRUSTEE FOR DIFFERENT TYPES OF TRUSTS

Revocable Living Trust

If you are forming a revocable living trust, the initial trustee is presumed to be easy, it's you. This is not always the best answer. If you are the sole grantor, trustee, and beneficiary, a legal doctrine of merger may apply. This could result in no trust being validly formed under state law because no different interests have been established. Apart from this possible legal issue, is it practical to be the sole trustee? A major goal in setting up a revocable living trust is to manage your assets and money if your are disabled. How will your trust make the transition from you as the sole and disabled trustee to the successor trustees? It is likely to be an easier and smoother transition if initially you name someone to serve with you as co-trustee. Then the co-trustee will have signed the trust, have a copy of the signed trust, be aware of his or her responsibilities, and will have signed the bank and brokerage signature cards in advance. In the event of an emergency or disability, no hurdles will block the co-trustee's efforts to assist you and your family.

It is prudent to name someone other than your spouse or partner as co-trustee because he or she likely travels with you much of the time and is likely to be with you if you are injured in an accident or other catastrophe. You can name your spouse or partner as the immediate successor. Thus, if an emergency affects you but not your spouse or partner, he or she will be immediately serving as successor trustee, the same position as immediate co-trustee. However, if your spouse or partner is incapacitated by the same emergency, the initial co-trustee will be in a position to help both of you with the least difficulty.

Trusts for Children

If you're setting up a trust for your children either now (inter vivos), or under your will, most likely your spouse who is the other parent of the children will be the initial co-trustee. It is generally preferable that a parent not be the sole trustee of a trust for a child. If the parent makes disbursements that discharge the parent's legal obligation to support the child, tax problems could be triggered. Thus, if the parent as co-trustee is prohibited from making disbursements that discharge a legal obligation of support, the other co-trustee can instead make decisions and take actions for those types of payment. Several successor trustees will have to be named since the trust will last for a long time if children are involved.

Qualified Personal Residence Trust

Since this is a grantor trust, you could be a trustee. However, if you wish to claim a lack of marketability and minority interest discount on you and your spouse transferring tenant-in-common interests to separate QPRTs, the trustees of the two trusts should differ (see Chapter 19).

Credit Shelter Trust

When setting up a credit shelter trust (bypass or "A" trust), your surviving spouse can be a co-trustee; however, exercise caution in making him or her the sole trustee because the primary objective of such trusts is to assure that its assets are not taxed in the surviving spouse's estate. If your spouse is co-trustee he or she can be prohibited from participating in decisions that could taint the trust as taxable in his or her estate. This can be further supported, if your estate planner advises, by limiting distributions to an ascertainable standard. See Chapter 8.

Qualified Terminable Interest Property (Q-TIP) Trust

This trust is intended to qualify for the estate tax marital deduction on the death of the first spouse. The value of this trust, however, is then taxed at the death of the surviving spouse (this is why second-to-die life insurance is often used in estate planning; see Chapter 16). Since the value of the trust will be included in the surviving spouse's estate in any event, there is less tax concern with naming the surviving spouse a trustee. The selection of trustees should address the powers given the trustees and the remainder beneficiaries (i.e., those beneficiaries who will receive the trust following the death of the surviving spouse). If it is a first and only marriage and common children will inherit the assets, there might be little concern other than assuring maximum comfort for the surviving spouse and meeting investment objectives. If a second or later marriage is involved, however, a conflict may be inherent in selecting as trustee the surviving spouse who is not a parent of the children who will inherit the remaining trust estate. Similarly, it is often not appropriate to have the children of a different marriage named as trustees.

Insurance Trust

If second-to-die insurance (pays only on the death of the second of two spouses) is to be held in a trust, neither spouse should generally be named trustee. Where insurance is purchased on your life, you should generally be the grantor and should not serve as trustee.

Other trusts will present their own unique problems in the naming of trustees. The preceding sections have summarized important points raised in several types of trusts. Because the selection of a trustee can be so complex from a tax perspective alone, it is essential to consult with an attorney specializing in estate planning. However, if you work through the discussions in this chapter, and begin your selection process with a well-thought-out list of persons to serve as trustees, you can and will save legal fees and speed the trust planning.

OTHER OPTIONS TO CONSIDER WHEN NAMING A TRUSTEE

If you are setting up an irrevocable trust, and concerned about how to address unforeseeable changes, especially changes concerning the conduct of trustees, the use of a trust protector or dual purpose trustees, may be the answer. Since these concepts are not commonly used, you should analyze them with an attorney who specializes in estate planning and who has had experience with them.

Trust Protector

If you are uncomfortable with the power and control given a trustee, perhaps you could consider the use of a trust protector to address some of your concerns.

This approach is common in many foreign jurisdictions. The protector serves as an intermediary between the beneficiaries and the trustee, with the primary objective of protecting the beneficiaries from, and representing them before, the trustee. A trust protector is, in some sense, a hybrid form of trustee because the protector can exercise certain limited powers that normally may be reserved to the trustees, or otherwise contained in the trust agreement.

A committee of advisers or protectors could be formed to advise the trustees on investments, administration, and distributions. This would allow the persons establishing the trust, the grantors, to maintain some level of control without usurping the powers of the trustees.

The trust protector may be a person or corporation that is not a trustee or beneficiary: a law firm or accounting firm, trusted friend, or family member who will not serve as trustee. The beneficiary should not be a protector since the unlimited power to remove the trustee (one of the key powers generally given to the protector) could cause the inclusion of the trust assets in the beneficiaries' estate.

The protector may exercise certain powers alone but, in other instances, must have the consent of the trustee. The trust protector may have the right to change characteristics of the trust that could expose its assets to risks in the event of a change in circumstances such as a change in the trustee, the situs of the trust assets (the state or country where the trust is based), and the choice of law provision (i.e., which state or country's laws are to govern the trust). If a host country's rules change, the ability to change any of these characteristics could be important to the continued protection of the trust assets. Some trusts provide the trust protector the right to add or change the beneficiaries of the trust.

An important power of the trust protector is the right to remove the trustee. Another common power is for the trust protector to change the jurisdiction of the trust to another jurisdiction. This is known as a "fight provision." The trust protector may wish to move the trust if it becomes threatened by litigation in the original jurisdiction, or if the governing jurisdiction enacts income, gift, or estate tax laws; becomes threatened by war or civil unrest; or as in the case of a foreign situs asset protection trust, enters into a treaty with the United States (which could jeopardize tax, litigation, or other benefits).

Divided Fiduciary Responsibility

When planning an irrevocable trust, you might lessen your concerns or discomfort about naming a trustee by dividing the responsibility of various trust functions, such as managing assets. A trustee skilled in real estate matters could be designated to make real estate decisions and assume primary responsibility for real estate matters, while a co-trustee with greater securities investment acumen could assume primary responsibility for security holdings. There are two general approaches for this plan. In the first case, each trustee, while assuming primary responsibility for a particular area, maintains involvement with, and responsibility for, all areas. In the second approach, there would be an actual division of responsibility. Legally, however, it is not clear that any trustee can delegate his or her fidiciary respnsibility. Thus, it may be possible to delegate work load but not the responsibility. The key is, that to accomplish this delegation of responsibility, your trust agreement must expressly provide for it.

POWERS THAT YOUR TRUSTEE SHOULD BE GIVEN

Your trustees need a broad range of powers to effectively discharge their responsibilities. There is some debate as to whether many of these powers need to be listed in the trust agreement. Since state law provides for certain trustee powers, these same powers should not need to be repeated in the trust document. In many situations, however, the all-inclusive approach seems to win out because few persons drafting trusts wish to risk not providing trustees with whatever powers they may need. Also, many grantors and trustees like the comfort of looking in the trust document and seeing an explicit statement authorizing them to take the particular action they are considering.

CAUTION: The trustee power provisions are quite long and often mistakenly dismissed as boilerplate. You should review the provisions and address any concerns. If the provisions are too broad, you may wish to limit them to better secure the beneficiaries. If certain provisions are too restrictive, you may wish to amend them to give the trustees the flexibility to address the beneficiaries' changing circumstances. Also, if you have any special goals or assets, the powers should address them. If you have farmland, real estate investments, closely held businesses, insurance policies, generation-skipping transfer tax concerns, and so forth, the trust power provisions should be tailored to assure the trustee has adequate powers to deal with these matters. In most cases, the attorney who is an estate planning specialist will modify your trust to address many of these situations. This is why you cannot feasibly expect an attorney to draft a trust in isolation of your business, personal, financial, and other estate planning considerations. Finally, if you fine-tune many of these provisions, you will incur additional professional fees since it will take considerably more time to complete your documentation than if you did not address such detail.

RIGHTS THAT YOUR TRUSTEE SHOULD BE GIVEN

The trustee may have the power to allocate income and principal among the various beneficiaries. This is called a sprinkle power. See Chapters 8 and 11. The trustee can be granted the power to reserve the right to withhold distributions of income to a beneficiary who is disabled or a minor. The trustee perhaps should not have the right to vote shares of stock in a closely held business in which he or she also has a significant interest.

Every trustee, unless the trust agreement specifically says otherwise, is entitled to compensation for serving as a trustee. Beyond immediate family members, no person is likely to serve without compensation. State laws, to prevent abuse, have set maximum fees that may be charged by trustees. Often, the trust agreement is silent and the permissible fees are charged. In some instances, you may wish to include a specific agreement as to fees in the trust agreement. An institutional trustee may require that approval of its standard fee schedule, and other provisions, be added to your trust. When naming an institution, even as a successor trustee, it is advisable to contact that institution before signing the trust and consider incorporating any requested language. This will facilitate services if they are eventually required.

To encourage the people or entities you name as trustees to serve, you may wish to exonerate them for liability where they have acted reasonably and in good faith. An honest error, or poor investment made after reasonable analysis, should not penalize your trustee. State law may affect the extent to which you can relieve a trustee of liability.

OTHER TRUST PROVISIONS AFFECTING TRUSTEES

The later chapters in this book contain further discussions of trustee powers, rights, and obligations in the context of specific trusts (see Chapters 10–20). These can be reviewed for further details of the concepts in this chapter. Discuss these rules carefully with your attorney because state law differs and powers that are appropriate for a particular type of trust, or in a particular situation, can all differ substantially. For tax-oriented trusts (e.g., QPRT, GRAT, CRAT, etc.), this is especially true.

TRUSTEE'S DUTIES AND OBLIGATIONS

Duty to Protect Trust Property

The trustee must take all reasonable steps to protect and conserve trust property. Importantly, this duty is not delegable. Where a family member or friend is named as trustee but does not have investment or other necessary expertise, that trustee should delegate investment or other activities. In general, however, the trustee will remain responsible and must monitor the person retained to assist the trust. Many trustees mistakenly assume that retaining a professional, such as a money manager, solves the problem. To the contrary, it will not. The family member trustee will still have a fiduciary duty to monitor and safeguard assets. Thus, when delegating as trustee, be certain to require periodic reporting sufficient to monitor activities.

Duty to Make Trust Property Productive

The trustee has a specific duty to make the property of the trust productive, unless the grantor indicated an intent otherwise, or it is impractical to do so. If you believe that the trust indicates the grantor's intent that you not make some portion or all of the trust estate productive, you may wish to obtain a legal opinion and the consent of the beneficiaries to avoid possible future claims. This obligation is independent of the requirements to make property productive to meet the requirements of qualifying a marital deduction trust for the unlimited gift or estate tax marital deduction.

Duty to Be Prudent

The duty of the trustee to be prudent can have an important impact on investment and other actions taken by the trustee. The trustee has a duty to act reasonably and competently in all matters relating to the administration of the trust. This is a standard of conduct, not performance. An amateur trustee is held to the standard of "such care and skill as a man of ordinary prudence would exercise in dealing with his own property." A trustee who holds himself out as a professional with special skills is held to the higher standard of employing those special skills. However, rather than relying on a lower standard being applied to you for lack of expertise, the safer and preferable approach will often be to retain an outside expert to advise you.

Duty to Carry Out Terms of the Trust

The duties of any trustee must be viewed not only in the context of the applicable state statutes and the general legal duties and responsibilities of the trustee, but in light of the governing trust document as well. Where these three are consistent, the trustee's course of action will be obvious. Where they are not consistent, problems will arise and legal advice should be sought.

Because the trustee's primary duty is to carry out the intentions of the grantor as communicated in the governing instrument, the first step any newly appointed trustee must take is to obtain a copy of the trust instrument, read it, and then discuss it with a trust and estate attorney. Without knowledge of the trust agreement, a trustee is unlikely to fulfill his or her obligations.

Can a trustee deviate from the terms of the trust instrument? Generally, unless there is impossibility, illegality, or change in circumstances, the answer should be no.

How can the trustee interpret his or her obligations where the trust agreement requires that distributions be made to the beneficiaries to maintain their lifestyle, provide for their comfort, and so forth? The trustee should have a periodic, at least annual, polling of beneficiaries. The input of the grantor is often not binding unless the grantor has expressly reserved the right and power to amend, modify, or revoke the trust (e.g., a revocable living trust). Thus, instructions of the grantor following the establishment of the trust may not be admissible to vary the terms of the trust. While polling the beneficiaries about their income needs, investment views, and other concerns may be useful in serving them, the primary duty of the trustee remains to the grantor (as the grantor's wishes are set forth in the trust document). While the trustee is not an agent of either the grantor or the beneficiary, the trustee should view him- or herself as an agent of the grantor more than as an agent of the beneficiary.

Can a Trustee Invest in Their Own Securities?

If the grantor designated an institutional trustee, or manager, or authorized the trustees to retain money managers, investments in such trustee or money manager's own securities can become an issue. This is most likely to occur where a pooled investment fund is used for many smaller trust funds. Where a trustee lends to itself without authority, it breaches the duty of loyalty it owes the trust. Even if borrowing is authorized, it can raise issues of impropriety. What if the trustee, an institutional fiduciary, invests directly in debt instruments issued by it or its parent company? What if the common trust fund makes such an investment? What should occur if the trustee receives stock of itself as part of a portfolio? Generally, it seems preferable for the trustee not to invest in its own stock, and if it receives stock to obtain an authorization from the grantor, if the trust is a revocable trust, to retain the stock.

Is a Trustee Permitted to Earn a Profit?

A trustee is in a fiduciary position (i.e., a relationship of trust and responsibility) with respect to the beneficiaries and the trust assets (corpus). As such, trust law has historically prevented the trustee from earning any profit from the trust, other than the trustee fees provided for under the trust agreement. This is one of the basis for requiring a trustee to account for all trust income and assets.

TIP: The trust agreement should address these matters explicitly. The trust should permit broad latitude to the trustee to retain consultants, advisers, money managers, and the like, and to compensate them and to make expenditures necessary regarding such activities. Where such persons may be related parties to the trust, this should expressly be addressed.

Trustee's Authority to Retain Agents

- *Authority to Retain Agents Generally.* The trustee is under a duty to the beneficiary not to delegate to others the committing of acts that the trustee can reasonably be required personally to perform. A trustee has the power to perform every act that a prudent person would perform for the purposes of the trust including employing persons such as attorneys, auditors, investment advisors, or agents, even if they are associated with the trustee, to advise or assist the trustee in the performance of administrative duties.

  A trustee may be permitted to appoint an associate as an agent. However, there is a general trustee's duty to avoid conflict-of-interest transactions when hiring agents. A court order may be required where the transaction involves a profit to the trustee.

- *Retaining Investment Advisers and Agents.* The Prudent Investor Act passed by many states will result in many trustees delegating investment authority to a money manager. How do a trustee's duties under law relate to this act of delegation? The consequences of improper delegation are that the trustee may be liable for the errors and omissions of the delegatee. The modern trend is to permit the trustee to delegate some investment discretion to investment advisers and others, provided there is adequate supervision by the trustee. This allows the trust to retain an investment adviser and to pay for the adviser's services from the trust. To be prudent in selecting advisers, the trustees should participate in setting trust investment objectives and routinely monitor the advisers' performance. Where this is properly done, the trustees should not be liable for delegating to advisers.

Duties Owed by Trustee to Trust and to Beneficiaries

The trustee owes a duty of loyalty to the trust and the beneficiaries. The trustee has a generic duty to administer. This means that the trustee should do what is necessary for the good of the trust and those interested in it. The general duty to administer is the source of other trustee duties including the duties of loyalty and impartiality.

Self-Dealing Issues Affecting Trustee

The risk of self-dealing is present whenever a trustee employs him- or herself, or a related entity to perform a service that an independent agent (e.g., a realtor, accountant, or attorney) could also perform. It is generally safer to employ a third party, unless the trust agreement expressly permits the employment of an agent. The language requested by many institutional trustees in trust agreements often includes express authorization for them to use related money managers, funds, and advisers in serving a trust.

CONCLUSION

Naming trustees is often the most difficult and important decision to be made when planning any trust. The powers and rights of the trustees, although often dismissed as boilerplate are extremely important and should all be reviewed with care to assure that your trust will function as closely as possible to your desires. If you contemplate accepting the position of serving as a trustee, not only must you be familiar with the trust instrument and your powers, but you must also understand your obligations and responsibilities as a trustee. This chapter has only outlined some of the many concepts affecting trustees. If any of the issues discussed could affect you, the safest course is to consult an attorney specializing in estate and trust work in your state.

Part Two

TAX CONSEQUENCES OF TRUSTS

7 PLANNING FOR THE GIFT AND ESTATE TAXES

TRUSTS AND GIFT AND ESTATE TAXES

Saving gift and estate taxes is a key goal for every taxpayer whose assets are large enough, or may grow large enough, to trigger these costly taxes, which start at 37 percent and quickly rise to 50 percent and more! In the war to minimize or eliminate gift and estate taxes, trusts can be one of your most potent weapons. A basic understanding of how the gift and estate taxes work will help you select tax, investment, and estate advisers—and once you have selected them—work with them in establishing the most effective plan.

This basic knowledge is especially important in trust planning to obtain tax benefits, because such trusts are almost always irrevocable (i.e., you do not have the right to change or revoke the trust after signing it). Therefore, both the gift tax and estate tax implications, as well as other aspects of the trust (e.g., who the trustees are, when beneficiaries should receive distributions, etc.) should all be carefully considered in advance. This chapter provides an overview of the gift and estate taxes, with an emphasis on how they affect trust planning.

What if taxes are not your primary concern? You can skip this and the next two chapters, but don't give up on trusts. Trusts are a valuable tool for achieving many personal, financial, estate planning, and other goals. Minimizing taxes is only one of these goals. Thus, even if your estate is not large enough for you to be concerned about gift and estate taxes, or if minimizing taxes is not your concern, trusts are still an essential tool. The Trust Finding Table that precedes Chapter 1 can help you find trusts to accomplish nontax goals.

OVERVIEW OF THE TRANSFER TAX SYSTEM

The transfer tax system consists of three separate, but related, taxes:

1. Gift tax, which is a tax assessed on gratuitous transfers of assets while you are alive. The gift tax is discussed in the following section of this chapter.

2. Estate tax, which is assessed on transfers of assets following your death (e.g., assets bequeathed under your will). The estate tax is discussed later in this chapter.

NOTE: The gift tax and the estate tax are largely integrated. They share many similar concepts, in particular a single unified credit. This credit can permit anyone to give away up to $600,000 in assets during their lifetime (as gifts) or at death (e.g., under your will). Because of this, these two taxes are discussed in the same chapter.

---

3. Generation-skipping transfer (GST) tax, which is assessed on certain gratuitous transfers made during your lifetime as well as certain transfers of assets following your death. This tax generally applies where the transfers are to people two generations below yours, such as grandchildren (or trusts for their benefit; see Chapter 8).

These three transfer taxes are all based on your transfer of assets. Unlike the income tax, which most taxpayers are all too familiar with, these transfer taxes are charged when you give away assets. While the tax rates for these taxes are extremely high, there are many exclusions, deductions, and other planning benefits. Much of your trust tax planning will be designed to take the most advantage of these benefits.

The three federal transfer taxes—gift, estate, and GST—can be distinguished from the inheritance tax assessed by many states. An inheritance tax is not a tax assessed on your transfer of assets. Rather, it is a tax on the recipient on the receipt of property.

THE GIFT TAX

What Types of Transfers Trigger the Gift Tax?

The gift tax is a tax charged on your right to give away, gratuitously, assets during your lifetime. The tax is not imposed to the extent you receive money or other valuable assets in exchange for what you transfer.

EXAMPLE: You sell your daughter jewelry worth $18,000. She pays you $6,000 for it. You have made a gift worth $12,000. The transaction is a part sale/part gift.

EXAMPLE: You sell your key employee a car for $6,000 although it is worth $18,000. You have not made a gift because the relationship is one of employer/employee. You have, however, paid additional compensation worth $12,000. The transaction is a part sale/part compensation. Your business should receive a compensation deduction.

The crucial difference in the preceding two examples is the relationship between the people involved. Anytime the people are related, expect the IRS to scrutinize the transaction much more closely for a gift.

Although in everyday usage the term "gift" implies a donative intent, tax law does not require that you had the intent to show this. All that the tax laws require to trigger the gift tax is your transfer of assets for less than full payment (consideration).

A Gift Must Be Complete for the Gift Tax to Apply

No taxable gift is made until the gift is completed. This means the donor must transfer beneficial interest in the assets to the recipient (donee) and must give up control over those assets. You must part with sufficient control so that the gift is completed and you cannot retract it. The gift must be beyond your recall. Delivery of the gift property should also be completed.

EXAMPLE: You give annual gifts of stock in a family business to each of your children at Christmastime. Each year, you sign gift letters (stating that your intent is to give the shares as a gift) and stock powers authorizing the transfer of the shares of stock. Your goal is to transfer the entire value of the business to your children through these annual gifts. However, you retain all stock certificates in a safe in your home. The IRS may successfully assert that the gifts are not complete.

If you make a gift to a trust for the benefit of your nephew, determining whether the gift is complete will involve not only analyzing whether you have consummated each of the steps necessary to transfer the asset to the trust, but evaluating the terms of the trust as well. The gift may not be complete if you have substantial control over the trust, are a trustee, or have reserved significant powers, such as the right to terminate the trust.

Is it better that the gift be completed or not completed for gift tax purposes? It depends on the circumstances and your goals.

NOTE: Incomplete gifts have been used as an intentional planning technique when setting up many different types of trusts. For example, transfers to a foreign situs asset protection trust may intentionally be structured so that you retain sufficient powers to avoid a completed gift. Without this arrangement, you may face, in addition to a gift tax, a substantial excise tax applicable to transfers of assets overseas (see Chapter 15).

If your goal is to remove the value of an asset from your estate, you will want the gift to be completed. Further, if your intent is to use the annual $10,000 gift tax exclusion described later in this chapter, you will want to be certain that the gift is completed in a particular tax year. Finally, there are different rules for determining whether a transfer is completed for income, gift, or estate tax purposes.

What Is the Value of the Gift Made?

Once you have determined that the transfer is a gift, and that the gift has been completed, you must determine its value. This is obvious for a gift of cash or stock in a publicly traded company (e.g., IBM, GM). In many situations, however, the value of the gift will not be simple. These more complex valuation situations can also present the best tax-planning opportunities.

The value of a gift is the fair market value of the asset given on the date the gift is completed. Fair market value is defined as the price that an unrelated buyer would pay for the asset when purchasing it from an unrelated seller, where neither the buyer nor seller was under any unusual pressure or obligation to consummate the transaction.

If the gift is residential real estate, a written appraisal from a local real estate broker is probably essential. If the gift is commercial real estate, a certified appraisal report should be obtained. In both instances, the reports should address comparable property sales, replacement cost, and the income capitalization method of valuation.

If the gift is an interest in a closely held business, a written analysis from a business appraiser should be obtained. The analysis should address each of the factors discussed in Revenue Ruling 59-60 of the Internal Revenue Service. The appraiser should be familiar with this ruling and other valuation law. The report should evaluate hard assets (accounts receivable, property, plant, equipment, etc.) and soft or intangible assets (goodwill, customer lists, customer loyalty, trademarks, patents, etc.). The analysis should also make adjustments for any transactions that were not arm's-length (on the same basis as if the parties had not been related). For example, if you control a family business, you might take a salary and perquisites (company car, travel, etc.) that are substantially more than that which an unrelated hired employee would have in a similar situation.

In all situations, a qualified professional should appraise the asset, providing sufficient documentation to demonstrate to the IRS that the value used was appropriate.

Once you have determined the value of the gift to be made, you can begin to address gift tax planning. The following sections will review the basic exclusions and other rules of the gift tax.

Four Exclusions to Avoid Gift Taxation

Four deductions or exclusions can be used to plan to minimize or avoid the gift tax. One or more of these may be a foundation for how you plan gifts to the trusts that you establish during your lifetime.

The Annual $10,000 Gift Tax Exclusion

You can give away up to $10,000, to any person, without incurring a gift tax. You can make this type of gift to as many people you want to during each calendar year. You can give away $10,000 every year to the same person so that over a number of years the gifts accumulate to a substantial amount. This is called the annual gift tax exclusion. For a large estate, the $10,000 limit may not sound large, but it can be impressive when used to the maximum extent feasible.

EXAMPLE: Tom and Tina Taxpayer have three children. Each child is married and has two children. Tom and Tina set up trusts for each of their six grandchildren. Tom can gift $10,000 to each of the six trusts every year; Tina also can gift $10,000 to each trust every year. Thus, the Taxpayers can gift $120,000 per year to trusts for their grandchildren. In two years, they can gift $240,000. Since the $10,000 gifts can be made in each calendar year, the Taxpayers could make gifts of $120,000 on December 31 and $120,000 on January 1. Thus, they could give gifts to trusts for their grandchildren of almost a quarter million dollars in two days.

Where gifts are made to a trust, rather than outright to the intended donee, however, special requirements must be met for the gifts to qualify for this exclusion. These complicated rules will be discussed later in the chapter.

Many transfers qualifying for the annual $10,000 gift tax exclusion are not subject to the generation-skipping transfer tax, which will be discussed in Chapter 8.

Exclusion for Medical and Tuition Payments

You can pay unlimited amounts to a qualifying educational institution without incurring any gift tax. A qualifying educational institution is one that normally maintains a regular faculty and curriculum and normally has a regularly enrolled body of students. You can also make unlimited payments for medical care if paid directly to the person or organization providing the medical services. Since tuition and medical payments must be made directly to the providers, this rule does not directly help your trust planning. Since neither of these payments count toward the $10,000 annual exclusion, however, this benefit can enable you to provide substantial benefits to your intended heirs and still leave plenty of opportunity to establish and funded trusts for the same beneficiaries.

Marital Deduction

Gifts made to a spouse, who is a U.S. citizen, or to a qualifying trust (Q-TIP) for a spouse, in any amount, are not subject to gift tax. There are three basic ways in which gifts can be made to a spouse and qualify for the unlimited gift tax marital deduction:

1. *Outright.* The gift is not in trust and not restricted in any manner.
2. *A Life Estate with a General Power of Appointment.* The spouse has the right to the income or use of the assets for his or her life, and also

has the right to designate who should receive the property following the spouse's death.

3. *A Qualified Terminable Interest Property (Q-TIP) Trust.* This trust is a key technique in your planning with trusts and is discussed at length in Chapter 11.

If your spouse is not a U.S. citizen, there is no unlimited gift tax marital deduction unless the gift is made to a special trust called a qualified domestic trust (Q-DOT) (see Chapter 11). If the gift is not made in trust, the maximum gift that can be made to the noncitizen spouse without incurring a gift tax in any year is $100,000.

If your partner is not legally your spouse, the unlimited gift tax marital deduction will not be available and a large transfer will trigger a tax. Special planning will be required (see Chapter 12).

Charitable Deduction

An unlimited gift tax charitable deduction can permit you to gift any amount of property to a qualified charity. For trust planning, large gifts to charities will usually be in one of the following forms:

- *Charitable Remainder Unitrust* (CRUT; see Chapter 14).
- *Charitable Remainder Annuity Trust* (CRAT; see Chapter 14).
- *Pooled Income Fund* (Not discussed in this book).
- *Q-TIP (Marital) Trust* (Remainder beneficiary after the death of the spouse is a charity; see Chapters 11 and 14).

The preceding gift tax deduction is independent of the income tax benefits of a charitable gift. If the gift meets the income tax requirements, and the various limitations on itemized deductions do not apply, the full amount of the charitable gift should generate an income tax charitable contribution deduction.

Special Rules Affecting the $10,000 Gift Tax Exclusion

The $10,000 annual exclusion is one of the cornerstones of planning for gifts to trusts. Many taxpayers only make gifts up to $10,000 per person each year to avoid taxable gifts (or as will be explained, to avoid using any of their $600,000 exemption). Thus, you must understand some of the nuances for applying this annual exclusion to obtain the maximum benefits when planning for your trusts.

Gift Splitting

Everyone can give away $10,000 per year per donee (recipient). Thus, a husband and wife can together give away $20,000 per year per donee. A special rule, called gift splitting, permits a couple to jointly give away

$20,000 per year without having to write out separate checks (or transfer assets separately).

The gift splitting technique enables either you or your spouse to make a gift and have the other nondonor spouse join in the gift so that two $10,000 annual exclusions can reduce the value of the gift. If the other requirements are met, gift splitting enables one of you annually to transfer up to $20,000 per recipient (donee) with the gift being deemed to be made one-half by each spouse. Each spouse's $10,000 annual exclusion is applied to eliminate any taxable gift.

To qualify for this valuable benefit, the two people making the election must be married; both must be citizens or residents of the United States; the spouse making the gift must not remarry during the remainder of the year; both spouses must agree (consent) to this tax treatment for the particular gift and for all gifts made by either of them while they are married during that particular year.

NOTE: If you choose to gift split, you must file a gift tax return, Form 709. Be certain to review this with your accountant before the April 15 due date.

Gifts to a Trust

Two issues are raised by gifts to a trust: Who are the donees, and does the annual $10,000 per donee exclusion from gift taxation apply?

Where a gift is made to a trust, the beneficiaries are considered to be the recipients, not the trust itself.

EXAMPLE: You pay $20,000 to an insurance trust that purchases insurance on your life. Your two children are beneficiaries. You can't then make gifts of $10,000 to each of your children and expect to qualify for the annual exclusion as well. You will have given more than the maximum $10,000 to each child in that year. The fact that one gift is direct, and the other indirect through a trust, is not relevant.

The $10,000 (or $20,000 for a couple) annual exclusions are only available to offset gifts that meet a technical requirement. They must be gifts of a "present interest" to qualify. This means that the recipient must have the current use and benefit of, and access to, the gift. If you receive $10,000 in cash, this is a gift of a present interest since you can take the funds and apply them in any manner you wish. Other gifts that do not as clearly meet, or fail, the present interest test do not qualify for the annual exclusion. This includes reversions and remainders—property received after the life beneficiary dies, or after a fixed number of years—that you will not have the right to possess or enjoy until some future date.

EXAMPLE: You transfer assets worth $10,000 as a gift to a trust established years ago for the benefit of your child. If the child cannot use or benefit from the gift until the money is distributed at some unknown future date (perhaps in the sole discretion of an independent trustee), the gift will not qualify as a gift of a present interest. Therefore, you won't be able to use the $10,000 annual exclusion to offset the gift's value. The result is that you will have to pay a gift tax on the $10,000 value, or use up a portion of your remaining unified credit, as will be explained. Had you transferred the assets directly to the beneficiary, you could have avoided paying a gift tax, or using up any of your unified credit. However, directly giving the cash to the child would not protect the money from the child's creditors or own spending habits.

It can sometimes be difficult to determine whether a gift to a trust is a present interest that qualifies for the exclusion. In many, if not most trusts, a major objective is to preserve the assets for future use by the beneficiary. Thus the trustee may be permitted to hold money in the trust and only make distributions when, in the trustee's judgment, it is appropriate. If you do not take an additional step (to be described), your gifts to the trust will not qualify as gifts of a present interest and will therefore trigger a tax or use of your unified credit. For most taxpayers, it is a mistake to use up your unified credit unless there is a compelling reason to do so. Even if your estate is well below the $600,000 in assets that can pass free of gift (and estate) taxes, it is usually best to preserve your unified credit for later use. What if your estate grows? You will then regret having wasted your credit through lax planning. Where feasible, you should plan your gifts to trusts for your children, insurance trusts, and so forth to assure they will qualify for the annual exclusion.

NOTE: Qualifying for the $10,000 exclusion is not relevant to many types of trusts. Assets of a revocable living trust are fully taxable in your estate (subject to the use of credit shelter and marital deduction planning) so qualifying for the annul exclusion would not make sense. Grantor retained annuity trusts (GRATs), grantor retained unitrusts (GRUTs), and qualified personal residence trusts (QPRTs) are structured so that the gift tax annual exclusion will not apply to gifts to those trusts. Thus, funding these trusts would consume a portion of your unified credit. Charitable trusts similarly do not qualify for annual exclusions.

The following are three rules for determining when a gift to a trust qualifies as a gift of a present interest, and thus the $10,000 annual exclusion is available: (1) The trust should generate an income flow; (2) some portion of the income must go to the trust beneficiaries; (3) the amount of income the beneficiaries will receive must be ascertainable.

EXAMPLE: You make a gift to a trust for your two daughters. The trust requires all assets be fully and productively invested and that all income be paid out to the two daughters each year. On the death of the last daughter, the trust is paid to your grandchildren. The income interest of your daughters, determined on an actuarial basis, might qualify as a gift of a present interest.

As a general rule, a gift in trust will not qualify for the annual gift tax exclusion if special provisions are not made. There are planning possibilities.

A gift to a special trust for the benefit of a minor child under age 21, which meets certain Code Section 2503(c) restrictions, does not require a notice to the beneficiary for the annual exclusion to apply (Chapter 13). The other alternative, and the one most commonly used, is to use an annual demand power, called a Crummey demand power. This power is named after the court case in which the court sustained the taxpayer's argument that a gift to a trust, where the beneficiary had an opportunity to withdraw the funds currently, but elected not to do so, qualified as a gift of a present interest, and hence for the annual gift tax exclusion.

If you are planning any irrevocable trust (e.g., life insurance trust or a child's trust) to which you will make gifts, you should carefully review these complex Crummey power rules with your estate planner. When you use a Crummey power, you will have to give a special notice to the beneficiaries following a gift to the trust. If this notice is required but is not provided to the beneficiaries, the transfers or gifts to the trust may not qualify for the annual $10,000 gift tax exclusion.

CAUTION: If you have existing irrevocable trusts to which you are making gifts, and you have not been issuing Crummey notices for each gift, consult your tax adviser immediately. Some tax advisers had their clients issue a single notice to the beneficiaries when forming the trust, and had the beneficiaries waive future notices. The IRS has ruled that this is not sufficient; annual notices are required. If you have not been making notices, it may be advisable to begin doing so for the current year's gifts.

A gift to a trust will qualify for the annual $10,000 gift tax exclusion up to the amount the beneficiary (e.g., your child in a children's trust) can withdraw each year from the trust. Even if the beneficiary does not exercise this right, so that the money or other assets remain in the trust, the existence of this right enables the person making a gift to the trust to avoid any gift tax or use of his or her unified credit.

The trustee must be careful to comply with the requirements of the notice, as contained in the trust agreement. Most trust agreements have a provision with a heading such as "Beneficiary's Annual Demand Power" that sets forth the requirements. The trust must give the beneficiary a reasonable opportunity to withdraw the money. The trustee accomplishes this by giving written notice to the child that the withdrawal right exists for monies contributed and that the child has some period of time, say 30 to 60 days, to send in a written request demanding the money be distributed (the actual term will depend on the requirements contained in the trust agreement). This period could end by December 31. Also, it is best to send the notice certified mail, which will provide proof it was sent. In addition, always have the beneficiary sign the notice acknowledging receipt.

Since an audit of a trust may not occur for many years, it can be difficult to keep track of all the Crummey notices you have sent. You may wish to provide your accountant a copy to retain in the permanent tax file for your trust (where he or she maintains a copy of the trust, tax election information, etc.). This will also alert your accountant to any gift tax return filing requirements. The donor should retain a copy in his or her gift files as well.

The Crummey notice system is complex and difficult for most taxpayers to understand. The key is, until Congress eliminates the "present interest" requirement in the law, everyone setting up a trust must comply with the IRS rules or trigger a potentially large and avoidable gift or estate tax. There are a host of complications to this type of planning, and the following discussion can merely highlight some of the concerns.

Care must be taken that the right of the child-beneficiary to withdraw funds does not create a problem called a "secondary gift-over." For example, assume that you set up a trust for the benefit of your son and daughter. Any monies not paid out or withdrawn are to be accumulated until the youngest child reaches age 35, then the monies are to be distributed equally to each child. A Crummey power is provided so that each child has the right to withdraw one-half of the amount contributed each year, up to a maximum of the $10,000 annual exclusion. The demand power that the son has is really a power of appointment over the amount not withdrawn to your daughter. When the son fails to exercise this power, he is deemed to make a gift to the trust. If the total gift you make to the trust for the year was $20,000, the son will be deemed to have made a gift back to your daughter of the $10,000 he does not elect to withdraw from the trust under his power. This is a taxable gift from your son to your daughter (and similarly, from your daughter to your son).

One solution to this difficulty is to limit the annual gifts to 5 percent of the trust principal or $5,000 so that the gift-over problem can be avoided under the special exclusion. This special rule provides that the end (lapse) of a power that is limited to the greater of 5 percent or $5,000 will not create any gift tax implications. Where the child beneficiary's right to withdraw exceeds this amount, a technique called a "hanging power" is used. A hanging power permits the child's withdrawal power to lapse only where it will not create a gift under the 5 percent or $5,000 rule. Under this approach, the beneficiaries' unexercised right to withdraw $10,000 of trust property each year (the amount you contribute each year, and on which you claim an annual gift tax exclusion) will lapse at the rate of $5,000 per year. The name "hanging power" reflects that the child's withdrawal right can "hang" until future years, and lapse at the rate of $5,000 per year long after you've stopped making contributions. The IRS is not particularly fond of this planning concept.

Another solution is to have separate trusts for each child. With this approach, the failure of the child to exercise his or her right to withdraw money will be a gift to the trust and not to a sibling. Separate trusts are generally preferable from a personal perspective as well, since children tend to mature, have different needs, and so on. Separate trusts enable the trustee to better meet each child's concerns.

This issue of Crummey and hanging powers is important to consider when establishing many types of trusts such as trusts for children (Chapter 13) and life insurance trusts (Chapter 16).

Unified Credit

In prior paragraphs, the method of determining whether a gift occurred, the amount of the gift, and the exclusions available to offset the value of that gift were all discussed. If you've made a taxable gift in excess of the exclusions available, one last, but substantial, tax break is available to offset any gift tax that would otherwise be due. This break is called the unified credit. This important tax break is the cornerstone of estate and trust planning for most taxpayers.

The unified credit is a tax credit of $192,800, which offsets the gift or estate tax on $600,000 of assets. It is called "unified" credit because it applies to the gift and estate taxes, which have been unified as a comprehensive transfer tax system. You can give away $600,000 of assets in taxable gift transactions while you are alive. But if you do, your estate will not have any unified credit left when you die to shelter your remaining assets from the estate tax. If you use the opposite approach and use none of your credit during your lifetime to offset taxable gifts (this doesn't mean you don't make gifts, just not taxable ones), your estate would have the full credit available to offset the tax on $600,000 of assets transferred at your death. Thus, the total amount of $600,000 is a single aggregate exclusion that you can give away, during your life and under your will following your death (or through a revocable living trust). The unified credit enables you to give away $600,000 worth of assets, over and above the exceptions previously discussed, before any tax is due. You can even give away up to $600,000 above the $10,000 annual exclusion amounts.

EXAMPLE: Paul Parent, a widower, has made no gifts before the current tax year. Paul Parent gives $10,000 to each of his three children on January 10. No gift tax is due and none of Paul's unified credit is used because Paul's gifts are each offset by the $10,000 annual exclusion available on gifts to each recipient. On June 1 of the same year, Paul Parent gifts each of his three children an additional $100,000. The annual exclusion has been used up. Therefore, he will use up $300,000 (3 gifts × $100,000 per gift) of the transfers which can be offset by his unified credit. In the next year, Paul pays $64,036 for tuition and medical expenses of his children and grandchildren direct to the educational institutions and medical care providers. No portion of his unified credit or annual exclusion is used because these gifts qualify for the special exception for medical and tuition payments. Paul dies four years later, having made no additional gifts. Paul's estate can use his remaining unified credit to offset the tax on $300,000 of assets passing under Paul's revocable living trust. Thus, during Paul Parent's life, and following his death, his entire unified credit has been used up, exhausting his right to transfer $600,000 of assets tax-free.

The preceding example also illustrates the integrated relationship of the gift and estate taxes. You cannot plan for one and not the other. In addition, when planning with trusts, you need to consider the impact of the gift tax rules, the nature of the trusts established, and the consequences to your overall plan.

EXAMPLE: Tom Taxpayer makes gifts to his partner of $250,000. The first $10,000 is tax-free as a result of the annual exclusion. The next $240,000 [$250,000 total gift – $10,000 exclusions available] is a taxable gift. Since Tom has not used any of his unified credit, no tax is currently due. However, Tom will have exhausted a portion of his unified credit so that $360,000 [$600,000 – $240,000] remains to be gifted away without a gift tax. In the next year, Tom establishes a grantor retained annuity trust (GRAT) for the benefit of his nephew (see Chapter 18). The gift tax value of the GRAT is $450,000. No portion of the annual exclusion is available for a gift to a GRAT so the full value of the gift offsets Tom's remaining unified credit. Tom will have thus made a taxable transfer to his trust of $90,000 [$450,000 taxable gift – $360,000 gift for which unified credit is still available to offset the tax]. A gift tax will be due. Tom will have to pay the gift tax and file a gift tax return, Form 709, by April 15 of the next calendar year. When Tom eventually dies, there will not be any unified credit remaining to offset any tax then due. If Tom was more concerned with benefiting his partner than his nephew, Tom could have considered establishing a trust for the nephew. He could have made $10,000 gifts for many years to the trust and used Crummey powers to preserve his unified credit. He could have also paid medical and tuition payments for his nephew without using any portion of his unified credit. The decision really depends on Tom's priorities, goals, size of estate, and so forth.

The gift tax is a vital consideration when planning most types of trusts. Although the tax can be extremely costly, careful planning and judicious use of the exceptions and other special rules can dramatically limit the tax.

THE ESTATE TAX

Understanding the Estate Tax Is Essential to Proper Trust Planning

Estate tax rates can reach as high as 55 percent (60 percent when certain phaseouts are in effect) and are even higher when state transfer taxes are considered. They climb higher still if the generation-skipping transfer (GST) tax is added on. Planning to minimize this tax burden is essential if you want to pass on the maximum amount of assets to your heirs. For many people, the proper use of trusts is a key to minimizing taxes. The following chapters describe many types of trusts that can help you minimize estate taxes, but you first need to acquire a general understanding of the estate tax. That is the goal of this chapter.

EXAMPLE: Most taxpayers can virtually eliminate estate taxes with the proper use of a credit shelter or bypass trust to fully utilize the unified credit available to both spouses, a marital trust (Q-TIP or Q-DOT), and perhaps an irrevocable life insurance trust. If you do not have a spouse, however, a QPRIT, GRAT, or other trust techniques may be needed to eliminate the estate tax burden. The basic estate tax rules are a prerequisite for working effectively with your tax adviser to determine which trusts meet your tax objectives.

EXAMPLE: You are considering using a grantor retained annuity trust (GRAT) to gift interests in a rental property to your children. The GRAT, as explained in Chapter 18, will discount substantially the value of the gift for gift tax purposes. However, if you don't survive the term of the trust, the entire value of the rental property will be pulled back into your taxable estate. As an alternative, your estate planner suggests transferring the rental property to a family limited partnership and making gifts to your children. Gifts made in this manner could be removed from your estate no matter how long you survive. To discuss these options with your estate planner, you need to understand how the estate tax works.

Overview of the Estate Tax

The estate tax is a transfer charge, or excise tax, assessed on property owned by you on your death. The actual tax, however, is much broader and more complicated than this simple explanation indicates. There are a number of exclusions and deductions. Also the definition of property you own at your death includes items that many taxpayers find surprising.

The following is an overview of the steps to determine your estate tax:

STEP 1.   Determine what is called your "gross estate." This is the sum of the values of all assets and other taxable interests you own at death.

STEP 2.   Any deductions permitted, such as for funeral and other expenses, are then subtracted. This is your taxable estate.

STEP 3.   Determine the adjusted taxable gifts and add this to the taxable estate. The rationale for this step is not as apparent as for the preceding steps but becomes understandable if you remember that the estate and gift taxes (as noted earlier) are a unified system. A single progressive tax rate applies to both gifts and estates. These rates are applied to the cumulative transfers you make during your lifetime and at death. Because the unified rate is progressive (higher rates apply to a larger tax base), the higher up the scale your cumulative life and death transfers are pushed, the higher the tax rate that will apply. Since a single gift and estate tax rate applies to all gifts during your life and assets transferred at your death, the IRS must add on to the taxable estate all prior taxable gifts. Once this is done, the progressive tax rate is applied to the entire amount of transfers. Including these prior gifts in the estate tax calculation would result in double taxation. This is not the intended result. The tax laws merely seek to assure that your lifetime transfers are taxed at the highest rate possible. To prevent a double tax on prior gifts, a credit is permitted for the tax paid on those prior gifts. The net result of this complexity is that in effect your estate could pay a surcharge on prior gifts of up to the difference between the maximum transfer tax rate and the lower progressive rate that applied to those gifts when they were taxed. Several of these latter calculations are part of the following steps.

STEP 4.   Apply the unified gift and estate tax rate to the sum of the taxable estate plus all prior taxable gifts. This is the tentative tax (it cannot be the final tax because, among other adjustments, it would result in paying a double tax on prior taxable gifts).

STEP 5.   Subtract the gift tax paid on prior taxable gifts (those after 1976). This step prevents any double taxation of the prior gifts. The net result is the estate tax due.

With this overview, the components of how the estate tax works can be reviewed in somewhat greater detail.

Assets Included in Your Gross Estate

The first step in calculating the estate tax is to identify all property and property interests included in what is called your gross estate.

NOTE: Don't confuse "taxable" estate with "probate" estate. Taxable estate means assets that will be subject to estate tax on your death. Probate estate refers to assets that must pass through the probate process on your death. Thus, if you set up a revocable living trust and transfer all of your assets to the trust, your probate estate may be nonexistent. However, your taxable estate may be substantial since it will include all assets in your trust. Insurance, IRAs, pension assets, and jointly owned property may all pass to your heirs without becoming part of your probate estate. However, each can be part of your taxable estate.

Your gross estate is the sum of the values of all assets or property owned or in which you have an interest on your death. Generally, your gross estate includes all property, whether real estate, personal property, or intangible property, to the extent the estate tax rules require that this property be included in your estate.

CAUTION: Many taxpayers substantially underestimate the size of their taxable estate and fail to take the steps necessary to avoid estate taxes. Most taxpayers simply do not feel as "rich" as the IRS and the estate tax laws view them. Your home may have appreciated substantially, but is not a spendable asset so long as you live in it. Life insurance can be included in your estate, but while you are alive, you certainly would not view the death benefit as an asset. Pension assets are often not felt to be as valuable as they actually are because they are seldom accessed before retirement, and postretirement they are often drawn down periodically and not viewed as a spendable asset. Thus, you could have a substantial estate for federal tax purposes without actually feeling wealthy.

Assets included in your gross estate include any interest that you had in property at the time of your death which is included in your probate estate. For example, a bonus you were entitled to at the time of your death is included in your gross estate. If you contracted to purchase real estate and died prior to consummating the purchase, the value of the contractual right to the property is included in your estate.

Property interests to be included in your estate are very broadly defined. Even property that you gave away during your life can be required to be included in your gross estate. For example, if you transferred property, but retained the right to the income, or even the right to designate who will obtain the income, these assets can be brought back into your gross estate. Where you transferred property to another person who could only obtain the right to use and enjoy that property after your death, the entire value of this property is included in your estate. If you transferred property but reserved the right to change who will have the right to enjoy that property, this will also be included in your estate.

If you formed a revocable trust, or retained sufficient control or powers over trust assets, those assets can be included in your taxable estate. If you use a revocable trust, the entire amount of assets in the trust will often be included in your estate. However, the rules are much broader and more complicated than this.

Where you had a general power of appointment over property (you could designate who would get the property), the value of that property is included in your gross estate. Powers of appointment can be extremely tricky to plan for. The rules are quite technical, and in some instances it is difficult even to identify whether and where you have been given such powers. These powers of appointment can exist not only in trusts you have created, but in trusts other people have created, even if you are not listed as a beneficiary.

EXAMPLE: Your uncle established a trust for his children. Following the death of the last of his children, he gave you the power to appoint the trust assets to any person or any number of people you designated by a clause in your will specifically referring to the power. Since you were not a beneficiary of the trust for many years while your cousins were alive, how can you find out about this power to even plan for it?

Joint property presents another costly trap for many taxpayers who mistakenly believe that joint ownership removes assets from their estate. It does not. Joint property is not included in your probate estate since it passes on the death of the first joint tenant to the surviving joint tenant by operation of law. It is, however, included in the taxable estate of the first joint tenant. In fact, the tax law presumes that where the joint tenants are not spouses, the entire value of the joint property is taxable in the estate of the first joint tenant to die, unless the surviving joint tenant can demonstrate that he or she contributed to the purchase of the asset. For a qualified joint tenancy with a spouse, only one-half of the property is deemed taxable in the estate of the first joint owner. This special rule is not applicable where the spouse is not a U.S. citizen.

Certain transactions that occurred within three years of your death are pulled back into your estate for tax purposes. These include:

- Gift tax paid on gifts made within three years of your death (the value of the gifts is not pulled back in unless one of the other special provisions pulls it back in).

- Life insurance policies that you transferred. This can occur when you set up an irrevocable life insurance trust but die within three years of transferring the policy to the trust.

TIP: When setting up an insurance trust, whenever possible, have the trustee on behalf of the trust apply for and take out the insurance. This avoids the transfer from you to the trust that could trigger the three-year rule.

- Life estate, reversionary interest or a power to revoke, amend, or terminate property interests where you revoke the power within three years of death.

EXAMPLE: If you form a trust but retain the unlimited right to revoke the trust or replace the trustee, the value of the trust assets will be included in your estate. If you revoke this power within three years of death, the value of the trust will still be included in your estate even though you did not hold this power at death.

Once the assets to be included in your taxable estate are identified, they must be valued.

Assets in Your Estate Must Be Valued

The fair value of the assets at the date of your death is the amount to be included in your gross estate. The value to be used is called the "fair market value." This is the price at which the property would change hands between a willing buyer and a willing seller, neither being under any compulsion to buy or to sell, and both having reasonable knowledge of the relevant facts.

- *Life Insurance.* Life insurance proceeds are taxable in the estate if the estate is a beneficiary of the policy, you owned incidents of ownership at death, or you transferred the property to a trust and died less than three years later. This includes, for example, the right to change the beneficiary and assign the policy. While in many cases, the life insurance will pass to a spouse so that the marital deduction can offset its value, this will not apply in all situations. If you own insurance on someone else's life, on your death the value of that policy is taxed in your estate. It is not, however, valued based on the face value.

EXAMPLE: Life insurance, contrary to what most taxpayers believe, is taxable for estate tax purposes. Many taxpayers, especially younger couples with children can have sufficient insurance to trigger a huge estate tax and never realize the tax problems in store for their heirs. The answer for many people is to transfer the insurance to an irrevocable life insurance trust, as discussed in Chapter 16.

- *Publicly Traded Securities.* Where a stock traded on a public exchange is included in your estate, the value is easily found in any major newspaper. Over-the-counter stocks are valued based on the mean between the highest and lowest quoted selling price on the date of valuation. The amount of any interest accrued from the last payment on a bond is added to the value. This latter item is called "income in respect of a decedent," or "IRD." IRD is subject to various special rules.

- *Mortgages, Notes, Cash.* These items are valued based on their face value. However, if it can be demonstrated that a particular note or mortgage is not collectible, the face value may be discounted.

- *Real Estate.* Real estate is generally valued based on an appraisal. If, as is quite common, the real estate is owned by an entity (partnership, S corporation, limited liability company, or trust) a two-step process is required. First, the underlying real estate must be valued. Second, the interest in the entity that owned the real estate must be valued. Real estate valuation can be a substantial point of contention between your estate and the IRS. This is why it is always best to have a thorough written appraisal supported by detailed income and cost analysis, comparables, and so forth. Real estate must generally be valued at its highest and best use. Thus, if you left land vacant, or used it as a parking lot, when it could readily be sold to a developer to build and sell condominiums, the value of the land as condominium land and not raw land or a parking lot is the relevant value.

- *Annuities.* These are generally valued using IRS tables.

- *Closely Held Business.* Business interests must be valued by a business appraiser. As with real estate, a thorough detailed report is essential. In some instances, a buyout agreement will determine the value so that no appraisal is necessary. However, if the buy-out value is not realistic or arm's length (what an unrelated person would pay), the IRS may not accept the value in the buy-out agreement.

EXAMPLE: Sam Shareholder owned a 50 percent interest in ABC Widget, Inc. The shareholder agreement required that his partner, Paula President, purchase his interest for $500,000. Further, the shareholders each owned insurance on the life of the other shareholder to fund this buyout (called a "cross-purchase arrangement"). On Sam's death, Paula purchased his stock from his estate for $500,000 using the insurance proceeds. This should probably be the value to be used for Sam's estate.

A number of special valuation rules should be considered:

- *Special Use Valuation.* As noted, real estate is generally valued at its highest and best use. This rule, however, can create hardships. What if the property is used in a family farming or business venture even though its best use might be condominiums? It would burden the family business excessively to require application of the general rule. Thus, the tax laws permit the executor to elect to value the land based on its current use, up to a maximum decrease in the value of the gross estate of $750,000.
- *Alternate Valuation Date.* The date at which the valuation must be made also has to be determined. In most cases, it is the date of death. However, if an asset is sold prior to filing the estate tax return, that value is often used as the best indication of the date-of-death value. Also, the executor has the option to elect to value all assets as of the date six months following the date of death. This is called the alternate valuation date. This election could be useful if there is a decline in the value of key assets following death (e.g., a stock market crash between the date of death and the date the estate tax return must be filed).

Certain Deductions and Expenses Are Permitted

Your estate is allowed deductions for:

- *Funeral Expenses.* Costs for clergy, monument, service, burial plot or place of interment, and, in some instances, even payments for perpetual care are deductible.
- *Estate Administrative Expenses.* The cost of paying executors is often one of the largest administration expenses. It is often a key component of the arguments for avoiding probate. In many instances, however, executor (also called personal administrator) expenses are paid to family members who are the beneficiaries of the estate anyhow. Thus, if the income tax cost to the executors of receiving executor fees (which are taxable to them as income) is less than the marginal estate tax cost that would have been incurred if the fee had not been paid and deducted by the estate, the family unit as a whole actually benefits from the payment.

    Interest expense paid on federal and state income tax deficiencies contested by the executor is deductible. Interest expense on money borrowed to pay estate and inheritance taxes is deductible. Interest expense paid to the IRS is deductible if the executor elected to defer estate tax under special provisions available where a substantial portion of the estate consists of interests in closely held businesses. However, these charges are only deducted when they become due.

    Reasonable legal fees are deductible. Court costs, appraisal fees (e.g., for determining the value of real estate or a closely held business included in the estate), accounting fees, storage costs, other costs of protecting and preserving estate assets, and so forth, are all deductible.

- *Casualty or Theft Losses*. Casualty losses include damage not reimbursed by insurance from fire, storm, theft, or other casualty that occurs during the administration of the estate and before the damaged property was distributed to heirs.

- *Claims against or Debts of Your Estate*. Debts of the estate or decedent can also be deducted. To be deducted, the debts have to be enforceable against the estate, personal obligations of the decedent at the time of death, and created in arm's-length transactions. Common examples include medical expenses, mortgages, notes, personal bank loans, unpaid income taxes, and so forth.

- *Charitable Bequests*. An unlimited deduction can be taken by your estate for qualifying bequests to charity. This could include the value of assets in a charitable trust (Chapter 14).

- *Qualifying Bequests to Your Surviving Spouse*. An unlimited marital deduction is available for qualifying distributions to a surviving spouse. This deduction is available where the value of the property passes from the decedent or the decedent's estate to a surviving spouse who is a U.S. citizen. To "pass," the property must be transferred under the decedent's will (or under the decedent's state's laws of intestacy if no will existed), as a result of joint ownership between the decedent and surviving spouse, pursuant to a general power of appointment in the decedent, or as a result of a beneficiary designation (e.g., the surviving spouse is listed as the beneficiary on an insurance policy). This could include trusts such as Q-TIP and Q-DOT trusts (see Chapter 11).

TIP: Some of the administrative and other expenses can be deducted on the estate's income tax return, Form 1041. No expenses can be deducted in both places. Discuss with your accountant where it would be better to claim the deduction.

An important concept to understanding the workings of these two marital trusts is called the "terminable interest rule." This rule provides that an interest that will terminate or fail on the lapse of time or the occurrence of some contingency will not qualify. The Q-TIP and Q-DOT trusts are an important statutory exception to this general rule. These special trusts are discussed in Chapter 11. However, there are two additional exceptions to the terminable interest rule, which in the appropriate circumstances can present alternatives to using the Q-TIP and Q-DOT trusts. The first is giving the surviving spouse a life estate and general power of appointment. If the surviving spouse receives assets under the following conditions, the marital deduction will be available:

- The surviving spouse must be entitled to all of the income from the property for life.

- The income must be payable annually or more frequently.
- The surviving spouse must have the right to convert nonincome-producing property to income-producing property (e.g., force the sale of raw land and the purchase of bonds).
- The power of appointment granted to the surviving spouse must give him or her the right to appoint the property to anyone following the termination of the spouse's life estate. This must include the spouse, the spouse's estate, the spouse's creditors, and the creditors of the spouse's estate.
- The surviving spouse must have the right, alone, to exercise the power. No one else should have the right to appoint the property.

The second exception is for what is known as an "estate trust." This type of trust will qualify for the unlimited marital deduction for a U.S. citizen where the preceding requirements for a life estate and general power of appointment are met, with one twist. The twist is that the income from the estate trust does not have to be paid to the spouse at least annually: it can be accumulated and added to the trust. However, the estate trust must require that the accumulated income and principal must be paid out at some future time to the surviving spouse, or to the surviving spouse's estate.

Credits to Reduce the Estate Tax

A number of credits may also be applied to reduce your estate tax including a credit for prior transfers, for death taxes paid to your state, and so forth. While the credits can be important for trust planning, they are beyond the scope of this book.

CONCLUSION

The gift and estate taxes are complex, broad transfer taxes that can substantially affect the type of trusts you choose to use. A properly planned gift and estate tax program is essential for any large estate. Even if your estate is small, it would be inadvisable not to consider gift and estate taxes when planning. Otherwise you could waste valuable benefits (e.g., your unified credit) that will be needed in the future if your estate grows. Planning is also important because many taxpayers simply don't realize how large the IRS views their estate.

The judicious use of annual exclusions, with particular attention to the problems created by gifts to trust, can enable you to transfer substantial assets out of your estate at little or no tax cost. The careful planning of assets transferred to irrevocable trust, and the proper restriction of the rights and powers that you retain in those trusts, can provide outstanding opportunities for reducing your potential estate tax cost while still providing you some comfort and assurance as to how those assets will be used.

Considering the complexities and what is usually substantial amounts involved, always review the gift and estate tax issues with your tax adviser.

For Your Notebook:

SAMPLE CRUMMEY POWER NOTICE

[TO REVIEW WITH YOUR ESTATE PLANNER]

*CO-TRUSTEE-NAME
*TRUST-NAME
*CO-TRUSTEE-ADDRESS

*MONTH *DAY, *YEAR
VIA CERTIFIED MAIL RETURN RECEIPT REQUESTED
*BENEFICIARY-NAME
[c/o *GUARDIAN-NAME] (if minor beneficiary)
*BENEFICIARY-ADDRESS

Re: *Notice of Limited Withdrawal Right From Trust*

Dear *BENEFICIARY-NAME:

Please be advised that a contribution of *$ _____ [fill in dollar amount or fair market value of property given as a gift to the trust] has been made to the above named trust. You have a limited power as a beneficiary of the above trust to demand the payment of any portion of the above contribution, not to exceed $10,000, be paid to you currently. You may request a distribution of this money only if you send a written request to me, as trustee, at the above address within _____ days [see the provision of your trust for the required time period; it is typically 30 days or 60 days from the date the funds are contributed and this notice given, but review the trust before deciding].

Sincerely,

*TRUST-NAME

By: _____
    *CO-TRUSTEE-NAME, Co-Trustee

[Having the beneficiary, or the guardian for a minor beneficiary sign and return the notice when the right to withdraw is not exercised is not required, but is recommended].

RECEIPT OF NOTICE HEREBY ACKNOWLEDGED:

By: _____
    *BENEFICIARY-NAME

If a guardian signs for a minor beneficiary the guardian should add ", by *GUARDIAN NAME" as follows:

By: _____
    *BENEFICIARY-NAME, by *GUARDIAN-NAME

NOTE: Be certain to save the original signed (by *both* the trustee and by the beneficiary) Crummey power notice for every gift made to each trust. The trustee should retain an original with the trusts records. You as the grantor, and donor of the gifts covered by the Crummey notice, should also probably retain an original as well in your records.

---

8 PLANNING FOR THE GENERATION-SKIPPING TRANSFER TAX

WHAT IS THE GST AND WHY DID CONGRESS ENACT IT?

The gift and estate taxes, described in Chapter 17, are not the only taxes involved when making gifts to trusts. The generation-skipping transfer (GST) tax—an expensive and complicated transfer tax contained in Chapter 13 of the Internal Revenue Code—can affect wealthy taxpayers making transfers by gift or at death to grandchildren or other people the tax laws consider two or more generations beyond the donor. The GST tax is charged on every gift or other transfer of property that meets the requirements of being a generation-skipping transfer. The GST tax is calculated as a flat 55 percent tax rate on the taxable amount of a generation-skipping transfer. While the GST will not affect most taxpayers, those it does affect can be shocked by its impact. Thus, if there is even a remote possibility the GST could apply to you, careful planning for it is essential. The tax can be quite tricky, applying where you might not expect it.

EXAMPLE: You transfer by gift assets to a trust to benefit your child and her descendants. A distribution from the trust on your grandson's 21st birthday could trigger a GST tax.

The purpose of the tax is to equalize intergenerational taxation of property transfers where planning is attempted to avoid the estate tax. The GST was designed to prevent the very wealthy from transferring assets through many layers of generations, tax-free, often through the use of trusts.

EXAMPLE: You become a grandfather and wish to make a gift of $1 million to your grandchild (cash, an interest in a property, or another asset). The GST tax, assuming you have used up your $1 million lifetime exemption, is in the maximum tax bracket, $550,000. Further, if the GST tax on a taxable termination is paid by you, the GST tax you pay is itself subject to tax! This is done by the tax laws treating the amount of GST tax you paid as another gift to your grandchild as well. So the gift tax to be paid on the $1 million transfer is based on a total gift of $1,550,000 [$1 million actual gift + $550,000 GST tax which is deemed to be a further gift]. At the 55 percent maximum gift tax rate, you will owe a gift tax of $852,500. To make the $1 million gift you will have had to pay taxes totaling $1,402,500 [$550,000 GST tax + $852,500 gift tax]. Thus the total cost of making the $1 million gift is $2,402,500.

To implement the many planning opportunities using trusts to minimize or eliminate GST tax, you must understand how the GST tax works. In this chapter, the basics will be explained first, and then the planning opportunities will be examined in detail.

HOW THE GST TAX WORKS

Calculating the GST Tax

Once it has been determined that a gift, bequest, or other transfer is subject to the GST tax, the GST tax must be calculated. The first step is to determine the value of the property involved. The property is generally valued at the time of the transfer. However, if the transfer was a direct skip (to be explained) and the property was included in your gross estate, the special valuation rules used by your estate will apply to the GST as well. These rules could permit your executor to value the property at the date six months following your death rather than at the date of your death, which is the general rule. Where the transfer also triggers a gift tax, the amount of GST tax paid by the donor is treated as a further gift subject to the gift tax.

The GST tax is assessed at a flat rate equal to the maximum estate tax rate, presently 55 percent. This tax rate is actually multiplied by the "inclusion ratio" defined later in this chapter.

Once the tax has been calculated, a credit for taxes paid to your estate may be available where the GST tax transfer occurs by reason of a taxable distribution or a taxable termination at the time of your death. You are also entitled to a $1 million exemption, which will be discussed later in the chapter.

Overview of Transfers That Trigger the GST Tax

The GST tax can apply to a broad range of property transfers, including transfers of property in trust (e.g., a gift to a trust established for a grandchild), life estates (e.g., a child has the right to income from the property for life and on the child's death a grandchild receives the property), remainder interests (e.g., a grandchild receives the property after the death of a child and the termination of the child's life estate), and so forth.

For the GST tax to apply, a taxable event must occur. This requires a generation-skipping transfer. The simplest example is where you give your grandchild property. More technically, the GST tax applies where there is a transfer of property (or income from property) to a person who is considered to be a member of a generation at least two generations below the generation of the person making the gift.

NOTE: You're generation 1. Your child is generation 2. Your grandchild is generation 3. Assume that your spouse sets up an irrevocable trust for one of your grandchildren and makes a gift to the trust of $45,000 of stock. This gift would trigger GST tax consequences because the gift benefits a person at least two generations below your generation. A gift from your spouse to your child of the same amount would not cause the GST tax to apply (but there could be a gift tax).

Some basic terms will be defined including the three events that can trigger the GST tax: a direct skip, a taxable distribution, and a taxable termination. First, however, it is necessary to understand the meaning of "skip person."

Who Is a "Skip Person"?

A skip person is a person who is two or more generations below the generation of the person making the gift or establishing a trust. This could include your grandchild, or a trust for the benefit of your grandchild. A trust is considered a skip person where no distributions can be made to nonskip persons. A nonskip person is someone who is less than two generations below the generation of the person making the gift (e.g., your child or sibling).

EXAMPLE: A credit shelter trust is formed under your will for the benefit of your surviving spouse and descendants including grandchildren who are skip persons. However, your spouse and children are not skip persons so that the trust is not a skip person. This doesn't mean that GST tax is not a consideration, but since the transfer is not to a skip person, the GST tax will not be due immediately.

While a grandchild or later descendant is obviously a skip person, the law is much broader and more complex. A skip person can include any individual (not only a direct descendant) who is more than a specified number of years younger than the person setting up the trust or making the gift. For nonlineal descendants, a generation is considered to be 25 years. A person born with 12.5 years (i.e., ½ of the 25 years) of your birthday will be treated as being of your generation. A person who is more than 12.5 but less than 37.5 (i.e., 12.5 + 25 years, which is considered a generation) is considered to be in the same generation as your children would be (assuming you had children). A person who is more than 37.5 years younger is considered to be in the same generation as your grandchildren would be (assuming you had grandchildren).

> **EXAMPLE:** Gary Grantor, age 73, never married and has no children. His will provides that his estate will be distributed to his four nephews. His nephews are ages 22, 23, 25, and 39 respectively. At Gary's death, the distributions to the first three nephews could trigger GST consequences. The fourth nephew, however, is deemed to be in the same generation as a child of Gary would be.

Taxable Transfer 1—A Direct Skip

A direct skip is a transfer of an interest in property, which is subject to the estate or gift tax, to a skip person (or to a trust for the benefit of a skip person). A direct skip occurs if your will leaves a car to a grandchild. If a trust is created and all trust income is accumulated for a number of years without distribution, but eventually the trust benefits only skip persons, a direct skip occurs and a tax is assessed.

The GST tax for a direct skip, when no trust is involved, is to be paid by the person making the transfer (the donor, or if it is a bequest under your will, your estate). If the transfer is made from a trust, then the trustee will have to pay the tax.

> **EXAMPLE:** You transfer property to an irrevocable (cannot be changed) trust for the benefit of your grandchild. If the transfer is a gift which is a direct skip, it will trigger the GST tax. If, however, you retain sufficient powers over the trust, or alternatively give sufficient powers to your children over the trust (so that the trust will be taxable in their estates), the GST tax won't apply. If you transfer assets to a revocable trust, the gift is incomplete for gift tax purposes and no GST tax can apply. These two planning techniques—(1) your retaining powers over the trust or having the trust revocable so that trust assets are taxable in your estate; or (2) giving your children (i.e., a nonskip person) sufficient powers over a trust so that it is taxable in your children's estate—can help you accomplish personal goals while avoiding the GST tax.

A direct skip is a "tax-exclusive" calculation. If you as donor pay the GST tax on a gift of assets (a direct skip) to your grandchild, the amount of GST tax you pay will not be considered an additional gift for GST tax purposes. While this sounds far from generous, for some GST transfers, as will be described, the GST tax is calculated on a "tax-inclusive" basis so that the payment of GST tax triggers more tax!

The recipient of the property may qualify for an increase in the tax basis of the property. The tax basis is increased by the portion of the GST tax attributable to the appreciation of the property given above the donor's tax basis.

There is a special exclusion from GST taxation as a direct skip where a child has died. If your child dies and you make a gift to the child of your deceased child (i.e., your grandchild), no GST tax will be assessed. Thus, your grandchild will not be considered a skip person for tax purposes, and the transfer won't trigger the GST tax.

CAUTION: This exception is very limited and does not apply in situations where logic and fairness might suggest its use. It only applies to a gift to a grandchild where the grandchild's parent, your child, has died. Say you set up a trust, a credit shelter sprinkle trust under your will, to benefit your surviving spouse and issue. If on the later death of your surviving spouse, your child has previously died so that the entire trust is distributed to your grandchild, the GST tax would apply. The taxable termination rules described later in this chapter could apply. The special rule for a deceased child applicable to direct skips would not be available.

Taxable Transfer 2—A Taxable Distribution

Where there is a distribution of property or money from a trust to a "skip person" the GST tax may apply.

EXAMPLE: Your spouse sets up a single trust for the benefit of your two daughters and their three children (i.e., your grandchildren). Any distribution by the trustee to any of the grandchildren will result in a GST tax. The grandchildren are all considered skip persons for purposes of the GST tax since they are two generations below you, the grantor of the trust.

The GST tax applies as a taxable distribution, and not as a taxable termination (to be discussed), if the child's (nonskip person's) interest ends for some reason other than death, for example, marriage.

EXAMPLE: You form a trust for the benefit of your child from your current marriage. The trust will last only until this child marries. Upon this child's marriage, the trust is distributed to the grandchildren from your former marriage. The GST tax, as a taxable distribution, applies when distributions are actually made to the grandchildren. Similarly, if instead of the trust terminating on the child's marriage, a distribution of $100,000 is made to each grandchild, these would be taxable distributions.

PLANNING TIP: Your GST and trusts' planning may encourage you to set up trusts for your children which can make taxable distributions to your grandchildren. This could occur where you've used up your $1 million exemption. If you set up a trust solely for the benefit of your grandchildren, the transfer would immediately trigger the GST tax. Since this tax is so onerous, it's always best to defer it. Deferral of the GST will let the assets in the trust continue to grow and earn interest. If the trust names your children and grandchildren as beneficiaries, and the trustee has the power to sprinkle income to any of these beneficiaries, the GST tax can be deferred until the trustee actually makes a distribution to one of the grandchildren (this is called a sprinkle trust). If you've set up a GST-exempt trust (to be described) to use your $1 million GST exemption amount, your trustee could be making generous distributions to your grandchildren from that trust before tapping the expensive (i.e., from a GST tax perspective) money in the sprinkle trust.

The GST tax on a taxable distribution is based on the fair value of the property transferred, reduced by any expenses incurred in connection with determining the tax. If paid out of a trust, the amount of tax paid is treated as an additional distribution subject to the tax. The GST tax on a taxable distribution is charged against the property that was given, unless specific provisions are made for a different treatment. The transferees (your grandchildren in the preceding examples), however, are liable to pay the GST tax.

When a GST taxable distribution occurs, the tax basis (what the grantor paid for the property transferred to the trust) is increased. The increase is for the portion of the GST tax attributable to the excess of the fair market value of the property above its tax basis. However, the increase cannot increase the tax basis to more than the value of the property.

If income from a trust is distributed to a skip person, the GST tax as a taxable distribution will apply. However, the recipient can deduct the GST tax paid on the income distribution on his or her personal income tax return.

Taxable Transfer 3—A Taxable Termination

A "taxable termination" is a transaction that will trigger the GST tax. This occurs when the interests of a beneficiary of a trust (the person entitled to receive income from a trust) terminate and a grandchild (or another person two or more generations below the person creating the trust) then receives the principal. This could occur as a result of a death, lapse of time (e.g. the trust lasts only until the child-beneficiary reaches age 60, at which time the trust ends and the grandchild receives the money), or release of a power (right). This will be considered a taxable termination resulting in a GST tax. If, however, someone other than a grandchild (or person two generations below the person setting up the trust) receives a portion of the trust, then the termination would not entirely be a taxable termination.

EXAMPLE: You create a trust. Income is paid to your child for his life. On your child's death, his interest terminates and the principal passes to your grandchild. A taxable termination will then occur triggering the GST tax. The GST tax would be in addition to any gift or estate tax paid when the trust was created. If the trust does not terminate but rather just makes a distribution to the grandchild, the rules for taxable distribution instead apply. There can be important technical differences (e.g., tax basis adjustments) depending on which rule applies, and these should be discussed with your tax adviser.

Several exceptions can prevent incurring the GST tax: (1) Immediately after the termination, a nonskip person has an interest in the property; or (2) no distribution can be made to a skip person.

EXAMPLE: If in the preceding example, your child was given a general power of appointment over the property (i.e., the right to designate who should inherit the property on his death), the property would be taxed in the child's estate and no GST tax would be due. This is because the power of appointment would constitute an interest in the property as required under the exception.

EXAMPLE: If in the example, the trust continued for the benefit of the spouse and issue of the deceased child, no taxable termination would occur and the GST tax would be deferred. If the trustee was given a sprinkle power to distribute income and principal to anyone in a class including your deceased child's spouse (no matter how young that spouse) and issue, no GST tax would occur on the death of your child. Thus, by including your child's spouse as a possible beneficiary, you will have deferred the GST tax. Later, if distributions are made to issue of your deceased child, the taxable distribution rules previously described will apply when those distributions are made.

The GST tax on a taxable termination is payable by the trustee of the trust. The amount is calculated based on the value of all property to which the taxable termination occurred, reduced by expenses, debts, and taxes. The tax is quite burdensome because it is a "tax-inclusive" transfer tax, which is similar to the estate tax. It means that there is no deduction for the tax paid.

EXAMPLE: If the trust were $1 million, and a 55 percent GST were to apply, the tax would be $550,000. Thus, the tax is assessed on the same dollars used to pay the tax (i.e., on the full $1 million, including the $550,000 of it which is tax). These are dollars that never pass to any beneficiary.

Of modest relief is that in a taxable termination, the tax basis of the assets is "stepped-up." This is similar to what happens when assets are included in an estate.

EXAMPLE: In the preceding example, if the donor/grantor who set up the trust had a $1,000 tax basis (investment) in the $1 million asset transferred to the trust, sale of the asset would result in a $999,000 taxable gain for income tax purposes [$1 million value – $1,000 tax basis]. When the child-beneficiary of the trust dies and a GST tax is incurred as a result of a taxable termination, the tax basis of the asset is increased (stepped up) to its $1 million fair value so that there is no income tax gain if the asset is sold. Note that if any portion of the GST tax is avoided by use of the $1 million GST exemption discussed later, the basis adjustment is reduced.

Disclaimers Can Trigger GST Tax

Disclaimers are a common postdeath estate tax planning technique. They can, however, trigger surprising and costly GST tax consequences. Any well-drafted will, depending on the testator's intent, may address what happens if a particular beneficiary dies. For example, if you bequeath your valuable antique gun collection to your son, your will might say that if your son is not then living or disclaims the bequest, the gun collection will be given to his son (i.e., your grandson). This type of flexible drafting is important. Obviously, if your son has died, you want to address where assets should be distributed. But it means more. What if your son is alive and well, but for other reasons does not wish to own the particular bequest. He might be in the midst of a divorce or lawsuit and not wish to expose the gun collection. He could then disclaim the bequest. This requires filing papers in the local surrogate's court (where wills are filed, in some places different names are used). Your will is then interpreted as if he had died before you. In this case, the gun collection would be given to your grandson. This disclaimer, while accomplishing important asset protection or personal goals, may have inadvertently triggered the GST tax. The gun collection now passes to your grandson, a skip person.

HOW TO PLAN TO MINIMIZE THE GST TAX IMPACT ON YOUR TRUST

Several basic GST planning techniques to avoid the harsh tax results previously illustrated need to be reviewed, particularly as to how they affect your trust planning.

Do You Even Want to Make Gifts to Grandchildren?

The GST tax generally applies to transfers that skip a generation, such as to your grandchildren. Most people seem to prefer to give most of their assets to their children, and to entrust their children with the responsibility of caring and providing for their own children (i.e., your grandchildren). The GST can be trickier, however. It can apply, as has been explained, to transfers to persons other than grandchildren simply based on the age differential between yourself and the donee. To the extent that you leave assets to children and nonskip persons, the GST tax will not apply. This can be done in less than obvious ways with trusts.

Your objective may be to pass certain amounts or assets to your grandchildren but you wish to avoid the GST tax. Assume that you set up a trust for your child providing that on your child's death the assets pass to your grandchild. This would be a taxable termination triggering GST tax. However, if you could cause the trust assets to be included in your child's estate (i.e., subject to estate tax on your child's death), no GST would be due. Why would you want to trade a GST tax for your child's estate tax? The estate tax is assessed based on graduated tax rates. The GST tax is charged at a flat 55 percent. Thus, the estate tax could be cheaper. The child's estate tax could be reduced by use of his or her $600,000 unified credit, deductions, or other planning options. But even if this saves the GST tax, if your goal was to benefit the grandchild with this particular amount of money, giving the trust principal to the child's estate would defeat your goal. This doesn't have to occur, however. You can set up a trust that will be taxable in your child's estate although neither your child nor your child's estate will not receive the principal of the trust. Instead, you grant the child a "general power" of appointment over the trust property. A general power of appointment is a right given to your child under the trust that is sufficiently broad that for estate tax purposes it will cause the trust principal to be taxable in the child's estate without necessarily causing the property to be distributed to the child's estate. The following sample clause illustrates a general power.

SAMPLE CLAUSE: The Trustee shall transfer the principal of the trust to such persons other than the Child, his or her estate, but including his or her creditors and the creditors of his or her estate, to such extent, in such amounts or proportions, and in such lawful interests or estates, whether absolute or in trust, as such Child may by his or her last will and testament appoint by a specific reference to this power.

Annual per Donee Gift Tax Exclusion

You can still give up to $10,000 per year to any person, including every grandchild, without triggering the GST tax. If your spouse joins you in the gift, you can give $20,000 per year. Thus, over a period of years, you can transfer substantial assets to your grandchildren with no GST tax cost. Again, however, the GST can be quite tricky. The requirements to qualify a gift to a trust for a grandchild or other skip person for the annual $10,000 GST exclusion are more stringent than the requirements discussed in Chapter 7 to qualify for the annual $10,000 gift tax annual exclusion.

Although the $10,000 annual exclusion is available for the GST tax, the requirements are different from those applicable for the gift tax. Thus, a transfer might qualify for the annual $10,000 gift tax exclusion, but not for the GST tax. The $10,000 annual exclusion is only available for GST tax purposes on a direct skip transfer. This is a gift directly to a grandchild (or later generation), or in some instances to a trust for a grandchild. It doesn't apply to a taxable termination or a taxable distribution.

To qualify for the GST tax annual exclusion, gifts to a trust must meet several requirements. During the life of the grandchild (other skip person) who is beneficiary of the trust, payments cannot be made to any other person. Thus, the commonly used sprinkle power (trustee has discretion to pay income and principal to anyone from a listed group of beneficiaries) will not be acceptable. This is why a single or pot trust for grandchildren will not qualify. This requirement does not, however, prevent the trustee from accumulating income in any given year rather than distributing it. An additional requirement is that if the beneficiary dies during the term of the trust, the trust assets must be taxable in the beneficiary's estate. The requirements to qualify for the GST tax annual exclusion are similar to the requirements for the Code Section 2503(c) minor's trust discussed in Chapter 13. They are dissimilar to those provisions typically included in a Crummey power trust, discussed in Chapter 7.

The requirement that the trust assets must be taxable in the estate of the grandchild can prevent gifts to a typical grandchild's education trust from qualifying. For example, assume that the trust provided that assets were to be held until the grandchild attained the age of 35, whereupon the assets would be distributed to the grandchild. If the grandchild died before the trust ended, the assets would be held in trust for the grandchild's children. This type of trust may not qualify for the annual $10,000 GST tax exclusion because the assets would not be included in the grandchild's estate. One solution is to give the grandchild a general power of appointment (see earlier discussion and sample clause). In some cases, you may prefer the certainty of control over where the assets will be distributed. In this case (i.e., the grandchild is not given a general power of appointment), you should be certain that your accountant files an annual gift tax return allocating a portion of your $1 million GST exemption to the trust each year a gift is made. This latter approach is often used if you are not planning on making multimillion dollar gifts to grandchildren (e.g., using the maximum $1 million GST exemption available to your estate and your spouse's estate).

CAUTION: This type of planning requires filing an annual gift tax return to allocate GST exemption even though no gift tax is due and a gift tax return would not otherwise have to be filed.

EXAMPLE: Grandmother has one child, a divorced daughter with two children (i.e., her grandchildren). Grandmother gives $30,000 of corporate bonds to a trust for the benefit of her daughter and two grandchildren. She may have a GST tax problem depending on the terms of the trust. If the grandmother transfers $30,000 to the trust, each beneficiary should have a Crummey demand power for Grandmother to qualify for the annual gift tax exclusion on the entire transfer. After the demand power lapses (which occurs if the child and grandchildren don't use it), the trustee can make distributions to the daughter and grandchildren. Where the trustee has a sprinkling power between generations, there is a potential GST tax problem. Even without such a power, if distributions will skip a generation when the interests of the middle generation—the daughter—terminate (e.g., the daughter's death, or a required distribution to the grandchildren upon her reaching age 35), a GST tax will be triggered. A better approach to avoid technical GST tax problems would be to have a separate trust for each beneficiary, if this approach is consistent with Grandmother's wishes.

Where a husband and wife elect to split their gift, the GST is deemed to have been made one-half by each. Thus, if wealthy spouse gives assets to grandchildren, a portion of nonwealthy spouse's GST tax $1 million exemption can be allocated as well.

Transfers for Educational and Medical Benefits

You can gift unlimited amounts of money to pay for a grandchild's education or medical benefits. A simple approach is for a grandparent with a substantial estate to set up a checking account. All children and grandchildren send any qualifying medical and tuition bills directly to the grandparent who then pays them directly. With a large family, and the high cost of quality medical care and education, tremendous amounts can be transferred for the benefit of later generations with no GST tax implications. This technique should be carefully reviewed before incurring the expense, and problems, of setting up trusts for grandchildren.

This exclusion for medical and tuition payments can protect distributions from trusts from the GST tax. For example, assume you established a credit shelter trust in your will permitting distributions to your spouse and descendants generally by the trustee under a sprinkle power. Since a distribution to a grandchild could trigger GST tax, this might not be desirable. Consider instead permitting the trustee to sprinkle distributions to your spouse and children without limit (if the trustee is independent, or perhaps under an ascertainable standard if the trustee is not) and to the issue of your children (i.e., skip persons) solely for qualifying medical and tuition payments. This approach could provide for maximum flexibility without triggering GST tax. See *The Beneficiary Handbook* (New York: John Wiley & Sons Inc., 1991) for suggestions on how to organize and maintain such checking accounts.

One-Million-Dollar Exemption

The primary protection from the GST is a one-time exclusion (similar to the use of the one-time gift and estate tax unified credit). You can gift up to $1 million to your grandchildren with no GST tax cost. Your spouse can similarly make a $1 million transfer to the grandchildren. Thus, a wealthy family can gift $2 million to grandchildren without the application of the GST. While this exemption can eliminate the GST tax for most taxpayers, it does not mean that taxpayers should ignore the GST; it can still be costly. Also, to use these large $1 million exemptions advantageously takes careful planning.

This exclusion must be irrevocably allocated to any property transfers you make. This allocation is generally made on your gift tax returns. This $1 million exemption can also be allocated by your executor on your estate tax return following your death to the extent not previously allocated on any of your gift tax returns. Many taxpayers plan to take maximum advantage of this exemption by setting up multiple trusts under their wills and granting their executors the authority to make certain decisions as to how these trusts will be funded, and how much GST exemption is to be allocated. However, the allocation once made, cannot be changed.

Once a portion or all of your GST exemption is allocated to a particular property transfer, the protection of that allocation will continue to stay with the property. Thus, if your GST exemption is allocated to property given to a trust, that trust will remain protected from your GST tax in future years.

To clarify the use of the $1 million exemption, another bit of jargon must be introduced, the "inclusion ratio." The GST tax exemption percentage (the inclusion ratio) is established when you make a gift and allocate your exemption (or when a trust is formed under your will and your executor makes the allocation). The inclusion ratio is: [1 – the "applicable fraction"]. The applicable fraction, where you make the gift to a trust, is determined as follows:

$$\frac{\text{Amount of GST Exemption Allocated to Trust}}{\text{Value of Property Transferred to the Trust}}$$

The numerator is the amount of your GST exemption allocated to the particular transfer. The denominator is the value of the property involved, reduced by any charitable contribution deduction and any federal or state estate or death taxes.

EXAMPLE: You set up a $1 million trust fund for your grandchildren and great-grandchildren. You allocate your entire $1 million GST tax exemption to the trust. The assets of the trust appreciate to $10 million before being distributed in a taxable distribution or termination. None of the transfers of the $10 million in trust property to your grandchildren and great-grandchildren is subject to the GST tax. This is because the applicable fraction is 1, and the inclusion ratio is zero. The applicable fraction is "1" because you allocated $1 million GST exemption to $1 million in assets. Had you instead only allocated $500,000 of GST exemption to the $1 million in assets, the inclusion ratio would be 50 percent and $5 million [50% inclusion ratio × $10 million taxable] would be subject to GST tax.

One approach to addressing this potential GST tax problem is to allocate some portion of your $1 million GST tax exemption to the trust. How much of your exemption to allocate is an extremely important decision and can be quite complicated. If you allocate any portion of your GST tax exemption to a trust, that portion of the exemption is considered used, whether or not a GST tax is ever incurred. So, if you make the allocation, and no GST tax is ever possible, you will have wasted that portion of your exemption. For example, assume that you allocate your $1 million GST exemption to a $1 million trust for the benefit of your child and grandchildren. However, the entire trust is exhausted making distributions to your child. Since no GST would have ever been triggered, the GST exemption was wasted. It may have been better to allocate the GST exemption to a trust solely for the benefit of grandchildren.

GST exemption can be wasted in other ways. If the trust in the preceding example declined to $600,000, instead of growing to $10 million, you would have wasted $400,000 of your exemption. Thus, in addition to the potential use of trust funds, you should also analyze all the investment and other relevant factors and estimate the likelihood of the trust incurring a

GST tax. If it appears likely that the trust will incur a GST tax, then you may wish to wager some of your exemption on the trust. If the likelihood of a GST tax appears small, you should preserve your GST tax exemption for other planning opportunities.

EXAMPLE: Grandpa has one son, who has two children. Assume Grandpa transferred $100,000 in trust with income to his son for life and the remainder to the two grandchildren on the son's death. Assume that Grandpa didn't allocate any of his GST tax exemption on the gift tax return. When the son dies, the trust property is worth $500,000. The inclusion ratio is 100 percent. The IRS will collect a $275,000 GST tax at the flat 55 percent rate. On other hand, had Grandpa allocated $100,000 of his $1 million GST tax exemption against the $100,000 transfer to the trust when he first made the gift, the inclusion ratio would be zero. Thus, the entire $500,000 would pass free of the onerous GST tax. Assume Grandpa makes the same gift; however, he allocates $50,000 of his exemption against the transfer. The inclusion ratio is 50 percent. Therefore, if a GST tax is imposed, it will be imposed at 50 percent of the usual rate because 50 percent of the trust is exempt. Thus, on the death of the son, the GST tax would only be $137,500.

Certain Transfers Are Exempt from GST

Transfers that meet the following three requirements are also excluded: (1) the property transferred was subject to the GST tax earlier; (2) the transferee (recipient) in that prior transfer was a member of the same generation as the current transferee; and (3) the transfer does not have the effect of avoiding the GST tax.

Comprehensive GST Planning Example

With proper planning over time, a substantial amount of net worth can be transferred to grandchildren without any GST tax.

EXAMPLE: You have four children, and nine grandchildren. You and your spouse set up separate trusts for each of your grandchildren, each properly structured so that $10,000 gifts will qualify for both the gift and GST tax annual exclusions. You and your spouse give, combined, $20,000 per year to each grandchild's trust. This amounts to $180,000 per year. Over a ten-year period (not even counting the earnings that would have made the trust balances grow substantially), you will have given away $1.8 million to your grandchildren. This is in addition to any amounts you could have given to each of your children and their spouses (which could have amounted to an additional $1.6 million over the same ten years). Finally, in each of your wills, you and your spouse each can provide for a $1 million GST-exempt trust (as will be explained). The two trusts will total, after the last of you and your spouse dies, $2 million. Thus, over a ten-year period, you have transferred $3.8 million to trusts for your grandchildren. Planning, however, is essential.

In the preceding example, if additional estate tax planning techniques are used in making the gifts to the trusts for your grandchildren, the amounts transferred can be increased substantially. For example, if stock in a closely held business, or interests in a family limited partnership (FLP), rather than cash is given to the grandchildren's trusts, the gifts may qualify for a lack of marketability and/or minority discount that can enable the transfer of more economic value than the equivalent cash amount. If the appropriate discount is 30 percent, then each $10,000 gift would be equivalent to a $14,286 gift [$14,286 – (30% × $14,286 = $4,286) = $10,000]. The $1.8 million of aggregate gifts could constitute $2,571,000 of gifts [$2,571,000 – (30% × $2,571,000 = $771,000) = $1,800,000). Without even considering any growth in the value of the stock given, or the $2 million GST exempt trusts under your wills, more than $2.5 million has been transferred without incidence of GST.

CAUTION: Exercise great care in undertaking gifts of minority interests in businesses. Be certain to obtain a proper appraisal, and have your tax adviser review the various gift tax valuation rules, including some complex rules under Chapter 14 of the Internal Revenue Code.

TAX ALLOCATION CLAUSES AND THE GST TAX

When planning for the GST tax, your attorney should, depending on your personal preferences, also consider the tax allocation clause in your will or trust. Taxes should be paid out of (i.e., should be allocated against) the assets creating the GST tax, and not simply against the residuary estate. While ideally, you may wish to allocate GST tax against the portion of your estate that does not qualify for the GST (to avoid wasting any of your GST tax exemption), this is not always appropriate. From a fairness perspective, the person receiving the assets causing the tax problem should generally pay the tax. From a tax perspective, having the GST tax (if any is in fact due) paid from property other than the generation-skipping trust can create additional GST tax problems. An issue can arise where the surviving spouse's estate, rather than the Q-TIP trust, bears the estate tax resulting from the inclusion of that trust in the surviving spouse's estate. If this occurs, the surviving spouse should be treated as the transferor for purposes of the GST tax, of the addition (i.e., the tax paid).

If your will is silent, the tax law (which is followed by many states' tax allocation laws) provides that the GST tax is to be paid by the beneficiary receiving the particular property subject to the tax. In the case of a trust, the trustee is to pay the GST tax out of trust property where there is a taxable termination or a direct skip from the trust. Where the donor makes a gift that is a direct skip, the donor pays the tax. In some instances, the payment of the gift tax could be deemed to be an additional gift.

TRUSTS AND THE GST TAX

GST planning can affect many types of trusts and the tax planning for those trusts. The use of a trust in estate and gift tax planning becomes more complex where the beneficiaries are, or could include, grandchildren (or other skip persons) instead of children (or other nonskip persons). The following situations summarize a few GST planning considerations for several types of trust. The planning ideas discussed in the preceding section, however, can be applied to a host of other trust planning situations as well.

Marital Trust (Qualified Terminable Interest Property Trust)

A marital trust can also be allocated your $1 million GST tax exemption. A marital, or qualified terminal interest property (Q-TIP) trust (see Chapter 11) would provide your surviving spouse the right to all the income, at least annually, from the trust for life. These mandatory income payments, as well as any principal invasions will reduce (waste) the GST tax exemption allocated to this trust. In a very large estate, it is preferable to preserve your full $1 million exemption by not invading that principal unless absolutely necessary.

Credit Shelter/Marital Trust Combination

A common GST planning approach is to establish two GST exempt trusts to which the $1 million GST exemption is allocated. The first trust would be equal to the amount of the unused unified credit (i.e., a credit shelter trust for $600,000 if none of your unified credit is used prior to death or elsewhere under your will). Your executor could then allocate $600,000 of your GST exemption to this credit shelter trust. This transfer would not trigger any estate tax because of the unified credit. The assets in this trust would be protected forever from your GST tax because of the allocation of $600,000 of your $1 million GST exemption amount in a manner to assure a zero inclusion rate. A second trust could be provided under your will to absorb the remaining $400,000 of your $1 million GST exemption ($1 million total less the $600,000 allocated to the credit shelter trust). This trust would be a Q-TIP or marital trust, which would avoid any estate tax because of the unlimited marital deduction. Finally, this plan would probably be completed with a third Q-TIP or marital trust for any remaining assets. The reason to have two Q-TIP or marital trusts is that one of the trusts would be GST-exempt and the other would be entirely subject to GST tax. The GST-exempt trust would be the last to be touched for principal invasion by your spouse. The non-GST-exempt marital trust would be spent down first. While the GST-exempt trust would waste some GST (e.g., by the requirement of paying income to your surviving spouse), it would waste less by virtue of the trustees first spending down the other marital trust.

EXAMPLE: The GST $1 million exemption can be allocated by your trustee (or executor if the transfer is under your will). It can first be allocated to each spouse's credit shelter or bypass trust (approximately $600,000). The trust will therefore have an inclusion ratio of zero and not trigger any GST. This means that the entire trust is GST-exempt since all of the assets transferred to it are covered by the GST exclusion. Securities most likely to appreciate should be allocated to this trust since it will not be included in the estate of the second spouse to die. If neither estate is significantly larger than the maximum $1 million GST exemption each spouse is entitled to use, only one additional trust will need to be set up, a Q-TIP trust to which the remainder of the GST is allocated (approximately $400,000); any remaining assets (i.e., above the $600,000 GST exemption used by the credit shelter trust and the $400,000 used in the Q-TIP/GST trust) are distributed out-right to the surviving spouse. This plan can avoid any GST tax, take maximum advantage of the $600,000 estate tax unified credit, and provide for the surviving spouse.

Planning for the use of the GST exemption when marital trusts are used presents an important, but somewhat confusing, planning opportunity. Assume the husband dies and his will establishes a Q-TIP trust for his surviving wife. On her death, the trust assets pass to the children. Generally, the surviving spouse (the wife in this scenario) who is benefiting from the Q-TIP trust would be considered the person transferring the trust assets to the children following her death. The husband who died first, and whose will established the Q-TIP trust, would not generally be considered the transferor of the Q-TIP property. Thus, only the wife's $1 million GST exemption can be allocated against this trust. The problem this creates is that the husband's $1 million GST exemption could be lost. The solution is a special tax election that treats the husband as the transferor of the assets in the Q-TIP trust for GST tax purposes. This election thus permits the husband to allocate his $1 million GST exemption against the trust. This election can be made by the executor of the husband's estate (or by the husband if the gift is made during his lifetime) for an income-only marital trust. This election is known as a "reverse Q-TIP election."

EXAMPLE: Husband dies leaving assets in a Q-TIP trust for benefit of surviving wife. A reverse Q-TIP election is made and the GST exemption of the husband, the predeceased spouse, is allocated to the Q-TIP Trust. The wife's estate then bears the estate tax that would otherwise have been allocable to the Q-TIP trust. This was done instead of applying the general rule under Code Section 2207A that the Q-TIP assets bear such estate tax. This payment of estate taxes by the surviving wife's estate raises the issue as to whether it constitutes an additional transfer by her estate to the Q-TIP trust for GST purposes. This argument would be based on the position that the failure of the surviving spouse's estate to require the available reimbursement of estate taxes from the Q-TIP would constitute a constructive addition to the Q-TIP trust for GST purposes.

Which is a better choice? Reverse Q-TIP to apply the husband's (first to die) GST exemption to the trust, or no special election so that the wife's (i.e., the second to die) GST exemption can be applied? One issue is when the exemption is applied. The husband's exemption would be applied based on the value of assets at the husband's death. Thus, if $1 million of assets are in the Q-TIP trust and the husband's $1 million exemption is applied, the trust assets will remain GST-exempt no matter how large they grow during the wife's lifetime. However, if the reverse Q-TIP election is not made and the wife's GST exemption is allocated on her death, the assets will have to be valued at that time. If the value of the assets has increased substantially, it would have proven wiser to have made the reverse Q-TIP election and applied the husband's GST exemption amount at his death.

Consideration must be given to the size of each spouse's estate. Will either or both spouses have adequate other assets to use up their GST exemption if this special election is not made?

Child's Trust

Where a single trust is established for both a child and a grandchild and the child dies, the death could trigger a "taxable termination" because of the transfer of the trust corpus to the grandchild as the sole remaining beneficiary. Thus, the GST tax would be due. When setting up trusts for grandchildren to whom you will make large gift transfers, it is often advisable to set up a separate trust for each grandchild.

Grandchildren Trusts

To take maximum advantage of the GST $1 million exemption, some trusts may be established solely for the benefit of grandchildren and other skip persons, while other trusts will be established solely for nonskip persons (e.g. children). The allocation of your GST exemption will be an important planning consideration. It will also be vital to address this allocation with the accountant completing your gift tax return for the gift.

EXAMPLE: Where there is no surviving spouse, the plan is somewhat different. Thus on the death of the second spouse, there is no need for a Q-TIP or credit shelter trust. This is because a Q-TIP trust, as explained in Chapter 7, is designed to hold assets in trust but qualify them for the unlimited marital deduction (which defers any estate tax). Similarly, the credit shelter trust is not necessary where there is no surviving spouse because the purpose of the credit shelter trust is to give the surviving spouse income but to keep the assets of that trust out of the surviving spouse's estate. On the death of the second spouse, that spouse's residuary estate (which is the entire estate after costs and taxes, and any specific distributions) can be dealt with in different ways, depending on the facts. Assume that the second spouse is survived by several children. Then one approach is put the remaining estate into a trust. All of the income from the trust could be distributed to the children and the remaining assets can eventually be distributed to the grandchildren.

> This trust can be divided into two parts—one exempt from GST and one not. Distributions of income to the children during their lifetimes should first be made out of the portion that is not exempt from GST so as to preserve the maximum GST tax-free portion for the grandchildren.

Insurance Trusts

Insurance trusts can be affected by GST planning. Should you allocate a portion of your GST exemption to gifts to the insurance trust? Since insurance offers one of the best methods of leveraging your $1 million GST exemption, an insurance trust intended to skip wealth to future generations is a powerful estate planning tool. You must allocate the GST exemption on a timely filed gift tax return. This can be a trap if your accountant is not aware of your estate plan; he or she may not be aware of the need to file gift tax returns. Also, many taxpayers overlook this filing requirement erroneously assuming that since no tax is due, and none of their unified estate and gift tax credit has been used, no filing is required.

Charitable Trusts

Charities are not considered skip persons for GST tax purposes. They are automatically deemed to be of the same generation as the donor, grantor, or other transferor. Thus, no GST tax is due on charitable gifts. This does not mean that transfers or trusts with charitable beneficiaries can always ignore the GST tax.

When planning a charitable lead trust, the choice of using a charitable lead unitrust (CLUT) or a charitable lead annuity trust (CLAT) may depend on whether grandchildren will be the ultimate beneficiaries (see Chapter 14). A special rule applies where a charitable lead annuity trust is used and the ultimate beneficiaries are grandchildren. To prevent an excessive leveraging of the GST exemption, it cannot be allocated when the CLAT is formed. The value of the gift for transfer tax purposes is reduced substantially at the CLAT's formation to reflect that a charity will receive an intervening interest before the grandchildren. Instead, the GST exemption is allocated when the charity's interest ends. A major goal of CLAT planning is to grow the value of the trust principal, and this will exacerbate the GST planning since the later allocation of GST exemption may not be sufficient to give the trust an inclusion ratio of zero.

Grantor Retained Annuity Trusts (GRATs)

A GRAT is intended to discount for gift tax purposes the value of assets given as a gift. This is accomplished by the donor retaining an interest in the trust, through an annuity payment, for the term of the trust (see

Chapter 17). At the end of the term of years, the assets of the trust pass to the beneficiaries named. However, if the grantor/donor dies before the trust term ends, the assets of the trust are included in the donor's estate. This period of time is called an "estate tax inclusion period," or "ETIP" for short. For GST purposes, the GST exemption cannot be allocated until this ETIP period ends at the termination of the trust, when the property is valued fully (i.e., without the discount the donor realized for gift tax purposes). Thus, just as for the CLAT (charitable lead annuity trust) previously described, the ability to leverage your GST exemption amount using this technique is quite limited.

The list goes on. As a result, if the GST could at all apply to any trust you are considering, review the potential GST consequences with your estate planner.

CONCLUSION

If the GST tax can affect your planning, it is important to carefully plan any trust transaction to avoid, or at least defer or minimize, the GST tax impact. With proper planning, substantial assets can often be transferred with no GST tax burden.

9 HOW TRUSTS AND BENEFICIARIES ARE TAXED

IMPORTANCE OF UNDERSTANDING TRUST TAX RULES

The manner in which trusts are taxed for income tax purposes is extremely complicated. For the brave reader, this chapter highlights several important principles of trust taxation. To properly plan and understand the uses of trusts, it is essential to have at least a general understanding of how trusts are taxed. This chapter demonstrates how important it is to obtain expert tax, accounting, and legal advice when planning, setting up, administering, and eventually terminating any trust. While many self-help books on using trusts alert readers to the benefits of trusts, these books are far too simplistic to help you do the job right.

Understanding the basics of trust income tax rules will enable you to better select beneficiaries for your trust. For example, since beneficiaries can be taxed on trust income when distributions are made to them, it can be advantageous to name children as beneficiaries of a credit shelter trust in addition to your surviving spouse. Trust income tax planning will help you best plan the investment strategy of your trust. It will also make you sensitive to how different investment strategies can affect the different beneficiaries and the tax consequences of all beneficiaries.

THRESHOLD ISSUE—IS THE TRUST A SEPARATE TAX ENTITY?

The threshold issue in determining how your trust will be taxed is to determine whether the trust income is to be reported on your income tax return, or on a separate tax return for the trust.

Where the trust income is reported on your income tax return, the trust is labeled a "grantor trust." For grantor trusts, the income tax consequences are generally the same as any other income you earn. Taxation as a grantor trust doesn't mean that there are no tax filing or other requirements you must be aware of. There are several. Also, determining when a trust is a grantor trust is not always a simple task. The next section will explain the tax consequences and tax-reporting requirements for grantor trusts.

Where the trust is to be taxed as a separate entity, it will file its own income tax return. Trust income tax returns begin in a manner similar to that for an individual. Simplicity doesn't last long as many unique concepts of trust taxation soon begin to apply. The remainder of this chapter will provide an overview of the consuming web of rules governing taxation of trusts that are treated as nongrantor trusts for income tax purposes.

GRANTOR TRUSTS ARE NOT TAXED AS SEPARATE ENTITIES

How Are Grantor Trusts Taxed for Income Tax Purposes?

If your trust is treated as a grantor trust, then all income and deductions of the trust are reported on your own tax return (if you were the grantor setting up the trust). The trust is disregarded as a taxable entity (it is not disregarded as a legal entity). For example, if a grantor trust makes charitable contributions, you would claim the contributions as itemized deductions on your personal income tax return. The deductions would be subject to the same limitations as any other charitable contributions reported by an individual taxpayer.

Many grantor trusts must obtain a tax identification number and file trust tax returns. This is usually required even though all of the income and deductions are reported on the individual grantor's personal tax return. There are exceptions, such as for revocable living trusts, which will be discussed later.

What Makes a Trust a Grantor Trust?

If you establish a trust but retain excessive rights, the trust will be classified for tax purposes as a grantor trust. In many situations, achieving grantor trust status is a major planning goal. For example, an unrestricted right under the terms of the trust agreement to remove and replace the trustee could cause you to be treated as though you retained the powers that the trustee had. If you have the right to obtain the assets of the trust for less than their fair value, the trust will be treated as a grantor trust taxable to you. If the trust will pay all of its income to you, or to your spouse, or accumulate the income for future payments to you or your spouse, the trust would be a grantor trust (at least with respect to the income) and would be taxable to you.

These rules can apply to a portion of a trust. It is not an all-or-nothing situation. So if you retain the right to appoint the income, but not the principal of the trust to anyone including yourself, the income will be taxable to you. The principal of the trust, however, may not be considered owned by you. Similarly, if you have the right to appoint one asset, such as a house, or certain bonds in a trust, but not the other assets, only the asset that you can appoint will be considered yours. This could be quite risky as the IRS may argue that the entire trust will be considered yours.

Any rights that your spouse has will be attributed to you for purposes of this test. Even if you have to have the permission of another person to get benefit from the trust property, you may continue to be taxed on the trust assets. This will not occur, however, where the other person whose permission you need is considered to have interests in the trust that are "adverse" to your interests. Someone who shares trust powers with you will only be considered adverse to your interests where (1) that person has a substantial beneficial interest in the trust and (2) that beneficial interest is adverse to yours.

EXAMPLE: Jones sets up a trust for the benefit of Jones and Wright. The unanimous consent of both trustees is required to make any distribution of income from the trust. If Jones needs the approval of Wright, the trust will not be characterized as a grantor trust (based on this rule) because Wright should be considered to have adverse interests to those of Jones. This is because every dollar that Wright authorizes for distribution to Jones means there is a dollar less in the trust that could be paid to him.

A trustee's rights to fees and commissions alone is not sufficient to classify the trustee as an adverse party.

There are certain powers that you, as grantor, can retain over the trust, without having the trust income taxable to you. You can have the power to distribute principal of the trust to any beneficiary in accordance with a reasonably definite (ascertainable) standard. You can have the right to withhold income temporarily, such as where a beneficiary is disabled or a minor. If these are the only powers you have over the trust, the trust will not be a grantor trust.

Where the trust principal may revert back to you (i.e., you have a reversionary interest) and where the terms of the trust agreement (or applicable law) provide that capital gains on the sale of trust assets must be allocated to the principal of the trust (rather than being allocated to the income of the trust and paid to the current beneficiaries receiving trust income), then you will personally be taxable on these capital gains. Any time that you have a reversionary interest in the income or principal of a trust, with a value of more than 5 percent of the total value of the trust (determined when the assets are first transferred to the trust), you will be treated as the owner of the trust (see also the discussion in Chapter 4).

What Trusts Are Grantor Trusts?

Many different types of trusts may be classified as grantor trusts. The following is a review of some of them:

- *Qualified Personal Residence Trust (QPRT).* If you establish a Qualified Personal Residence Trust, you will want to assure that it is a grantor trust (see Chapter 19). If the QPRT is a grantor trust, you will continue to be able to deduct property taxes, mortgage interest, qualify for a tax-deferred rollover of any gain if the house is sold, and so forth. In the past, this trust was generally treated as a grantor trust because the grantor had the right to substitute property of equal value for trust assets. Now, the trust may be planned to assure that the grantor has more than a 5 percent reversionary interest. This means that there is more than a 5 percent probability of the trust assets being distributed back to the grantor setting up the trust as a result of him or her dying before the trust term ends. Other options can be discussed with your estate planner.

EXAMPLE: You establish a QPRT to remove the value of your house from your estate at a discounted cost. The trust term is 12 years. If you die before the 12 years elapse, the house is distributed back to your estate. If there is more than a 5 percent chance of this occurring, based on your age and life expectancy, the trust is a grantor trust.

- *Revocable Living Trust.* These trusts are formed for nontax reasons; classification as a grantor trust makes matters simpler. There is no intent to remove assets from your estate with a living trust, or to form an entity to file separate tax returns. The objectives are probate avoidance and management of assets. Since you will retain the right to revoke, terminate, alter, or amend a trust, you will be taxable on the income from the trust. When forming a revocable living trust, you will retain total control to modify the trust, it will be characterized as a grantor trust.

  There are important advantages to the fact that a revocable living trust remains taxable to you as a grantor trust. This tax status can permit you to transfer, for example, your interests in your home to a revocable trust. When the home is sold, the special tax rules of rolling over a gain on the sale of a personal residence and the ability to exclude up to $125,000 of gain for taxpayers age 55 and older should continue to be available. If your home were transferred to other types of trust, these benefits could be lost. This is vitally important to taxpayers wishing to use revocable living trusts as a tool to manage assets, avoid probate, and so forth.

Because these trusts are so popular, and the tax-reporting requirements somewhat complicated, they are discussed in detail in this book:

- *Grantor Retrained Annuity Trust (GRAT).* If you establish a grantor retained annuity trust (GRAT) or a grantor retained unitrust (GRUT), the trust will be planned to be a grantor trust (see Chapter 17).
- *Child's Trust.* If you establish a trust for the purposes of holding assets for your child and removing those assets from your estate, you would assume that the trust should also be a nongrantor trust. However, the rules for when a trust is a grantor trust for income tax purposes differ from the rules governing when assets are removed from

your estate. What some clever taxpayers have done in the past is arrange for a child's trust to be taxed, for income tax purposes, (but not for estate and gift purposes) as a grantor trust. This can be tricky, because they must assure that the trust is not pulled back into their estates for estate tax purposes. When the strategy was successful, the taxpayer parent would pay income tax on the earnings of the child's trust. This served as another way of transferring value to the child. Further, these taxpayers then argued that their payment of tax on the income of the child's trust was not a further gift to the child. Thus, this additional transfer (i.e., equal to the amount of tax paid) was not reported for gift tax purposes. The IRS, needless to say, has not looked favorably on this type of planning.

Where the trust income is used to discharge your legal obligations, such as the education of your minor child, the trust income could be taxable to you (see Chapter 13).

EXAMPLE: You set up a trust for the benefit of your child. Your spouse is the sole trustee. All of the income from the trust is used to pay for your child's education in a private school and related expenses. The laws of your state make a parent responsible to pay for these types of expenses. The income from the trust used to meet these expenses should be taxable to you. The trust assets may also be taxed in your estate.

- *Insurance Trust.* Most insurance trusts are classified as grantor trusts because if income of the trust can be used to pay for insurance premiums on policies on the grantor's life, the trust is classified as a grantor trust. This is why insurance trusts, before the insured's death, should not generally hold any assets other than the insurance policies and a nominal cash balance (see Chapter 16).

Special Tax Filing Rules for Revocable Living Trusts

Because revocable living trusts are so popular, the tax filing requirements for them deserve special attention. This section will summarize the various tax filing requirements. The reporting requirements for revocable living trusts can generally be handled in one of three ways. No matter which option you choose, the trust income will be reflected on your Form 1040. The first option is available to trusts created in 1981 or later years. The second and third options became available on or after January 1, 1996:

1. You may file a "skeleton" Form 1041—U.S. Income Tax Return for Estates and Trusts, with an information statement attached. You do not report the trust income on Form 1041.
2. In your capacity as co-trustee, you furnish certain information regarding the trust to all payors and are not required to file any return. In your capacity as grantor, you must complete Form W-9.

3. In your capacity as co-trustee, you furnish certain information regarding the trust to all payors and file Form 1099.

Alternative 1

Under this option, a skeleton Form 1041, "U.S. Income Tax Return for Estates and Trusts," with an attached information statement, is filed. Form 1041 is filed together with the grantor's individual income tax return (Form 1040). The income is not reported on Form 1041 but instead is reported on Form 1040. The box in Section A of Form 1041 is checked to indicate that the trust is a grantor trust. Attached to the Form 1041 is the following statement:

SAMPLE PROVISION:

Attachment to *YEAR Form 1041
John Taxpayer Revocable Living Trust
EIN: ———-——————

The John Taxpayer Revocable Living Trust is a grantor trust. The income of the John Taxpayer Revocable Living Trust is taxable to the grantor, John Taxpayer, whose Social Security Number is 123-45-6789 and who resides at 123 Main Street, Any Town, Wisconsin.

The income taxable to the grantor and the deductions and credits applied to the income are reported on the grantor's *YEAR Form 1040, Schedule E.

Alternative 2

Under Alternative 2, the trustee must provide to all payors of income and proceeds during the tax year the following information:

- Grantor's name.
- Grantor's Social Security number.
- The address of the trust.

If this information is furnished to all payors, the trustee is not required to file a Form 1041 with the IRS.

If the trustee is not the same person as the grantor, then the trustee must provide to the grantor a statement that includes the following information for each taxable year:

- All items of income, deduction, and credit of the trust.
- Identification of the payor of each item of income.
- The information necessary to compute the grantor's taxable income.
- A statement that the preceding items must be included in the grantor's income.

The grantor is required under this method to provide the trustee with a completed Form W-9, "Request for Taxpayer Identification Number and Certification." Generally, a copy of Form W-9 should not be given to a payor because Form W-9 contains the address of the grantor and this method of reporting requires the trustee to provide the address of the trust.

Alternative 3

Under Alternative 3, the trustee must furnish to all payors of income and proceeds during the tax year the following information:

- Trust's name.
- Trust's taxpayer identification number.
- Trust's address.
- The trustee must file with the IRS the appropriate Form 1099s reporting each type of income and each item of gross proceeds paid to the trust during the tax year, showing the trust as payor and showing grantor as the payee.

If the trustee is not the same person as the grantor, then the trustee must provide to the grantor a statement that includes the following information for each taxable year:

- All items of income, deduction, and credit of the trust.
- The information necessary to compute the grantor's taxable income.
- A statement that the preceding items must be included in the grantor's income.

By furnishing this statement, the trustee satisfies the obligation to furnish statements to recipients with respect to Forms 1099 filed by the trustee.

Changing Reporting Methods

- *Changing from Alternative 1 to Alternative 2 or 3.* A trustee who has filed a Form 1041 for a tax year and later changes to reporting under one of the alternative methods, must file a final Form 1041 for the tax year that immediately precedes the first tax year for which the trustee reports under one of the alternative methods. The trustee must write on the front of the final Form 1041, "Pursuant to Regulation Section 1.671-4(g), this is the final Form 1041 for this grantor trust."
- *Changing between Alternatives 2 and 3.* A trustee can change from furnishing the taxpayer identification number of the grantor (Alternative 2) to that of the taxpayer identification number of the trust (Alternative 3) by furnishing the necessary information to each payor.

To change from furnishing the taxpayer identification number of the trust (Alternative 3) to that of the taxpayer identification number of the grantor (Alternative 2), the trustee must provide the necessary information to each payor. In addition, the trustee must indicate on each Form 1096, "Annual Information Return Summary and Transmittal Return," that it files for the final taxable year for which the trustee so reports that this is the final return of the trust.

- *Changing from Alternative 2 or 3 to Alternative 1.* A trustee filing under Alternative 2 or 3 can elect to instead file a Form 1041, with the attached statement under Alternative 1. A trustee who filed under Alternative 2 (furnished the name and taxpayer identification number of the grantor to all payors) must furnish the name, taxpayer identification number, and address of the trust to all payors for subsequent years. A trustee who filed under Alternative 3 (furnished the name and taxpayer identification number of the trust to all payors) must indicate on each Form 1096 that it files for the final taxable year for which the trustee so reports that this is the final return of the trust.

TRUSTS REPORTING INCOME ON THEIR OWN TAX RETURNS

Calculating Trust Income

Generally, when a trust is required to report its income on its own tax return, it will be taxed in a manner that is similar to the way in which an individual taxpayer, like yourself, is taxed subject to several modifications discussed later. The gross income of a trust is generally determined in the same manner as gross income of an individual is determined. Then several modifications, which will be discussed, are made.

A trust is generally required to report its income and deductions using a calendar year.

A trust, like any taxpayer, must use a method of accounting that clearly reflects its income. Trust income determined under the trust's accounting methods includes all income received by the trust during the tax year, including income accumulated in the trust, income that is to be distributed currently by the trustee to the beneficiaries, and income that, in the trustee's discretion, may be either distributed to the beneficiaries or accumulated. The IRS has held that where a trustee waives or refunds trustee fees and commissions, that this amount should also be treated as income to the trust.

One of the most important concepts of trust taxation is that the trust will generally only pay tax on income which it accumulates. When the trust distributes its income to its beneficiaries, the trust will be treated as a conduit for tax purposes. The trust will not pay tax on distributed income; instead, the income and deductions will be taxed to the beneficiaries to the extent the income is passed out of the trust to them. This result is achieved by giving the trust a tax deduction for the income actually distributed (or required to be distributed) to the beneficiary. The trust is effectively treated as a conduit passing income to the beneficiaries.

A trust, however, is not a perfect conduit since several items are affected by special trust tax rules. For example, all losses do not generally pass through the trust to the beneficiaries until the year in which the trust terminates. Capital losses are not deducted in the calculation of a trust's distributable net income (DNI). Thus, where a trust has a capital loss (e.g., from selling stock) but no capital gain, the loss is not passed through the trust to be reported on the beneficiaries' income tax returns. Capital losses, however, can be offset against capital gains of the trust.

The determination of the extent to which the trust or beneficiary bears the actual tax liability on any income depends on the calculation of distributable net income (DNI), which is explained in some detail later in this chapter.

Deductions and Losses Available to Trusts

Trusts are entitled to certain tax deductions in calculating their income. Generally, trusts are allowed the same tax deductions and credits as are individual taxpayers. Trusts are not, however, permitted to claim the standard deduction that individual taxpayers are entitled. The 2 percent floor on miscellaneous itemized deductions applicable to individuals, is similarly applicable to trusts. A number of trust expenses may be subject to this limitation, including tax return preparation fees, safe deposit box rentals, legal and accounting fees, investment counsel fees, and so forth. A trust must make special calculations to determine its adjusted gross income. For example, distribution deductions and the expenses paid or incurred to administer the trust are deductible in arriving at adjusted gross income.

EXAMPLE: A trust has $10,000 of adjusted gross income. It incurs $1,000 of expenses, which are chargeable against income and which are subject to the 2 percent floor rule. The first $200 of these expenses are therefore not deductible [$10,000 × 2%]. Trust income is therefore $9,200 [$10,000 − ($1,000 + $200)].

The special reduction of itemized deductions which individual taxpayers are required to make does not apply to trusts.

A trust is permitted to deduct expenses which are ordinary necessary business expenses incurred in its business, expenses incurred in the production of income, and expenses to determine its tax liability. Where a trust owns a house occupied personally by a beneficiary, the trust may not be able to deduct maintenance and similar costs. Instead, these personal type expenses may be treated as a distribution to that particular beneficiary. Reasonable amounts incurred for trustee fees are deductible. The deductions, however, are only allowed for items that are obligations of the trust. Where a beneficiary pays a trustee fee instead of the trust, no deduction is allowed to either the beneficiary or the trust.

A trust is not permitted to claim any deductions for the expenses allocable to tax-exempt income. The rationale for this rule is simple: If the trust is not taxed on the income, it should not be able to deduct expenses incurred to generate that income.

EXAMPLE: A trust earns the following income:

Ordinary stock dividends	$12,400
Tax-exempt bond interest	4,500
Total income	$16,900

The trust incurs the following expenses:

Office expenses	$ 1,000
Account fee—brokerage firm holding tax-exempt bonds	$ 250

The expenses allocable to the tax-exempt income, and which are not deductible by the trust, have two components. The $250 account fee relates solely to the tax-exempt bonds and is therefore not deductible in its entirety. The office expense fee, it is assumed, was incurred in earning all income and in managing all assets. So this amount can be allocated ratably between the ordinary stock dividends and the tax-exempt bond interest, as follows:

$$\frac{\$4,500 \text{ Tax–Exempt Bond Interest}}{\$16,900 \text{ Total Income}} \times \$1,000 \text{ Office Expense} = \$266$$

Thus, the $266 of the Office Expenses is not deductible. The total expenses that relate to the tax-exempt income and that are not deductible are $516 [$250 + $266].

Depreciation deductions are allowed, but may have to be allocated between the beneficiaries and the trust based on the allocation of trust income. Bad debt deductions, net operating losses, and casualty losses are also permitted, but may not all pass through to the beneficiary in each tax year.

Charitable contribution deductions are permitted for amounts paid to recognized charitable organizations under the terms of the trust. The rules for trusts are more generous than those for individuals. Individual taxpayers are only permitted deductions for contributions up to certain percentages of their income. These rules do not apply to trusts. The contributions, however, must be made in a manner consistent with the terms of the trust agreement and must generally be paid out of trust income (not principal).

Trusts, like individual and certain other taxpayers, are subject to the complicated passive loss rules, which can limit the ability to deduct losses from rental real estate and other passive investments. The passive loss limitations are applied to beneficiaries on the passive income or deductions distributed to them, and to the trust on the passive income or deductions that it does not distribute.

Special Deductions for Trusts

Trusts are entitled to several special deductions that differ from those available to individual taxpayers as previously described.

Classifying the Trust as Simple or Complex

The rules for determining the deductions available to a trust vary depending on whether the trust is characterized as a simple or complex trust. These same rules are necessary to understand the DNI deduction discussed in the next section.

A simple trust is one that is required by the trust agreement to distribute all of its income currently and make no distributions other than of current income, and that has no provision for charitable contributions. The fact that the trustee may not distribute all of the income as required will not affect the characterization of the trust. That capital gains must be allocated to principal rather than income, under applicable state law or the trust provisions, will also not affect the characterization of the trust as a simple trust.

Any trust not characterized as a simple trust under the preceding rules is characterized as a complex trust. A complex trust refers to any trust not required to pay out all of its income currently.

The rules for complex trusts are more difficult because complex trusts may accumulate income (i.e., when a trust doesn't pay out all of its income currently, that portion is "accumulated," or kept by the trust for distribution in later years). Where income is accumulated, then some portion of the distributions in any year may be made from principal amounts. This can be principal from the original assets given to the trust, or from accumulations in prior years.

NOTE: Most of the trusts described in this book will be complex trusts. To provide your trustee with the most flexibility, and to give the beneficiaries of your trust the most rights, many of the sample trust provisions illustrated in this book empower the trustee to accumulate income, or make distributions out of principal of your trust.

Exemption Deduction

Every trust is entitled to an exemption deduction. Simple trusts are entitled to an exemption of $300, complex trusts $100.

DISTRIBUTABLE NET INCOME (DNI) DEDUCTION FOR TRUSTS

DNI Deduction Is Essence of How Trusts Are Taxed

The most important deduction available to a trust is the deduction for distributions to beneficiaries. This deduction is the key to avoiding double taxation of the same income to the trust and its beneficiary. It is also the basis of a trust being characterized as a conduit for income tax purposes. To understand these rules, you must understand a tax concept unique to the taxation of trusts: Distributable Net Income (DNI).

DNI accomplishes three purposes: (1) It determines the maximum amount that a beneficiary of the trust will be taxed on in any year; (2) it determines the maximum amount that can be deducted by a trust for distributions made by the trust to beneficiaries in any year; and (3) it provides for the character (e.g., tax-exempt income or non-tax-exempt income) of the income that the trust passes to a beneficiary.

In the most basic terms, DNI is roughly equivalent to the trust's taxable income (rather than its income determined under trust accounting concepts), though there are modifications and adjustments. The rules for DNI are different for simple and complex trusts (not that the rules are simple for "simple" trusts). These differences, which are very important, will be explained in general terms.

The trust's deduction for distributions is limited to its DNI. DNI also limits the amount taxable to the beneficiary. Distributions to a beneficiary in excess of DNI are generally subject to income tax. Also, the DNI concept preserves the character of income distributed out of the trust.

Calculating DNI

For a domestic trust, DNI is calculated based on the following modifications of the trust's taxable income:

- Any deduction claimed for distributions to beneficiaries is added back.
- The personal exemption is added back.
- Tax-exempt interest, less deductions allocated to it, is added back.
- Capital gains that are allocated to the principal of the trust and that are not paid or required to be distributed to a beneficiary, are subtracted.
- Capital losses that aren't used to offset capital gains are subtracted.

DNI Deduction for Simple Trusts

A simple trust is generally entitled to deduct the lesser of DNI or the amount of income required to be distributed currently to the beneficiaries of the trust. The concept behind a deduction for the trust's DNI is that a trust, when it distributes current income to its beneficiaries, is treated as a conduit, passing tax consequences to those beneficiaries. For a simple trust, the DNI deduction is available even if the actual distribution is made after the close of the tax year.

EXAMPLE: You are the only beneficiary of a trust required to distribute all of its income each year. Because all income must be distributed currently to you as the beneficiary, the trust is considered a simple trust. Therefore, the trust, in addition to any other business deductions, will be entitled to a $300 deduction for its exemption.

The trust had the following income and expenses:

Dividends and interest (ordinary income)	$13,556
Expenses relating to ordinary income	2,350
Capital gain (allocable to principal)	4,500
Expenses relating to capital gain income	1,250

You would receive a current distribution of $11,206 [$13,556 of ordinary income – $2,350 of expenses relating to ordinary income].

The trust's DNI is $9,956 [$13,556 ordinary income – $2,350 expenses relating to ordinary income – $1,250 expenses relating to capital gain income]. Note that capital gains are not included in the calculation of DNI since the trust document requires that they be allocated to the principal of the trust and that they not be treated as income.

The amount that you, as beneficiary, would have to report on your tax return for the year is limited to the $9,956 of the trust's DNI.

The trust would receive a tax deduction for the amount actually distributed to you. Thus, the trust's taxable income would be:

Dividends and interest (ordinary income)	$13,556
Capital gain (allocable to principal)	+4,500
Total trust income	$18,056
Expenses relating to ordinary income	–2,350
Expenses relating to capital gain income	–1,250
Exemption amount (simple trust)	–300
Deduction for distribution to beneficiary	–11,206
Trust's taxable income	$ 2,950

NOTE: The capital gain in the preceding example will be taxed to the trust at its tax rate. However, where the trust realizes a taxable gain on property within two years of receiving that property (e.g. by way of a gift) special rules may apply. These are discussed below.

DNI Deduction for Complex Trusts

Where complex, as opposed to simple, trusts are involved, two different categories of trust distributions must be considered. The first category is distributions of current income of the trust required to be distributed to the beneficiaries in that year. This is similar to the concepts that will be discussed for simple trusts. The beneficiaries are taxed on this first category of income to the extent of DNI.

The second category that must be addressed to understand the taxation of complex trusts includes all amounts, other than those included in the first category, which are paid, credited, or required to be distributed by the trust to its beneficiaries. These beneficiaries will only be taxed on the amount they receive if the distributions to the first category of beneficiaries does not use up all of the trust's DNI for that year.

A complex trust may deduct the amount of income required to be distributed during the year. This can include any amount that must be distributed, whether paid out of income or principal, to the extent that it was actually paid. Where different types of income are distributed, the deduction available to the trust for the distribution is allocated in the same proportion as each type of income bears to the total DNI, unless state law or the trust instrument provides for a different allocation method. Rules for allocating the different deductions and classes of income to the amounts received by the beneficiary are also provided.

For a complex trust, the trustee can elect on an annual basis to treat any distribution made to a beneficiary within the first 65 days after year-end, to be treated as if made in the prior year.

Special Rules When You Have Several Trusts

Because each trust has some income taxable at the lowest tax rates, and has its own exemption amount, there can be a tax advantage to having several trusts. To prevent abuse of the tax benefits of using multiple trusts, the tax laws provide that in certain situations, multiple trusts will be treated as a single trust. This will occur where the trusts have substantially the same grantors and beneficiaries and a principal purpose of having multiple trusts is tax avoidance. A husband and wife are treated as the same beneficiary for purposes of determining whether the grantors are the same.

EXAMPLE: Carried to the extreme, it would seem advantageous to set up many trusts so that income would always be taxed at the lowest tax bracket. There are restrictions to prevent this abuse: Where there are multiple trusts, special rules may apply to deny the benefits of repeated use of lower tax brackets and other trust-splitting benefits.

Trust Tax Return Filing Requirements

General Requirements

The trustee must file a federal income tax return, Form 1041, where the trust has gross income of $600 or more. For many of the trusts described in this book, the trust will be considered to be a separate taxpayer for federal income tax purposes and must file its own tax return. For example, a trust was treated as a separate tax entity where its purpose was to transfer title of property to the trustees to protect and preserve property for the beneficiaries. Such a trust will generally result in a separate tax entity so long as the grantor does not retain any impermissible powers. Foreign trusts are subject to a host of filing requirements beyond the scope of this book.

Estimated Tax Returns

Many trusts are also required to file estimated tax returns, similar to those of individual taxpayers. An important exception is provided for certain trusts that are primarily responsible for paying the debts, taxes, and expenses of a decedent; they are exempt for two years from the requirement to pay estimated taxes. Where a trust makes estimated tax payments and these payments exceed its tax liability, the trustee can elect to give the benefit of these excess tax payments to the beneficiaries. To do this, the trustee should attach Form 1041-T, Transmittal of Estimated Taxes Credited to Beneficiaries to the trust's tax return.

Income Tax Planning for Trusts

If the income of the trust is reported in part by the trust, and in part by the beneficiary, there may be some benefit gained from taking advantage of the lower tax brackets of each. Lower income tax brackets occur because the income tax rate is graduated; the more income, the higher the rate at which it is taxed. If the trust will be taxed at a higher income tax rate than the beneficiary, consider directing (or at least permitting) the trustee to make distributions of income to the beneficiary. Where the beneficiaries are children subject to the kiddie tax, this will be less likely. The kiddie tax is explained in Chapter 13. In brief, the kiddie tax requires that income of a child under 14 years of age be taxed at his or her parents' tax rate.

Changes in the tax law have limited, but not eliminated, this benefit. The first $1,500 of trust taxable income is taxed at the lowest 15 percent income tax rate. Thus, if the beneficiary were in a 39.6 percent tax bracket, there could be a tax savings by the trust accumulating, and not distributing, $1,500 of income.

The accumulation of income, however, can later trigger a complex tax on accumulated distributions. How and when income accumulated by the trustee in one year, and distributed in a later year, should be taxed is quite complex. The answer is found in a confusing set of rules that apply when income accumulated by the trustee in one year, is distributed to a beneficiary in a later year (in tax jargon, an "accumulation distribution"). The tax rules that apply to accumulation distributions are called "throwback" rules. The idea is to tax the trust's income as if it had been paid to the beneficiary in the year it was earned, rather than held by the trust. This result is estimated by throwing-back the income to the beneficiary's tax return for the year in which the income was earned by the trust and in which it could have been distributed. The tax laws contain several modifications and assumptions that distort this process to make the required calculations.

CAUTION: For a trust to accumulate income to be taxed at a lower bracket, or alternatively for the trust to distribute income to the beneficiaries to be taxed at their lower tax brackets will depend on the authority given to the trustee under the trust agreement. When you are having a lawyer prepare a new trust, weigh the pros and cons of leaving the trustee substantial flexibility to distribute or accumulate funds. This can provide the opportunity to plan for maximum tax benefit under the Clinton Tax Act rules, and for future changes. A sprinkle power can give the trustee the right to distribute income or principal to any one or more of several named beneficiaries based on need or other criteria. Providing the trustee the flexibility of a sprinkle power may also enable the trustee to distribute income to the beneficiaries in the lowest tax brackets.

Another planning technique used in past years has also been substantially curtailed. Trusts chose to use tax years ending on January 31 of each year to defer the amount of income to be reported by the beneficiaries. However, with the exception of certain charitable trusts, this is generally no longer possible.

Where a trustee wishes to distribute income to avoid the high trust income tax rates, he may be concerned about the beneficiary having access to cash. An alternative, if the trust agreement permits, is to consider distributing property. In some instances, a property distribution can carry out to the beneficiary some of the taxable income that would have otherwise been taxed at a high rate to the trust. Also, careful selection of the type of property may make distributions possible that are less liquid than cash so as to discourage a beneficiary from making undesired expenditures.

EXAMPLE: A beneficiary receives a distribution of stock from a trust worth $35,400. The trust's tax basis in the stock was $23,000. Assuming that the trustee does not make a special election to recognize gain or loss on the distribution, the beneficiary's tax basis in the stock will also be $23,000. The distribution will be considered to carry out to the beneficiary income (DNI) to the extent of the lesser of the adjusted basis in the property or the fair value of the property. In this case, $23,000 would be considered to be distributed.

Another planning consideration for trusts where income cannot be distributed to a lower taxed beneficiary is to restructure the investment portfolio of the trust to favor tax-exempt securities, growth stocks, and other investments that do not produce ordinary income taxed currently at the highest tax rates.

CAUTION: Trustees must be careful in pursuing these strategies. First, the trust agreement must authorize the trading necessary and permit the types of investment that will achieve the intended tax results. Consider the different tax and economic consequences to the beneficiaries. The results may not be obvious. Many trust agreements provide how income, dividends, gain, loss, and so forth should be divided between income and principal. If the trust agreement is silent, you will have to consult local law. For many trusts, the income beneficiary may differ from the beneficiary who ultimately will receive all the trust property (the remainder beneficiary). A substantial change in investment posture to reduce income could favor a remainder beneficiary at the expense of the current income beneficiary and expose the trustee to claims. Consider your liability as a trustee in light of both local state law and the provisions of the trust agreement. Could you be challenged legally for violating your fiduciary responsibility as trustee if you invest all the trust's assets in municipal bonds? How will the state prudent investor rules applicable to the trust affect this?

HOW NONGRANTOR TRUSTS ARE TAXED ON PROPERTY SALES AND DISTRIBUTIONS

How a Trust Is Taxed on the Sale of Property

The gain or loss to be realized by the trust, or a beneficiary who receives property distributed from a trust, depends on the determination of the investment in the property (called the "tax basis").

The calculation of the gain or loss realized on the sale of property acquired by a trust or beneficiary is made under special rules for determining the investment in the property. The determination of the tax basis depends how the property was acquired, and the nature of the property sold. If the trustee acquired the property as a gift, the trust uses the grantor's adjusted tax basis for calculating any gain.

EXAMPLE: Grandparent gives stock that cost $70,000 and that is worth $95,000 to a trust for the benefit of a grandchild. The trust's tax basis in the stock, assuming no gift tax is paid, is $70,000.

The calculation of adjusted tax basis becomes more complicated where the donor/grantor (person making a gift of property to the trust) incurs a gift tax as a result of making the gift. In this event, the adjusted tax basis in the property is increased by the amount of gift tax paid.

EXAMPLE: Assume that in the preceding example, the grandparent pays $20,000 of gift tax to make the gift of the stock to the trust for the grandchild. The trust's tax basis in the stock is increased to $90,000 [$70,000 + $20,000].

The amount by which the adjusted tax basis in the property can be increased as a result of the gift tax paid by the donor/grantor is subject to a cap. The gift tax paid is only used to increase basis to the extent that it is attributable to the appreciation in the property given to the trust. This is the excess of the fair market value of the property as of the date of the gift over the grantor's adjusted tax basis in the property.

EXAMPLE: Assume that in the preceding example, the grandparent incurred a gift tax at a 50 percent rate. The gift tax incurred on making the gift to the trust would be $35,000. If the full gift tax were added to the grandparent's (i.e., the donor's) tax basis, however, the trust's tax basis would be $105,000 [$70,000 + $35,000]. This amount exceeds the fair value of the property, so the basis to the trust is limited to the $95,000 fair market value of the property.

TIP: Since the general rule for capital gains is that they are allocated to the principal of the trust and are not considered part of current income, they will be taxable to the trust at the trust's tax rates. It can be advantageous in some situations to include a provision in the trust document permitting the trustee to allocate certain capital gains to income, rather than principal. This could enable the trustee to distribute the capital gains to beneficiaries who may be taxed at a lower tax rate than the trust. This is because the lowest tax rates are phased out at very low income levels for trusts—at much lower amounts of income than those at which the low tax brackets for individuals are phased out.

Where a loss is realized by the trust on the later sale of property, the trust's adjusted tax basis (investment) is the lower of (1) The donor/grantor's adjusted tax basis in the property; or (2) The fair market value of the property at the time of the gift to the trust.

EXAMPLE: Assume that in the preceding example, the trustee of the grandchild's trust sold the stock four years later for $50,000. Since the property was sold at a loss, the amount of tax loss for the trust is $20,000 [$50,000 sales price – $70,000 lower of cost or value on transfer]. The second figure is the lower of (1) the $70,000 tax basis of the Grandparent; or (2) the $95,000 fair market value of the property at the date of the transfer.

Where property is received by a trust from an estate (i.e., under a will) the trust's tax basis is the fair market value of the property in the estate. This is the fair market value on the date of death, or at a date six months after the date of death if the estate elected to value all assets at that date (the alternate valuation date).

Where do you find the information for these calculations? In most cases, the trustee will have maintained the proper records. If the records are not readily available, consider any of the following:

- If a gift tax return was filed by the grantor or other person giving property to the trust (donor), a copy of the gift tax return should provide the necessary information. If the trustee, the donor, and the accountants for the trust and donor do not have copies, the IRS may be able to provide one on request. It is also important to determine whether a gift tax was paid when the gifts were made to the trust. For example, if the gifts qualified for the unlimited marital deduction (there's no gift tax on transfers to your spouse), or if the amount given to your trust was within the remaining $600,000 unified credit of the donor, then no gift tax cost may have been paid on the transaction of setting up your trust.

  Without the gift tax return filed when the initial transfers were made, it may be impossible to correctly determine any adjustment that may be required to calculate the appropriate tax basis for the property, inclusive of adjustments for gift tax purposes.

- If the property was transferred to the trust under someone's will, the adjusted tax basis of the assets transferred from the estate to the trust will generally be the fair market value of the assets as of the date of death. The best approach is to obtain a copy of the decedent's federal estate tax return. If no federal estate tax return was filed, a state inheritance or other tax return may have been filed.

Tax Consequences of Property Distributed from a Trust to a Beneficiary

General Tax Rules on Property Distributions

Generally, no gain or loss results from a transfer of property from a trust to a beneficiary under the terms of the trust instrument. There are several exceptions. Where the distribution is of appreciated property distributed in satisfaction of the beneficiary's right to receive a specific dollar (pecuniary) amount, or where the distribution is of specific property other than the property that is required to be distributed, gain may be recognized.

EXAMPLE: Grandparent transfers various assets to a trust for the benefit of several grandchildren. When each grandchild reaches age 35, he or she is to receive $35,000. When the first grandchild reaches age 35, the trustee transfers stock with a tax basis of $24,000 and a fair market value of $35,000. The trust must report a gain of $11,000 [$35,000 – $24,000].

Thus, a trust must recognize taxable gain or loss where a cash bequest is satisfied by distribution of other appreciated property.

Where a stated percentage of the principal of a trust is distributed to a beneficiary before the termination of a trust, it is not considered to be a satisfaction of an obligation of the trust for a definite amount of cash or equivalent value in property. The transaction is simply treated as a partial distribution of a share of the trust principal. Therefore, no sale or exchange is deemed to have occurred, and no gain or loss can be recognized. The beneficiary's tax basis will be the same as the tax basis of the trust. Any gain or loss is thus deferred until the beneficiary disposes of the property involved.

EXAMPLE: Beneficiary receives a distribution of stock from a trust worth $35,400. The trust's tax basis in the stock was $23,000. Assuming that the trustee does not make an election under Code Section 643(e) to recognize gain or loss on the distribution, the beneficiary's tax basis in the stock will be $23,000. The distribution will also be considered to carry out to the beneficiary DNI to the extent of the lesser of the adjusted basis in the property or the fair value of the property. In this case, DNI of $23,000 would be considered to be distributed.

Distributions of property, such as stocks, bonds, or other trust assets (in tax jargon, "distributions in kind") are also subject to the preceding rule. The amount of income to be recognized by the beneficiary depends on whether the trustee makes an election under Internal Revenue Code

Section 643(e) to recognize income on the distribution of property. The result of this election is as if the property had been sold for its fair market value at the date it was distributed. This election is to be made on the trust's income tax return for the year in which the distribution occurs. The election must apply to all distributions made by the trust during the entire tax year. The trustee can't choose to make the election for some property but not for other property.

Where this election is made, the beneficiary's basis in the distributed property is the trust's adjusted tax basis prior to the distribution, increased (decreased) by the gain (loss) recognized by the trust. Thus the tax basis to the beneficiary becomes the fair market value of the property on the distribution.

EXAMPLE: Your trust purchased stock in XYZ, Inc., years ago for $1,000. The stock is now worth $5,000. If the trust distributes the stock to you, your tax basis in the stock is $1,000, the same as the trust's. Thus, if you sell the stock, you would realize the gain. Your tax basis will be stepped up, or increased, to the $5,000 fair value of the stock only if the trustee makes a special election to recognize the $4,000 of gain in the trust. Where the trustee makes this election, the trust will receive a deduction for a distribution to you of the $5,000 value. When should a trustee consider making an election to pay a tax? When the tax cost to the trust of reporting the gain on the property distributed would be less than the tax cost to the beneficiary. This could occur, for example, where the trust had capital losses from other stock sales that could offset the gain, or if the trust had not realized enough income to use up the lower tax brackets available to it.

Special Rule Where Trust Sells Property Quickly

A special tax is imposed on a trust that sells or exchanges property within two years after the property was transferred to the trust. Under this special rule, the trust is taxed at the grantor's tax rate on certain gains from property that is sold within two years of its transfer to the trust, and before the grantor's death. The idea behind this rule is to prevent anyone from gaining a tax advantage by transferring property he or she intends to sell to a trust and then having the trust make the sale. The amount of gain that the trust has to recognize is the lesser of the actual gain the trust recognized on its sale of the property and the excess of the fair market value of the property over the trust's tax basis immediately after the transfer of the property to the trust. This special rule treats the transaction as if the grantor sold the property and then transferred the proceeds, net of the applicable tax cost, to the trust. Several situations are exempted from this special rule. Where the trust is formed on death or is a charitable remainder trust (Chapter 14), this special tax does not apply. Special rules apply in several circumstances, such as where the kiddie tax (Chapter 13) applies, where there is an installment sale, and where there are net operating losses.

TAXATION OF TRUST BENEFICIARIES

Beneficiaries Face Complex Tax Rules

A beneficiary of a simple trust is taxed on the income required to be distributed, whether or not distributed during the tax year. The income, however, cannot exceed distributable net income. Where the income distributed exceeds distributable net income, then each class of income is allocated so that only a proportionate amount is included. Each item of income retains the same character as it did to the trust, unless applicable state law or the trust instrument provides for a different allocation.

A beneficiary of a complex trust must include in income his or her allocable share of trust income required to be distributed, whether or not such income is actually distributed. In addition, any amounts that are properly paid or credited during the year to the beneficiary are also included in income. Where the trustee makes the election to include in income the amount paid within 65 days following the close of the tax year, the beneficiary must include income in the earlier year in conformity with the trustee's election. Where the amount of income required to be distributed exceeds the allocable share of distributable net income, the beneficiary includes in income a proportionate amount. Ordering rules are provided for making these allocations.

Where a trust has more than one beneficiary and is to be administered as distinct shares with respect to each beneficiary, then such separate share treatment is required to be followed for calculating distributable net income.

Trusts must also calculate alternative minimum tax and the amount allocable to each beneficiary. This is referred to as distributable net alternative minimum taxable income. This concept is so complex that you must discuss it with your accountant.

How Different Types of Trust Income Are Allocated to the Beneficiaries

Yet another important concept of basic trust taxation must be understood to work properly with trusts. As noted earlier, trusts are generally treated like a conduit passing taxable income and deductions to their beneficiaries.

EXAMPLE: A simple trust distributes all of its income currently in equal amounts to Jane and Tom. The trust earns a total of $6,000 during the year, with no expenses. $3,000 is distributed to each Jane and Tom. However, the analysis cannot stop here. Of the $6,000 of income earned by the trust, $2,000 was interest on tax-exempt bonds, and $4,000 was interest on CDs. Jane and Tom should each be allocated $1,000 of tax-exempt income, and $2,000 of ordinary income to comprise each of their $3,000 shares.

There can be advantages, however, in allocating different types of income to different beneficiaries. For example, if one beneficiary is in a low tax bracket, and another beneficiary is in a high tax bracket, it could be advantageous to allocate taxable income to the low bracket beneficiary, and tax-exempt income to the high bracket beneficiary. For example, the kiddie tax (see Chapter 13) could make it advantageous to allocate tax-exempt income to a child beneficiary under age 14, while older children who are beneficiaries would receive allocations of taxable income.

As is usually the case, there is a cost and restriction on obtaining any tax advantage. The trust document must specifically make the desired allocation. This makes it difficult to achieve the optimal tax result because you will have to anticipate events when you first sign the trust, not an easy task. Further, there must be an economic effect independent of the income tax benefits of the allocation for the IRS to recognize it.

EXAMPLE: Assume in the preceding example, Jane was allocated the entire $2,000 of tax-exempt income and $1,000 of taxable income. Tom would then receive $3,000 of taxable ordinary income. The trust agreement must provide for this in advance. What if the trust agreement provides that when the tax-exempt and non-tax-exempt bonds are sold, the gain is divided equally between Jane and Tom? This would make it appear that the only consequence of allocating tax-exempt income to Jane was the income tax benefit. The IRS would probably not accept such an allocation. If, however, any gain or loss on the tax-exempt bonds was allocated 100 percent to Jane, and she was allocated only one-third of the gain or loss on the other bonds, then Jane would bear the economic risks and rewards of the tax-exempt income allocated to her and the allocation may be accepted.

How Is a Beneficiary Taxed on the Receipt of Income Accumulated by a Trust?

Consequences of Trust Accumulating Income

Trusts may accumulate, rather than currently pay out, income for several reasons. The primary reasons are personal, not tax. Most parents would not want a trust for a minor child to pay the child all of the income as earned. Rather, most parents would want the income accumulated, for example, added to principal until a later date, such as when the child is in college. Tax reasons could include the fact that the trust may be in a lower tax bracket than the beneficiary. The phase out for the low tax brackets which trusts have, however, will often limit this benefit. This limited benefit was discussed above. There are important non-tax reasons to accumulate income. Where the current beneficiary does not need the money, and the remainder beneficiary will likely need the money, the trustee may choose to hold income rather than distribute it, assuming the trust agreement gives him or her the power to do so.

EXAMPLE: You set up a trust for the benefit of your spouse. On your spouse's death, the income and eventually the principal of the trust will go to your child.

Your spouse is the current beneficiary. Your child is called the remainder beneficiary. Since your spouse has substantial income, you authorize your trustee, in the
trust agreement, to distribute income to your spouse if necessary. You do not however require distribution. This could be a credit shelter trust described in Chapter
17 rather than a Q-TIP/marital trust described in Chapter 11. Your spouse does ex-
ceptionally well in the stock market and has no need for any income from the
trust. Rather than expose the income to your spouse's creditors, especially when
there is no need for the money, your trustee saves the money for future distribution to your child.

Although the tax laws affecting income accumulated by trusts are quite
complex, the economic and personal benefits of trusts that can accumulate
income outweigh the difficulties of dealing with the tax rules.

Theory of How Accumulation Distributions Are Taxed

How and when should income accumulated by the trustee in one year, and
distributed in a later year, be taxed? The answer is found in another confusing set of rules that apply when income saved (in tax jargon, "accumulated") by the trustee in one year is distributed to a beneficiary in a later
year (in tax jargon, an "accumulation distribution"). These rules are called
"throwback" rules. The idea is to tax the trust's income as if it had been
paid to the beneficiary in the year it was earned, rather than held by the
trust. This result is, in theory, achieved by "throwing back" the income to
the beneficiary's tax return for the year in which the income was earned
by the trust and in which it could have been distributed.

This is the result "in theory" because several modifications and assumptions contained in the tax laws distort this process to make the required
calculations easier. The tax laws provide what is called a "shortcut
method" for making this throwback calculation. The approach is to average the amount of income involved over the years during which the income
was earned by the trust. The average income earned by the trust is added
to the beneficiary's income for a five-year period, with the lowest and
highest years being dropped from the calculation. Thus, three years of the
beneficiary's income (as reported on the beneficiary's personal tax return) is used in the calculation of the additional tax on the accumulation
distribution. The average tax for this three-year shortcut period is multiplied by the number of years during which the trust accumulated income.
This is the preliminary tax due, which can be reduced by any tax credits. A
more detailed explanation of these concepts is necessary to understand
the application of the throwback rules.

Definitions of Key Terms

To properly understand the concepts of an accumulation distribution and
the throwback tax calculation, which are essential aspects of the tax rules
affecting many of the trusts you will wish to work with, the formal definition of these terms must be reviewed. First the technical definition will be

presented, then each of the technical terms will be defined, and then examples illustrating the calculations will be presented.

DEFINITION: A throwback calculation is a method of tax calculation that is only required where (1) there is an "accumulation distribution"; and (2) in at least one "preceding tax year" there was trust income that was not distributed (called "Undistributed Net Income").

Each of the technical phases in the definition can be analyzed:

- *Accumulation Distribution.* This is the excess of (1) the nonrequired (extra) distributions from the trust; over (2) the trust's DNI reduced by the required distributions made to the trust's beneficiaries in that year. For example, when a child begins college a distribution of income accumulated in prior years may be used to meet tuition. It is not uncommon, in the final year of a trust, for an accumulation distribution to occur.
- *Preceding Tax Year.* This includes only the five tax years prior to the year in which the accumulation distribution is made.
- *Tax Imposed on the Trust.* These are taxes that are allocable, under the IRS rules, to the undistributed portion of the trust's DNI.
- *Undistributed Net Income.* This exists where the trust's DNI for the year is greater than the amounts distributed to the beneficiaries and any "Tax Imposed on the Trust" on the income not distributed.

EXAMPLE: A trust has DNI of $25,000. The trust makes distributions to its beneficiaries of $15,000, leaving $10,000 of undistributed income. The trust pays income taxes of $1,750 on this amount. The trust's undistributed net income is $8,250 [$25,000 – ($15,000 + $1,750)].

Example: Taxation of an Accumulation Distribution

With this background, an example can be presented showing the calculation of an accumulation distribution:

EXAMPLE: You set up a trust years ago for the benefit of your children. A friend is the trustee. The trust has total income in 1992 of $22,500. Administrative expenses are $1,750. Thus, the distributable net income, or DNI, of the trust is $20,750 [$22,500 – $1,750]. The trust agreement requires the trustee to distribute $15,000 to the beneficiaries. In addition, the trust agreement gives the trustee the discretion to distribute principal for certain purposes. The trustee exercises this right and distributes an additional $15,500 to one of the beneficiaries to use as a down payment on the purchase of a new home. The accumulation distribution is calculated as follows:

Amounts other than required distributions distributed to the beneficiaries		$15,500
DNI	$20,750	
Distributions required to be made currently to beneficiaries	−15,000	
Taxes paid by trust on undistributed DNI	−1,200	
Undistributed net income		−4,550
Accumulation distribution for the year		$10,950

Once it has been determined that an accumulation distribution has occurred, and the amount has been calculated, the next step is to calculate the tax that is due as a result of the required throwback calculation. The following paragraph will explain the calculation.

Example: Allocation of Accumulation Distribution to Prior Years

When an accumulation distribution occurs, the amount of the accumulation distribution is allocated to each prior tax year of the trust that had undistributed net income.

EXAMPLE: In 1992, a trust has an accumulation distribution of $10,950, as calculated in the previous example. Undistributed net income for the trust for the prior five years is as follows:

Year	Undistributed Net Income
1986	$3,401
1987	1,540
1988	0
1989	2,909
1990	2,875
1991	1,331

The $10,950 is allocated to each of the prior years up to the amount of the undistributed net income in each of those prior years:

Year	Undistributed Net Income	Accumulation Distribution Allocation
1986	$3,401	$ 3,401
1987	1,540	1,540
1988	0	0
1989	2,909	2,909
1990	2,875	2,875
1991	1,331	225
		$10,950

Only $225 was allocated against the 1991 undistributed net income since that was all that was necessary to allocate the entire $10,950 of the accumulation distribution. The remaining 1991 undistributed net income of $1,106 [$1,331 − $225] would remain for allocation of future year accumulation distributions.

If the accumulation distribution exceeds the amount of undistributed net income of the trust's prior years, then the excess is treated as a tax-free return of the investment made in the trust.

The next step is to calculate the taxes that were attributable to the undistributed net income of the trust in each of the prior years. The idea behind this step is quite reasonable. The trust reported certain income on its tax return and paid a tax on that income. One of the underlying concepts of trust taxation is that the trust is a mere conduit that should pass income and deductions to the beneficiaries who should pay the tax on that income. Since the trust had accumulated income, it originally had to pay the tax. Now that the income is distributed, to get back (roughly) to the intended scenario of the beneficiary bearing the tax burden, a calculation is made as to what tax cost the beneficiary should pay. However, since the trust has already paid some tax, the beneficiary should get some credit for the tax paid. If this were not done, the IRS would be taxing the same income twice—once to the trust in the year the trust accumulated the income, and a second time when the beneficiary received an accumulation distribution. This was not the intent.

So the next step of the calculation is to determine the tax that was attributable to the undistributed net income of the trust in each of the prior years to which the accumulation distribution is allocated. One more step must be taken, however. The goal is to achieved a result equivalent to what would have occurred had the beneficiary paid the tax originally. If the trust had not paid a tax, the trust would have had more income to distribute. So the tax paid by the trust and attributable to the undistributed net income in each prior year is added to the undistributed net income to arrive at the amount the beneficiary could have received as a distribution. This is called the "total deemed distribution." This step must also be taken because, as illustrated in a prior example, the tax paid by the trust was subtracted from DNI in calculating the undistributed net income of the trust.

EXAMPLE:

Year	UNI*	Tax Attributed to UNI	Total Deemed Distribution
1986	$ 3,401	$1,023	$ 4,424
1987	1,540	352	1,892
1988	-0-	-0-	-0-
1989	2,909	544	3,453
1990	2,875	512	3,387
1991	225	92	317
	$10,950	$2,523	$13,473

*UNI = Undistributed Net Income. This is limited to the amount of UNI used up by the carryback of the Accumulation Distribution, as illustrated in the prior example.

Next, it is necessary to calculate the tax that the beneficiary must pay on the total deemed distributions, as calculated in the preceding example. This calculation also requires a series of steps:

STEP 1.   Determine which of the trust's prior tax years to which the accumulation distribution is to be allocated.

STEP 2.   Deduct from the accumulation distribution amounts that would not have to be included in the beneficiary's income if it had been distributed (e.g., tax-exempt income).

STEP 3.   Divide the result in Step 2 (i.e., the accumulation distribution less tax-exempt income) by the number of years identified in Step 1. This is an average accumulation distribution amount.

STEP 4.   For the five tax years immediately preceding the year of the accumulation distribution, take the beneficiary's income, and eliminate the highest and lowest years.

STEP 5.   Add to the beneficiary's taxable income for the three years remaining after Step 4, the average accumulation distribution amount calculated in Step 3.

STEP 6.   Calculate the income tax that the beneficiary would have paid in each of the three years involved with the addition of the average accumulation distribution amount to each of those years.

STEP 7.   Subtract from the recalculated tax, the actual tax paid by the beneficiary in each of those years. The net result is the additional tax that would have to be paid in each of those years.

STEP 8.   Average the additional taxes due for each of the three years.

STEP 9.   Multiply the average tax increase by the number of years in Step 1.

STEP 10.   Subtract from the total tax calculated in Step 9 the total taxes deemed distributed to the beneficiary (taxes deemed distributed was explained and illustrated earlier in this chapter). The net amount is the additional tax that the beneficiary must pay on receipt of an accumulation distribution.

Although it may be hard to believe, this method of calculating the beneficiary's tax is referred to as the shortcut method.

Accumulation Distributions: Exceptions

An important exception to these complicated throwback rules exists. Where income was accumulated before the beneficiary was 21, this tax will not apply. This is particularly important in the context of trusts of children (see Chapter 13).

Several complicated exceptions and special rules can affect a throwback calculation. These can apply where there are multiple trusts, a foreign trust is involved, or the trustee's records are inadequate. In all cases where an accumulation distribution is involved, seek qualified professional help.

152 TAX CONSEQUENCES OF TRUSTS

CONCLUSION

The tax rules for taxing a trust and beneficiary are extremely complicated. You should rarely be deterred by this complexity because the benefits of using trusts to properly protect you, your family, your privacy, and your assets will usually outweigh the costs of complying with the trust tax rules. It is almost essential, however, to retain specialized professional accountants or tax advisers.

Part Three

TRUSTS FOR DIFFERENT PEOPLE AND ORGANIZATIONS

10 TRUSTS FOR YOURSELF

WHY SET UP A TRUST FOR YOURSELF?

The reasons to set up a trust for yourself are many of the same reasons you would set up a trust for others: providing for management of your assets in the event you need assistance or are disabled, protection of your assets from creditors, avoiding probate (or at least ancillary probate in states other than the one in which you permanently reside), and so forth. Estate tax benefits are generally not one of the key benefits you seek when setting up a trust for yourself. This is not to say, however, that a trust you set up for yourself will not provide tax benefits.

EXAMPLE: You set up a living (inter vivos) revocable trust for yourself, naming yourself as the trustee during your life and prior to your disability. On your death, the first $600,000 of your assets held in your trust are transferred to a credit shelter trust for the benefit of your surviving spouse (see Chapter 11). Where the combined estate of you and your spouse exceeds $600,000, this approach can reduce, and perhaps eliminate any federal estate tax. However, these tax benefits do not require you to use a living trust. They can be provided under a will.

There are several types of trust you may consider setting up for your own benefit. This chapter will consider one—the revocable living (sometimes called loving) trust. Two asset protection trusts—the foreign situs asset protection trust (APT) and the Medicaid qualifying trusts—are discussed in Chapter 15.

REVOCABLE LIVING TRUST

What Is a Revocable Living Trust?

A revocable inter vivos (living) trust is one of the most talked-about estate planning techniques. While it can be a useful estate planning tool, much of the talk is hype. Learning how to properly use this trust, and when, is thus quite important to enable you to make the right decision and avoid unnecessary legal fees and complications.

A living trust is a trust that you set up during your lifetime. You retain complete control over the assets in the trust while you are alive and prior to your becoming disabled. For tax purposes, the trust is generally ignored and all income and deductions are reported on your own tax return (see Chapter 9). If you become disabled or infirm, an alternate trustee takes over managing your assets (although it can be preferable to have that successor trustee serve as a co-trustee before you become disabled). On your death, provisions that serve the same purpose as a will apply to govern the disposition of your assets. Since there is no current tax benefit of setting up a living trust, the format can be quite flexible to meet a broad range of personal objectives. This section will explore the benefits, as well as possible drawbacks, of using living trusts.

In appropriate circumstances, these trusts can be an ideal vehicle to accomplish many essential planning goals. In inappropriate circumstances, they can be an unnecessary waste of time and money, and create some unnecessary hassles and complications in managing your affairs. In the worst-case scenarios, you may use a revocable living trust when another technique would have been more appropriate. The results could be disastrous.

EXAMPLE: Assume you live in New Jersey and have a rental vacation property in New York. A living trust will avoid probate for the New York property. However, a living trust will not avoid New York estate tax. A living trust will not facilitate making gifts of interests in that property to reduce your estate tax cost. As explained earlier in this book, the use of a limited liability company (LLC) can achieve these two goals. Using a living trust instead of an LLC would be less than ideal. But it gets worse. If you use a living trust and are sued for more than your insurance coverage by an injured tenant, your entire estate could be jeopardized. An LLC would have prevented this. In this latter scenario, the use of a living trust instead of an LLC could be disastrous.

Whatever your final decision is, it should be made with full awareness of all of the benefits and costs of setting up a living trust. The following discussions will provide a summary of many of these factors and dispel the myth that a living trust will solve all of your problems. It won't. But that doesn't mean that they are not useful estate and financial planning tools. The goal of this chapter is to help you cut through the hype and determine when you will really benefit from a revocable living trust.

CAUTION: The most important point to remember is that no single estate planning step can solve all your problems, or solve everyone's problems. Whatever the hot item of the day, whether it's a living trust, a second-to-die insurance policy, a charitable remainder trust, or any other technique, no single step can possibly address all of your needs. The only approach to use, no matter how much money you have, or how simple your situation may be, is a comprehensive estate, financial, insurance, and tax plan. Nothing less will provide you with the comfort that you have best addressed all of the possible needs of you and your loved ones.

Is a Living Trust Really Better than Probate?

A living trust is primarily touted for its use as a method of avoiding probate. A living trust can also enable you to avoid having your assets disclosed to the public, a result that a will cannot. Reality, however, can be quite different.

Probate is not necessarily the evil and excessively expensive process many people fear, although it sometimes can be. A living trust is not necessarily the simple and inexpensive document many people expect. The truth, as often is the case, is somewhere in between. You can achieve benefits with a living trust that far outweigh avoiding probate and supposedly maintaining privacy. One of the most important is the management of your assets in the event of advanced age or disability.

The proper approach is to evaluate the costs, benefits, and objectives of using a living trust in the context of a review of your overall financial, estate, and tax planning situation. The following factors should be considered in deciding whether a living trust is appropriate for you.

Cost of Setting Up a Living Trust

A rule of thumb for revocable living trusts could be that if your estate (with your spouse) is worth more than $2 million, the net benefits afforded by a revocable living trust should probably be obtained. If your estate is worth less than this amount, you should find more specific reasons to justify the cost. To properly set up a living trust, you must retain a lawyer to properly prepare a trust document. The trust document, if properly done, is not a simple matter. It should be tailored to address your personal goals and objectives, estate tax, and other needs. Be certain that the attorney coordinates the tax allocation clause in your will with the tax clause in the trust. Make sure the trust addresses each of the phases in a living trust described in this chapter, as they pertain to you. Carefully provide for successor trustees. Be certain the document defines exactly when and how you are deemed disabled so that the successor trustees can take over.

The trust document, however, is only the first step. You must then arrange to transfer assets to the trust. For real estate, you will need to execute a deed, and depending on where you live, complete various tax and other forms. If the property has a mortgage, you will have to review it for a "due on sale" clause and most likely notify your bank. Insurance policies on real estate and art will have to be changed to the name of the trust to be effective. The title insurance company that insured any real estate you want to transfer may require a new policy in the name of the trust. Personal property will require a bill of sale to transfer. These steps to create a living trust can be time consuming, can require the assistance of an attorney, and can create additional fees and charges. New bank accounts may have to be opened (see Chapter 3). A separate tax identification number may have to be obtained and tax and other filings may be required (see Chapter 9). For tips on how to organize all these documents, see

Shenkman, *The Beneficiary Handbook* (New York: John Wiley & Sons, 1991).

Living Trust Costs Are Incurred Now, Probate Costs Are Incurred in the Future

If all of the preceding are actually cheaper than probate costs, it still doesn't mean that setting up a living trust is the low-cost option. Remember, the costs of setting up your living trust will be incurred now, whereas the probate costs may not be incurred for 10, 20, or more years in the future. There is a time value to money. The money you spend today on all these costs is not available to invest for future needs. If you instead invest the money you would have spent to set up a living trust, the value at the date of your death may exceed the cost of probate. Thus, although the actual dollar cost of setting up a living trust, and having your trustees transfer assets after your death under the trust, may be less than the cost of a probate (assuming that with a living trust you avoid probate completely), on a present value basis, the cost of probate may easily be less. However, as noted previously, for large estates the extra benefits of a revocable living trust should be considered in any event.

A Will Is Needed Whether or Not You Have a Living Trust

A living trust is not a substitute for a will. You should always have a will because there is no assurance that your trust will own every asset of yours at your death. Omissions could occur because of the improper or incomplete transfer of assets, acquisitions for which there was inadequate time to complete a transfer, assets that could not be assigned, and finally assets that you may not be aware of. Your will should not be the typically overly simple pour-over will providing that all assets under the will are simply to be transferred to (poured over into) your living trust. The will should go on to state how your estate assets should be distributed if for any reason the trust is invalid or unable to accept property. If you're concerned enough to minimize legal and other problems by having a living trust, you should be concerned enough to insist on a complete will. If not, and if for some reason your trust is not valid, a pour-over will into a nonexisting trust is probably as bad as dying without a will or any document. Also, your will should have all the detailed power provisions assuring your executor the authority to do all necessary acts, even if the will is a pour over.

So by using a living trust, you won't eliminate the cost of a will; in fact, you've increased your legal costs by needing two documents where one would have sufficed. A will is often necessary to designate a guardian for minor children. A complete will is necessary to authorize your executor to take the actions that might be necessary if circumstances change.

In unusual instances, it may be possible for a person to possess the testamentary capacity to sign a will, but to lack the required legal capacity to sign a living trust. Because a trust is a legal contract, it can be valid only if the person establishing it has the comprehension, understanding, and state of mind required to create a binding legal contract. The standard accepted by some courts for a person to sign a will has been lowered. This standard requires the person signing to be aware of his or her descendants (called "bounty") and the extent of his or her assets. Thus, if a disabled or infirm person is perhaps incapable of signing a contract but has sufficient capacity to sign a will, a will and not a living trust should be used.

Confidentiality: Avoiding Probate through a Living Trust

The confidentiality you hope to obtain with a living trust may not be realized. If your will contains a pour-over provision, it is going to be probated. If the will pours over into your living trust, the probate process may require that your living trust be recorded in the public record in a manner similar to the will. If there are any legal disputes between beneficiaries or other persons claiming an interest in your assets, or if your living trust is contested, these events might easily wind up in court records that are open to the public. Some courts require that anyone who would have inherited property from you if you had died without a will must be notified, even though you have a will. Thus, people you may seek to disinherit could be notified of your estate if any of your assets pass through probate. The result is that a living trust may offer little additional secrecy. Also, unless you're a well-known public figure, it is unlikely that the media would have any interest in your will even if it is probated and thus available to the public records.

If your successor trustee is not certain how to interpret a provision in your living trust, the trustee may petition the court to interpret your trust agreement and advise the appropriate action. This will obviously defeat any confidentiality your living trust may have provided. Similarly, where any beneficiaries, or persons who believe they should be beneficiaries, challenge the disposition of your assets, the ensuing litigation and court proceedings could make the terms of your living trust public information.

If you transfer real estate to your trust, depending on the customs in your area, you may have to record the trust, or a summary (called a Memorandum of Trust) in the public records to transfer the deed. Again, anonymity could be defeated.

Legal Fees Will Be Incurred on Death Whether a Will or a Living Trust Is Used

When a person with a living trust dies, the assets in that trust must still be transferred to the designated beneficiaries. Thus, whether assets pass through probate or under a living trust, steps will still have to be taken to transfer those assets. Where the property is real estate, stocks, or other assets, the paperwork may not be that different. Also, it is often possible to probate an estate for far less in legal costs than many popular books and articles in financial publications indicate. Numbers like 5 percent of total assets are often suggested as typical legal fees, but in many instances, this is a gross exaggeration. The size of the estate often has little to do with the work necessary. The nature of the assets, cooperation of family members, and organization of necessary financial and personal records are important factors in determining the legal work involved. Also, the particular probate court that will handle the estate can have a significant effect on the overall cost. Some probate courts are extremely efficient, helpful, and professional, which can drastically reduce the cost and time delays involved. If your estate is taxable, a federal estate tax return will have to be filed. Using a living trust does nothing to reduce the costs of this filing.

Court Costs Are Not Always Significantly Less with a Living Trust

Even with a living trust, it may not be possible to completely avoid probate. Many of the forms and court filing fees are about the same even if your probate estate (your assets that go through probate in the event of your death) has been reduced with a living trust. Also, the court costs are not that significant in many jurisdictions, and for most estates.

Executor and Trustee Commissions

State law provides for a maximum amount that can generally be charged by persons serving as executors under your will and trustees under your trusts. In some instances, however, additional fees and administrative costs may be permitted. On the other hand, in many situations, close family or friends serve as executor or guardian for no additional fee. So will your fiduciary (i.e., executor and trustee) fees be lower if you use a living trust than if you rely fully on a will and the probate process? It depends.

Simple and Inexpensive Steps Can Reduce Probate Expenses

A significant cost in administering many estates is the time and effort necessary to ascertain exactly what assets and liabilities the decedent has. Carefully maintaining accurate and complete records during your lifetime can provide substantial savings in professional fees later. This simple step is ignored by the majority of people.

When a lawyer or accountant is hired to handle your probate matter, insist on detailed bills itemizing all steps taken. Obtain estimates in advance and request regular billing and quick notification if actual costs may exceed any budgeted costs. Don't be shy about questioning a bill, retainer agreement, or budget that doesn't make sense. For detailed instructions and sample forms on how to reduce probate costs, see Shenkman, *The Beneficiary Handbook* (John Wiley & Sons, 1991).

Durable Powers of Attorney May Be a Lower Cost Solution

In some instances, particularly if you're young and healthy, the cost of a living trust to provide for disability may be excessive when compared with a durable power of attorney, which is simple and inexpensive to complete. The preparation of a living trust to avoid probate, even if warranted based on an analysis of the other considerations listed here, would be a premature expenditure at such a young age.

For older or infirm taxpayers, however (depending on the laws and customs in your area), a revocable living trust may help avoid the need for a guardianship proceeding in the event of disability. The combination of a revocable living trust governing your financial matters and a living will/healthcare proxy, which governs medical and healthcare decisions, will probably assure that you can avoid the need for a formal court guardianship proceeding.

A Living Trust Does Not Avoid Estate Taxes

A living trust can offer estate tax benefits only if the other planning techniques and trusts discussed in this book are incorporated into it. A living trust itself does not provide any tax benefit.

NOTE: You establish a living trust that helps you avoid probate on your $1 million estate entirely. On your death, your living trust provides that your entire estate passes outright to your children. Although you've avoided probate, your living trust will do nothing to save estate taxes.

EXAMPLE: Assume the same facts, except your living trust provides that the first $600,000 of your assets will be transferred to a bypass, or credit shelter, trust (see Chapter 11). The remaining assets are transferred to a Q-TIP trust for the benefit of your wife. A revocable trust can be used to create a Q-TIP trust providing an income interest to a surviving spouse. Your living trust, with these provisions, may have enabled you to entirely avoid any estate tax. However, these same benefits could have been obtained at less cost under your will.

A Living Trust Can Create Additional Tax

One of the most basic estate planning techniques is to make gifts of $10,000 or less per year to as many heirs as possible. Gifts not in excess of this amount do not reduce your once-in-a-lifetime $600,000 unified credit and do not generally create a gift tax cost. However, where the gifts are made through your living trust, the interplay of complex tax rules could result in these gifts being added back to your estate, potentially creating an expensive estate tax cost. Where a trustee of your revocable living trust makes gifts, the property given away could be equivalent to you (i.e., the grantor) relinquishing the right to revoke the living trust to the extent of the property given away (a partial release). If you die within three years of a partial release of such a power, the value of the release could be included in your gross estate and be subject to estate tax. By making the gifts yourself directly, instead of through your trust, you can avoid this problem and save substantial estate taxes. Although the IRS has backed off this position somewhat, caution is still in order.

TIP: This problem can be avoided by having the trustee of your living trust make distributions solely to you as grantor; you can then make the gifts yourself. This eliminates the potential tax problem. If you are disabled, the trustee could make the distributions to your agent under your durable power of attorney, and the agent could then make the gifts on your behalf. It is important, however, that your durable power of attorney have a specific clause enabling your agent to make gifts.

Trusts must generally file tax returns using the calendar year (i.e., January to December). An estate can choose a fiscal year (any 12-month period, such as March to February). This gives an estate more flexibility than a revocable living trust following your death, which can provide tax savings opportunities. Trusts get a smaller personal exemption than estates. Passive losses, and other losses of trusts are subject to more severe restrictions than losses by estates.

Other Probate Avoidance Techniques Are Available

If avoiding (minimizing is a more realistic goal) probate is an important goal, the use of a living trust is not the only approach to accomplishing your objective. For example, if you own property as a joint tenant with the right of survivorship (JTWROS), this form of ownership will pass the asset to the surviving co-owner without probate. This simplistic approach, however, may not permit implementing some of the estate, legal, and other planning discussed in this book.

Trustee Actions May Be Subject to Less Scrutiny than Executor Actions

The successor trustee under your living trust may not operate under any court supervision. There may be no reporting requirements. Depending on your trust and confidence in the successor trustees named in your revocable living trust, this may be positive or negative.

Outright Gifts or Irrevocable Trusts May Be Better Options than Either a Living Trust or a Will for Certain Assets

Probate and a will, or a living trust and avoiding probate, are not the only choices. Again, a thorough review of all estate, financial, insurance, and other goals and circumstances is essential. If your estate is large enough, giving away certain assets as gifts to your adult children, to remove them from your estate, may be better than transferring into a living trust that won't remove them.

EXAMPLE: Your estate is valued at over $2 million, and $600,000 of your estate is stock in a closely held business. If the value of the stock exceeds 35 percent of your adjusted gross estate, your estate will qualify for favorable estate tax deferral provisions. These can permit your estate to pay out any estate tax on an installment basis over a period of about 14 years. This can be a tremendous benefit and perhaps minimize the need for expensive insurance coverage. However, for your estate to qualify, the stock must exceed the percentage threshold of 35 percent. If you transfer your nonbusiness assets to a living trust, or retain your assets in your estate (to pass under your will), this valuable estate tax deferral will not be available.

Alternatively, if you gave away nonbusiness assets to your adult children, or transferred to trusts for the benefit of your minor children and grandchildren

$285,715 [$2 million − ($600,000/35%)] of assets other than the stock in the business, your estate will qualify for this favorable tax benefit. If you have five married children, each with four of their own children, you and your spouse could give away $300,000 in a single year using your $10,000 annual gift exclusions. If your family is smaller, the same gifts could be completed on a tax-free basis over several years. In this situation, limiting your decision to probate versus living will could miss an important point that would reduce and pay for the potential federal estate tax cost.

If your estate is modest in size, and your liquid savings inadequate, a living trust may not be worth the expense, particularly if you and your spouse are relatively young and in good health. A preferable approach may be simply to sign durable powers of attorney, living wills, and simple wills. When your ages and assets increase, a living trust may become more worthwhile.

Benefits of Using a Revocable Living Trust

With all the previous caveats, is there any reason left to use a revocable living trust? Absolutely. It remains a vitally important and useful estate planning technique.

EXAMPLE: You're a widower, age 78, and have few family members other than your children and minor grandchildren. They all live several hundred miles away. A living trust is likely to make sense unless the other facts and circumstances are very persuasive against such use. Considering the age and scarcity of those who can help in a financial emergency, a living trust may be ideal to provide protection against disability. If you have no fully trusted people to name as successor trustees, you could name an institution to serve as a co-trustee with friends or family members. The institution is subject to substantial regulatory scrutiny and safeguards and thus gives comfort that your assets will be looked after for your benefit. Institutions will not generally serve as agents under a durable power of attorney, so a living trust may be necessary.

EXAMPLE: You're in your mid-70s and have a substantial estate. Other than your house and some bank accounts, a diversified securities portfolio located in three major brokerage firms comprises your entire estate. A living trust to avoid probate (considering the size of your estate), and to provide for disability is almost certainly the appropriate decision. For probate avoidance alone, a living trust is almost assuredly the desired option. The estate is substantial and the assets are so easy to transfer to the trust's name—simply advise your broker what is necessary.

A review of the many real benefits that a living trust can provide, however, will help you better understand how it should be used and what provisions it can contain.

Living Trusts Are the Best Vehicle to Plan for Disability

A power of attorney is a simple approach to enable someone to act in your behalf if you are disabled. However, a living trust can be a far more effective vehicle. Unlike the typical durable power of attorney, a living trust can provide detailed provisions and contingency plans for dealing with disability.

The authority of an agent under a durable power of attorney could be less certain than that of a successor trustee under a revocable living trust. The successor trustee (the trustee who takes over as trustee when you become disabled) has legal ownership (title) to the assets in the trust, so the line of authority of the trustee is perhaps stronger than an agent under a power. Banks and other financial institutions may more readily accept the authority of your trustee than of your agent.

NOTE: The two documents, a living trust and durable power of attorney, are not mutually exclusive. A durable power of attorney should always be signed as part of any estate plan. There are few exceptions. When a living trust is determined to be an appropriate tool for your estate and financial goals, you still should consider signing a durable power of attorney. Your durable power of attorney should give your agent the right to make gifts (this addresses the gift tax issue discussed earlier) and most importantly, should have an express provision giving your agent the authority to transfer assets to your living trust. Rarely does anyone transfer every asset they own to their living trust when they set it up. A checking account, gifts received after the trust was formed, personal property acquired after the trust was formed, and assets that are costly, inconvenient, or difficult to transfer (perhaps a car) are often not in your trust. If you become disabled, the only mechanism to get these assets into your trust is for your agent, acting under a durable power of attorney, to transfer these assets.

A living trust is an excellent vehicle for a single person who can't rely on immediate family to handle financial matters in the event of disability. A comparison should also be made with another option for financial management of a disabled or incompetent person—having a court appoint a guardian, conservator, or committee. The definitions and functions of each differ under each state's laws.

Avoid Probate

Probate can be time consuming. Thus, unless your family has sufficient assets of their own to sustain them during the probate process (or at least until interim distributions can be made), a living trust can prove (but won't always) a simpler and quicker method for getting needed cash and other assets to your heirs.

Avoid Publicity

Subject to the many caveats previously discussed, a living trust can minimize the publicity and public availability of information concerning your assets and bequests.

NOTE: If you are part of a relationship with a nonmarried partner that is not acceptable to your family, a living trust may help minimize scrutiny, interference, and potential challenge. Your revocable living trust may have a degree of confidentiality that a will does not. If you transfer only a portion of your assets into the trust, retaining the remaining assets in your estate, family members adverse to your relationship may not even realize that a trust governing some portion of your estate exists. This can be an effective planning technique.

Professional or Organized Management

You can use a living trust to establish a range of procedures to govern the management of your assets. Unlike other methods, a living trust can provide an ideal tool to test your procedures. If you are not satisfied with how things are working, you can always modify the provisions governing management.

Four Stages in the Life of Your Living Trust: How Does a Living Trust Work?

The best way to understand how a living trust would work for you is to review the four stages in the life cycle of a typical revocable living trust.

Phase 1: Formation

After a complete review of your tax, estate, financial, and personal goals and status, a comprehensive plan should be formulated. Where a revocable living trust is an appropriate component, you should retain a lawyer to draft the trust. The trust should be signed, witnessed, and notarized, and copies should be given to your professionals, accountant, financial planner, broker, and insurance adviser. These people will be helpful, if not critical, in assisting you to properly transfer assets to your trust, as described in detail in Chapter 3. Your accountant should include a copy of your trust in the permanent file of your important documents. Also, your accountant will likely be involved in helping your family in the event of your death or disability, and then will need a copy of your trust.

Phase 2: Management Prior to Your Disability

You will continue to manage the assets in your trusts as if they were your own, with one exception—transactions affecting trust assets will be completed in the name of the trust. You will sign trust checks and buy stock in your trust's name.

NOTE: John Doe sets up the John Doe Revocable Living Trust on January 14, 1999. When John buys assets, or signs checks on the trust checking account, this should be done as "John Doe, Trustee of the John Doe Revocable Living Trust dated 1/14/99." Signature lines must be signed in the following manner:

JOHN DOE REVOCABLE LIVING TRUST

By: _____
John Doe, Trustee

[You then sign on the above line. This formality is important for all trusts. If the document you are signing has only a single signature line, you should then write in the necessary information and lines using the illustrated approach.]

Phase 3: You Become Disabled

When you become disabled, your successor trustees will take over the management of your trust assets. If you instead named an initial co-trustee, that co-trustee and the next successor co-trustee appointed in the trust document will then serve. At this time, your agent, acting under your durable power of attorney (as discussed earlier) may transfer to the trusts any assets you own that were not already transferred to the trust.

Your living trust should contain detailed provisions stating how and who should take over including how it should be determined that you are disabled so that your successor trustees can take over. Further, it should make it clear how to determine when you are no longer deemed disabled so that you can take back control over your financial management. This is important to consider since disability can frequently be short term, not permanent. These provisions should be reasonable to implement. For example, if a court determination is required, it could be expensive and time consuming to demonstrate whether or not you are disabled. If the trust simply refers to state law definitions of disability you will have to hire a lawyer to research the issue. The better approach is to have a detailed definition and mechanism for determining if that definition is met right in the trust document.

An important part of the disability provisions of your living trust is detailed instructions as to how you should be cared for in the event of disability. Many of the "form" trusts simply do not provide this type of personalized detail. Do you want to avoid being placed in a nursing home as long as possible? Do you prefer a certain type of health care facility if placement becomes absolutely necessary? If location or family proximity is important to you, you should specify in your living trust that in the event of disability you would wish to be placed in a facility located in a certain part of the country (or near your family); if religious preferences are important, you may wish to specify that the health care facility be near a church, mosque, or synagogue so that you could attend services, or so that the facility could meet your religious dietary requirements. Do not assume that your trustees "will know." Specifying such details may be vital depending on who the trustees are and can also enable them to defend their decisions and expenditures if challenged by your heirs.

Phase 4: After Your Death

Once you die, your trust will no longer be revocable, and its provisions will be implemented by your successor trustees. These provisions could include the outright distribution of property to intended beneficiaries (such as adult children), or the establishment (or continuation) of one or several trusts. Several of the trusts described in this book can be incorporated into your living trust.

EXAMPLE: The only way to know which of the many different trusts are appropriate for inclusion in your living trust is to complete a comprehensive analysis of your overall estate, financial, insurance, and personal planning. The diversity of trusts, and combinations of different trusts, is why relying on "self-help" trust books can be dangerous. No single form that purports to be adaptable by all readers of a book could possibly give everyone the optimal combination of trust arrangements to meet each person's unique goals.

At this point, any assets that were not already transferred to your trust (either by you when you formed it, at a later date by you or by someone making a gift to you, or by your agent under your durable power of attorney after your disability) can be transferred under what is known as a pour-over will. The key provision of this will provides that any assets you may have owned at your death, which were not already in your trust, should be transferred (or poured over into) your trust.

CONCLUSION

Living trusts are an important and flexible estate and financial planning tool. Their benefits can be substantial. Where a living trust is to be used, however, all of the benefits and costs should be carefully considered. Further, the living trust should be completed as part of an overall estate plan, including durable power of attorney with authority to make gifts and transfer assets to the living trust, a living will/health care proxy with guardian appointment, and a pour-over will.

Other trusts you may establish for yourself are discussed in Chapter 15.

For Your Notebook:

SCHEMATIC OF LIVING TRUST

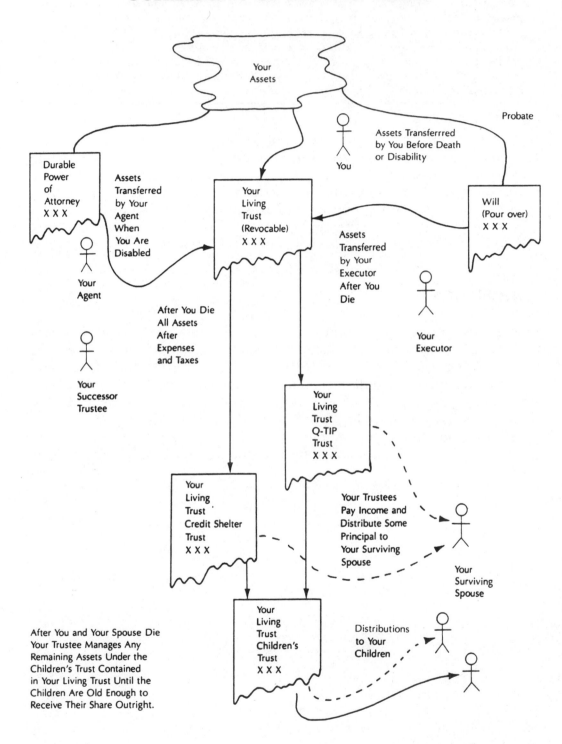

11 TRUSTS FOR YOUR SPOUSE

TRUST PLANNING FOR YOUR SPOUSE

Many of the trusts described in this book can be used in some manner to benefit your spouse:

1. *Charitable Remainder Trust.* You can contribute appreciated (or other) property to a charitable trust in exchange for an annuity for the joint lives of you and your spouse. See Chapter 14.

2. *Irrevocable Life Insurance Trust.* This is one of the most common trusts used to benefit a spouse. The trust holds insurance on your life to protect it from estate tax on the death of the last of you and your spouse when the unlimited marital deduction will not be available. If the insurance is on your life alone (as contrasted with second-to-die insurance) the proceeds can provide for your spouse. See Chapter 16.

3. *Revocable Living Trust.* This is a common tool used to protect the designated person in the event of illness and disability. You can also benefit your spouse under your revocable living trust by including a credit shelter or marital/Q-TIP trust under your living trust for your spouse's benefit. See Chapter 10.

4. *Qualified Personal Residence Trust (QPRT).* This trust is used to reduce estate taxes. You may transfer the house into tenants-in-common (you and your spouse each own a one-half interest in the property) and thereafter you each transfer your one-half interest into separate QPRT trusts, with your spouse reserving the right to live in the portion of the house in his or her trust. See Chapter 19.

The list goes on. However, when planning for marital trusts, all the other trusts and steps in your overall estate plan should be considered. These are important, since it is the aggregate benefit of all planning that your spouse will receive, not just the results of one component of that planning. For example, if your spouse is the sole beneficiary of an insurance trust with a $2 million insurance policy on your life, you may be less concerned about providing for her under other trusts you form.

The focus of this chapter will be on those trusts uniquely and specifically intended for spouses. In most cases, the focus of a spousal trust (and the factor that distinguishes a spousal trust from other trusts) is qualification for the unlimited estate and gift tax marital deduction. This deduction permits you to transfer unlimited assets to your spouse without any tax cost, if the applicable requirements are met. When the term "spouse" is used in this chapter, it refers solely to a person whose relationship under local law is that of a marital partner. A nonmarital partner will not qualify for these tax benefits (see Chapter 12). The term spouse should also be limited to a spouse who is a U.S. citizen unless special provisions discussed next are met.

An important point must be considered when planning for marital deductions and marital deduction trusts. The use of a marital deduction is not a tax savings. It is a tax deferral. Thus, although the marital deduction remains a cornerstone of planning for married couples, it should not be relied on to the exclusion of estate tax reduction planning techniques (e.g., CRTs, QPRTs).

GIFT TAX MARITAL DEDUCTION

Gift tax planning for spousal trusts can be quite important. It may be advantageous to establish an inter vivos (i.e., while you are alive, rather than under your will) marital (Q-TIP or Q-DOT) trust.

For Spouses Generally

There is a gift tax marital deduction available for gifts outright to your spouse. In addition, the gift can be made in trust if it meets the requirements of a Q-TIP or Q-DOT. Why would you wish to establish and fund a marital trust while you are still alive? If your spouse has few assets, he or she will not be able to fund a credit shelter trust, thus wasting the $600,000 unified credit he or she is entitled to. If you make a gift while you are alive to a Q-TIP marital trust for the benefit of your spouse, there will be no current gift tax cost as a result of your qualifying the gift for the unlimited gift tax marital deduction. You will have to elect to qualify the gift to the trust for the marital deduction on a gift tax return. Further, on your spouse's death (if he or she should predecease you) the $600,000 Q-TIP trust would be taxed in his or her estate. Since your spouse has little other assets, his or her entire unified credit of $600,000 may be available to offset the estate tax on this amount. Thus, this trust could pass to your children (or other heirs designated in the Q-TIP trust you formed) without any estate tax. This will ultimately save your family $225,000 in federal estate taxes. In addition, assets taxed in your spouse's estate will receive a step-up in basis to the fair value on death.

TIP: This technique can be carried further. Say the wife is in favor of transferring $600,000 to a marital trust for her husband so that his $600,000 unified credit will be used for the family's betterment. However, the wife would like to receive the income from that property if her husband predeceases her. Can she? Yes. The Q-TIP trust can be structured to become a credit shelter trust (using the husband's unified credit to avoid tax on his death) for the benefit of the wife.

Is $600,000 the optimal amount to gift to your spouse in an inter vivos Q-TIP trust? Maybe. However, if your estate is so large that you want to take maximum advantage of the $1 million generation-skipping transfer (GST) tax exemption available to each of you and your spouse, perhaps enough assets should be transferred to assure that your spouse's estate will have $1 million (see Chapter 8).

Why use the Q-TIP approach rather than an outright gift? The children who are ultimate beneficiaries may be from a different marriage. Your spouse might be a professional concerned about malpractice. The Q-TIP trust will make the assets available but outside the reach of malpractice claimants.

For Noncitizen Spouses

The gift tax rules applicable where your spouse is not a citizen present a trap to your trust planning. The unlimited marital deduction is not available for a gift to a noncitizen spouse. However, a gift of up to $100,000 per year can be made to a noncitizen spouse without incurring a gift tax. The mechanism for this is to provide that the annual per donee gift tax exclusion is increased from $10,000 to $100,000. To qualify, the gift must be one of a present interest. This provision is quite valuable in that substantial assets can be transferred to the noncitizen spouse during your life. However, this restriction must be carefully considered in setting up any trusts for the benefit of your spouse.

ESTATE TAX MARITAL DEDUCTION

You or your estate can qualify for the gift or estate tax marital deduction in several ways. In planning the use of this deduction, review with your estate planner the pros and cons of deferring estate tax. In some instances, it may be advantageous to use less marital deduction and actually incur some tax on the death of the first spouse. This could be done, for example, to take advantage of the lower graduated estate tax brackets.

General Tax Rules Governing Bequests to Your Spouse

An unlimited marital deduction is available for qualifying distributions to a surviving spouse. This deduction is available where the following requirements are met for a transfer to, or for the benefit of, your spouse:

- The property that is intended to qualify for the marital deduction must pass from you to your surviving spouse. This means that the property must be transferred under your will (or under your state's laws of intestacy if you died without a will, or under a revocable living trust), as a result of joint ownership between you and your spouse, pursuant to a general power of appointment, or by a beneficiary designation.
- The rights and property transferred to your spouse cannot be what is called a terminable interest. This is an interest that will terminate or fail as the result of the passing of time, the occurrence of an event or contingency, or the failure of an event or contingency to occur. A life estate (my spouse shall have our home for her life) or a bequest for a term of years (my spouse shall have my yacht for 15 years) are terminable interests and do not qualify for the marital deduction. A number of exceptions from this rule are important to the use of trusts for your spouse and will be discussed. The most commonly used exception to this rule denying a marital deduction for property interests that may terminate, however, is the exception provided for Q-TIP property.

Where the following requirements are met, your estate will qualify for the estate tax marital deduction, but you will be able to exert important controls over the use and ultimate disposition of the property:

- Your spouse is given a life estate in particular property.
- The property must pass from you.
- No person has a power to appoint any part of the property to any person other than your surviving spouse.
- The necessary election is made by your executor to have the property qualify for the marital deduction. This is done on your estate tax return.

Outright (i.e., No Trust) Gift or Bequest

Where your estate makes a transfer to your spouse (who is a U.S. citizen), outright and free of any restrictions or trusts, which qualifies for the marital deduction, the amount transferred to your spouse is deducted from the value of your gross estate. The simplest wills generally bequeath all assets of the first spouse to die, to the surviving spouse. The problem with this simplistic approach is that it wastes the $600,000 unified credit available to the estate of the first spouse to die. It results in "doubling-up" assets in the estate of the surviving spouse. Thus, on the second death, all of the family's net worth becomes taxable in the estate of the second spouse to die, where there is only one $600,000 unified credit to offset it. The better planning approach is to use a credit shelter trust for the first approximately $600,000 of assets in the estate of first spouse to die. This trust is explained in Chapter 7, and again briefly in a later section of this chapter ("Classic/Marital Credit Shelter Estate Plan").

The primary issue in evaluating the use of an outright (i.e., not in trust) marital bequest is whether you are comfortable losing control of the proceeds of your estate to the surviving spouse. What if your spouse remarries following your death? Where will your assets ultimately be distributed? Personal concerns are often paramount. The estate plan should be tailored to meet these objectives with the least tax interference possible. In most cases, this requires the use of one or more trusts.

Another factor to consider in evaluating an outright marital bequest versus a transfer of assets to a Q-TIP trust is that the marital deduction must be claimed if the assets are distributed outright. If the assets are distributed in trust, your executor has the option to claim, or to forgo, the marital deduction. This additional flexibility can be important.

Q-TIP Marital Trust

The qualified terminable interest property, or Q-TIP, trust is the most popular form of marital deduction after the simple distribution of assets outright to the surviving spouse. The key advantage is that the assets transferred to a Q-TIP trust qualify for the unlimited estate or gift tax marital deduction, but you can control where the assets are ultimately distributed following the later death of your spouse (e.g., your children from another marriage). Thus, your estate can qualify for the estate tax marital deduction without your having to give complete control over the assets to your spouse.

To qualify for Q-TIP tax benefits, the trust must meet the following requirements:

- The surviving spouse must be entitled to all income from the trust for life.
- No person can have the power to appoint the trust assets to any person other than your surviving spouse prior to his or her death.
- Income from the trust must be paid to your spouse at least annually.
- Your executor must elect to qualify the trust for the marital deduction.

On the death of the surviving spouse, the entire value of the Q-TIP property is included in your surviving spouse's gross estate. These assets will be taxed at his or her top marginal tax brackets. Your surviving spouse cannot give away these assets to avoid this tax result. An attempt to do so will trigger a gift tax for the entire principal balance given as well as for the value of the income interest.

Life Estate Coupled with a General Power of Appointment

If you give your surviving spouse a life estate coupled with a power of appointment in the property, this qualifies for the unlimited gift or estate tax marital deduction. This requires that you give her the right to all of the income from the entire property (or from a specific portion of the property) for life. This income must be payable at least annually. If the property is held by a trust for the surviving spouse's benefit, she must have the right to require that any non-income-producing property be converted into income-producing property. In addition, your surviving spouse must have a general power of appointment (i.e., to designate where the property will be distributed on her death), exercisable by your spouse alone, to appoint the entire interest in the property as he or she chooses. This power must include the right to appoint the property to herself or her estate. No other person can have the right to appoint the property involved to any person other than your spouse.

Estate Trust

The estate trust is another method of qualifying a bequest for the unlimited estate tax marital deduction. It is another exception to the terminable interest rule described earlier, which would otherwise prevent this deduction from qualifying for the estate tax marital deduction. This type of trust will qualify for the unlimited marital deduction for a U.S. citizen where the requirements for a life estate and general power of appointment are met and the income from the estate trust that is not required to be paid to the spouse at least annually, can be accumulated and added to the trust. However, the estate trust must require that the accumulated income and principal be paid out at some future time to the surviving spouse, or to her estate. Thus, your spouse may receive no income from this trust, but on her later death, the entire trust will be paid to her estate and distributed as she directs.

Marital and Charitable Trusts Combined

There are a number of ways you can combine marital and charitable trusts. You could have a Q-TIP marital trust and provide that on the death of your surviving spouse the entire trust is paid to charity. The result will be no tax in your estate as a result of the marital deduction. On your spouse's later death, there will be no tax in her estate as a result of the charitable contribution deduction. This can be a better approach then using a charitable remainder trust (CRT) because the surviving spouse will receive all income of the trust rather than just the specified annuity or unitrust amount under the CRT. Principal can be invaded for the surviving spouse.

Charitable remainder trusts (CRTs) can be combined with marital deduction planning. Your spouse can be the sole noncharitable beneficiary of a charitable remainder trust. This would entitle her to a unitrust or annuity payment each year (month, or quarter) during her lifetime. The interest she has will qualify as a marital deduction and thus not be taxable (see Chapter 14).

Marital Deduction for Spouse Who Is Not a Citizen

If your spouse is not a United States citizen, the unlimited estate tax marital deduction will not be available if special steps are not taken. Thus, the Q-TIP trust will not defer estate tax. While a credit provision can mitigate this result to some extent, the best answer, short of becoming a U.S. citizen, is to use a special trust for noncitizen spouses.

The credit works as follows: If you bequeath property to your spouse, who is not a citizen, the property transfer is subjected to the estate tax. Since it would not have been taxed had your spouse been a citizen, a credit is given later. On the death of your spouse, her estate will receive a credit for the tax paid by your estate on the earlier transfer to her, which did not qualify for the marital deduction.

If your spouse is not a citizen, the key planning opportunity involves the proper use of trusts. Where the assets are passed into a qualified domestic trust ("Q-DOT"), the marital deduction will be available without limit. To qualify, a Q-DOT, must meet the following requirements:

- *Trustees.* At least one of your trustees must be either a United States citizen or corporation. This requirement must be contained in the trust documents. Provisions should be made for alternate trustees to assure compliance with this requirement. For example, a final alternate should be a United States bank or trust company.

- *Income.* The surviving spouse must generally be entitled to all of the income from the trust, payable at least annually.

- *Regulations.* The trust must meet additional requirements prescribed by IRS regulations which are intended to assure that the trust assets will not escape United States taxation.

- *Election.* Your executor must make an irrevocable election on the U.S. estate tax return with respect to the trust. This rule provides flexibility in that your executor is not required to make the election. The executor's right to make, or not make this election, should appear in your will or the Q-DOT trust.

Estate tax will be levied on distributions of principal (corpus) from the Q-DOT other than annual income distributions. This tax will be calculated as if the amount distributed had been included in your estate (i.e., the first to die, the citizen spouse). This calculation adds all prior distributions from the Q-DOT to your taxable estate to push the tax on the Q-DOT distributions into the highest federal estate tax brackets. This calculation and tax requirement also will somewhat complicate the administration of the Q-DOT. An exception is provided for certain hardship distributions. In addition, a tax will be assessed on the property remaining in the Q-DOT on the death of the second spouse. This tax is calculated in the same manner. Where a trust does not meet the requirements of a Q-DOT, the IRS may provide the flexibility of reforming the trust so it does qualify. However, it is always preferable to plan properly in advance and not rely on the IRS's generosity.

CLASSIC MARITAL/CREDIT SHELTER ESTATE PLAN

The classic zero tax approach using trusts for a married couple is to combine a credit shelter trust and marital trust.

Credit Shelter Trust Funded on First Spouse's Death

You and your spouse provide for a credit shelter (since the assets in it are sheltered from estate tax by the unified credit) or bypass (since it bypasses the surviving spouse's estate) trust under each of your wills. Some books refer to this trust as the "B" trust (the marital trust below is usually referred to as the "A" trust). Be certain that ownership of marital assets has been divided so that each spouse has as close to $600,000 in his or her name alone (joint property cannot fund the credit shelter trust since it passes on death to the joint owner, never the trust under the will). On the death of the first spouse, approximately $600,000 of assets are placed in the credit shelter trust, protected from tax by the unified credit. The trustee of the credit shelter trust is given the right to pay income to the surviving spouse (and children if desired), and certain principal invasion rights (perhaps limited by an ascertainable standard) are given to the surviving spouse, or to a co-trustee of the credit shelter trust.

Whatever assets are placed into the credit shelter trust remain free of estate tax in both your estate and your surviving spouse's estate. It does not matter how large they grow. If the $600,000 grows to $2 million by the time your spouse dies, it remains estate-tax-free. Less than the full $600,000 is typically placed into such a trust because the amount that can be used is often reduced by the estate's administrative expenses, which are deducted on the estate's income tax return or other bequests which do not qualify for the marital or charitable deduction (e.g., $1,000 to your old army buddy).

Remaining Estate Distributed to Q-TIP/Marital Trust

The remainder of the estate is to be given either outright and free of any trust (i.e., in a manner that qualifies for the unlimited estate tax marital deduction), or in a Q-TIP trust to your spouse (which benefits the surviving spouse but can qualify for the unlimited estate tax marital deduction or a Q-DOT). No estate tax will be due on the first death because any assets not sheltered from tax by the unified credit to which your estate is entitled, will be sheltered from tax by the unlimited marital deduction.

The "Disclaimer" Option

Not sure which approach to use? Perhaps you are weighing the simplicity of giving all assets to the surviving spouse, and letting the children worry about the taxes (after all, they will inherit so much anyway). If your estate is only somewhat over the $600,000, say $735,000, you may not be convinced that the paperwork (e.g., annual trust income tax returns after the credit shelter trust is funded following your death) are worth it. Alternatively, you might be debating having all assets over the credit shelter amount given outright to your surviving spouse versus holding them in trust to protect them from a new spouse. There is an option. Instead of your will or trust forcing the funding of either the credit shelter trust or the Q-TIP marital trust, have the document give the assets outright to your surviving spouse. If the surviving spouse disclaims them (files required papers in the surrogate's court within nine months of your death declining to accept the assets), the document can then transfer the assets to the appropriate trust. This mechanism gives the survivor of you and your spouse until nine months after the first death to determine which approach to use and to what extent.

How Do You Divide the Estate between the Credit Shelter and Marital Trusts?

Once you have determined that your will or revocable living trust should take the classic estate-planning approach, these documents must include a mechanism to divide your estate between these two trusts. There are two choices.

Fractional Share Method

This approach divides your remaining estate into two shares and places the appropriate proportion in each trust. Your will or living trust might say: "The fiduciary shall transfer to the Q-TIP trust that fractional share of my residuary estate which, when added to all other assets passing to my spouse which qualify for the unlimited estate tax marital deduction, is the minimum amount necessary to reduce the federal estate tax as close as possible to zero using the unlimited estate tax marital deduction. The remaining fractional share shall be distributed to the Credit Shelter trust."

This method has several important characteristics. Any appreciation or depreciation in assets is shared proportionately. There is no income tax cost to funding the trusts.

Pecuniary Share

This method transfers a specified dollar amount (as contrasted with a share, as in the preceding method) to one of the trusts, such as the credit shelter trust, with the balance to the other trust. All appreciation or depreciation in the value of assets from the date of death through the date of funding the trust inures to the residuary trust (either trust can be in the residuary depending on how your lawyer prepares the document): "I give to the Trustee, in trust, a pecuniary sum equal to the largest amount

178TRUSTS FOR DIFFERENT PEOPLE AND ORGANIZATIONS

which will not result in any federal estate tax payable after giving effect to the unified credit to which I am entitled, as well as the state death tax credit and other credits applicable to my estate." There can be an income tax cost if the pecuniary share is funded with appreciated assets.

SPOUSAL RIGHT OF ELECTION

In planning for marital and other trusts to benefit your spouse, you must carefully consider the implications of any premarital or postnuptial agreement. These agreements can have a substantial impact on what you can accomplish with your trusts. In addition, many states have laws giving a surviving spouse the right to demand a specified percentage of an estate if less is left to him or her under the will of the deceased spouse. These laws can be quite complex in how they determine this percentage, and what assets of the deceased spouse are to be considered in the calculations. The goal of these laws is to assure a surviving spouse a minimum inheritance. These rules can be important to address when planning to transfer assets to trusts.

For example, under state statute, a surviving spouse may have the right to elect to take a forced share (called "elective share") of one-third of the decedent spouse's estate. This elective share may be more than the amount left to the surviving spouse in the decedent spouse's will. A Q-TIP (marital) trust under your will may qualify as part of the bequests to your spouse under some state laws, but not under others. In some states, assets bequeathed to the surviving spouse in trust are only counted in part toward meeting the surviving spouse's minimum inheritance. Finally, state laws could even give the surviving spouse the right to demand distributions from a trust you formed to meet the minimum inheritance. In some states, a surviving spouse can take outright from a Q-TIP trust enough to satisfy the statutory right of election and defeat the deceased spouse's tax and estate plan.

When calculating the "estate" against which the surviving spouse can exert an elective right to a minimum inheritance, the estate may be increased by:

- The value of property transferred by the deceased spouse at any time during the marriage to or for the benefit of any person other than the surviving spouse, to the extent that the decedent did not receive full consideration in money. This is generally any gifts made.
- Any transfer under which the decedent retained the possession or enjoyment of, or right to income from, the property, at the time of death.
- Any transfer to the extent the decedent retained at the time of his or her death the power, either alone or in conjunction with any other person, to revoke or to consume, invade, or dispose of the principal for his or her own benefit.
- Any transfer whereby property is held at the time of decedent's death by decedent and another with right of survivorship.

Several planning possibilities may exist, depending on the laws in your state. Where the surviving spouse gave a written consent to the transfer, or joined in the transfer, the property transferred may not be included in the augmented estate. Where the estate plan provides for a surviving spouse to receive less than the elective share statute would provide, a method of assuring that the disposition scheme will be respected is to have the spouse waive the right of election. The waiver may be wholly or partially effective. It may be completed prior to, or after, the marriage.

To determine whether the surviving spouse has received the one-third share of the augmented estate that the statute provides for, the following transfers/assets may be considered under some states' laws:

- The value of all property owned by the surviving spouse in his or her own right at the time of the decedent's death from whatever source acquired as a result of decedent's death.

- An interest in a trust created by the decedent spouse during his or her lifetime, property appointed to the spouse by the decedent's exercise of a general or special power of appointment, insurance proceeds, and so forth.

Always make sure your estate planner has addressed these rules by assuring that your spouse will receive the minimum inheritance required under your state's laws, or that appropriate steps have been taken for your spouse to waive those rights.

ALIMONY TRUST

In some divorce cases, trusts are used to fund alimony payments. This can be done to minimize the contact and interaction you will have with your ex-spouse, and to give greater certainty to the receipt of alimony payments.

EXAMPLE: Charles and Laura divorce. Charles places $5 million in a trust. Laura is to receive the income for her life. On her death, the trust assets are to be distributed to their children. The trust eliminates Laura's worry over receiving alimony payments when due.

Alimony trusts face a special tax problem. If you form a trust and then use the trust money to pay an obligation of yours, all trust income will be taxed to you. This is the same problem faced by some children's trusts, as discussed in Chapter 13. You cannot use a trust to discharge your legal obligation of support without incurring tax. There is an exception to this rule for certain alimony trusts. If you set up an alimony trust to pay income to your former spouse, and the marriage was ended by a court-issued divorce decree or a decree of separate maintenance, your spouse will be taxed on the income instead of you. This rule is flexible in that the divorce agreements don't have to require the formation of the trust. If you had previously formed a trust for your spouse even before the divorce, it can still qualify.

CAUTION: This special tax rule for alimony trusts is not available for payments to children.

CONCLUSION

For married couples, the gift and estate tax marital deduction can be the most important planning technique to minimize the overall gift and estate tax burden on transfers to living trusts or trusts that become effective on your death. However, simply claiming the maximum marital deduction (all my property to my spouse on my death, and vice versa) is almost never the optimal approach where you and your spouse have significant assets (in excess of $600,000). Where one spouse is not a United States citizen, planning is imperative to avoid what could otherwise be a substantial estate tax. The spouse can either become a citizen or use a special trust, called a Q-DOT, to defer the tax.

12 TRUSTS FOR NONMARRIED PARTNERS

IMPORTANCE AND DIFFICULTIES OF TRUST PLANNING FOR NONMARRIED PARTNERS

Nonmarried couples, whether gay, lesbian, or an unmarried heterosexual couple, face several difficulties in planning for their estates that traditionally married couples do not. These additional problems stem from the bias that the tax and property laws have in favor of married couples. There is no right to transfer unlimited assets without gift or estate tax cost to a nonmarried partner as there is for a spouse. State laws that "fill in" where wills are inadequate or nonexistent do not provide for distributions to nonmarried partners in the manner that they do for a spouse. As a result, the use of trusts, although somewhat different, is even more important for nonmarried couples. This chapter will address some of these issues and trust planning opportunities.

The goals of nonmarried couples are similar to those of married couples:

- Assure the availability of the personal residence and other specified property to the surviving partner.
- Provide for personal protection in the event of illness or disability.
- Minimize estate and gift taxes.
- Protect your desired beneficiary against a lawsuit or other type of challenge or problems created by people to whom you are not leaving your assets.

For the nonmarried couple, in contrast to the married couple, these goals are more difficult to achieve and require more advance planning.

LEGAL PROBLEMS AFFECTING NONMARRIED PARTNERS

Because state laws are generally extremely biased against couples living together outside marriage, nonmarried couples face several potential problems compared with married couples. These problems, however, can be avoided through proper planning.

Intestacy Laws Differ for Nonmarried Couples

If you die without a will (and haven't used a revocable living trust or other alternative technique) what happens to your assets? Your state's laws will answer this question. These laws, called laws of "intestacy," determine who inherits your property if you die without a will. Although different from state to state, on the death of one spouse, the surviving spouse will generally inherit a substantial portion of the estate, even without a will. If there is no spouse, then other relations will inherit. If a nonmarried partner dies, no consideration of the partnership is made by state statute. Therefore, planning is essential. This effort includes a properly drafted will providing for distributions to the surviving partner, tax planning, properly planned ownership (title) to assets, and trusts. If these steps are ignored, the property will pass on death to the deceased partner's family members, and not the surviving partner. This could have devastating financial consequences to the surviving partner. It can also create substantial personal conflicts where the family members succeeding to the property did not approve of the relationship.

No Spousal Right of Election Available

A surviving spouse has the right, under the laws of most states, to make an election against the will of a deceased spouse. This can permit the surviving spouse to obtain a statutory minimum amount of property even if the deceased spouse had changed his or her will to disinherit the surviving spouse. This right is not available to a surviving partner if the state does not recognize the partnership as a legal relationship. If your goal is to provide for your surviving partner, you must take specific steps to prepare a will, living trust, or other arrangements. Absent this, the fallback position of intestacy laws that a married couple can rely on not only will be unavailable, but will serve to transfer property to family members instead.

ESTATE AND GIFT TAX DIFFERENCES FROM THE MARITAL SITUATION

Estate Tax Considerations for Nonmarried Partners

Because the tax laws provide especially favorable treatment to married couples, every couple can readily avoid any estate tax on the death of the first spouse. Any husband or wife can transfer on death to the surviving spouse unlimited assets without any tax cost. The concept behind this favoritism is that married couples are viewed for tax purposes as a partnership, a single economic unit. All assets of the marital economic unit will be subject to the estate tax after the death of the two spouses. This same principle is behind the filing of a joint income tax return by a married couple. While there is logic and equity in this concept, these same benefits are denied to any couple whose relationship is not under state law a marriage. Although nonmarried couples may be as much of a single economic entity as a married couple, the tax laws do not recognize this. There is no unlimited "partner" deduction equivalent to the unlimited marital deduction even though nonmarried partners are often as much of a single economic unit as married couples.

A spouse can generally make unlimited transfers of property to the other spouse during life as gifts, or after death through intestacy or under a will. All these transfers are free of federal and state gift and estate taxes. However, this right is not afforded to nonmarried partners presenting them with substantial and costly problems. Nonmarried or married couples alike can bequeath up to $600,000 (the value of assets exempted from estate tax by the unified credit) to anyone they choose without any estate tax cost. If your estate is not in excess of this amount, you will not face any federal estate tax problem (although there can still be significant state level transfer tax costs). If your estate exceeds this amount, the federal tax cost will be substantial. You cannot transfer unlimited assets above this amount to your partner (as you could if the relationship were treated like a marriage). Other tax planning steps must be taken to protect assets in excess of $600,000 to avoid horrendous tax consequences and to assure that your partner will in fact receive the assets.

Possible suggestions to address the potentially costly problem of a significant estate tax on the death of the first partner include:

- The partner with the most significant assets should purchase life insurance to cover this estate tax. The insurance should be owned in an irrevocable life insurance trust to remove the proceeds from the reach of creditors, and to keep the proceeds out of the taxable estate of the first nonmarried partner.
- Begin an aggressive gift program to reduce the wealthier partner's taxable estate.
- Use the tax-oriented trusts and other techniques discussed throughout this book: grantor retained annuity trusts, charitable remainder trusts, and so forth.

Gift Tax Considerations for Nonmarried Partners

Married spouses are permitted to make unlimited transfers to each other without triggering any gift tax. For partners other than a husband and wife, the maximum amount that can be transferred in any year to any one donee (recipient) is $10,000. Unlimited amounts may be paid for tuition and medical care for any person, including a partner (if paid directly to qualifying providers). Any transfers above this amount will first be applied to reduce the $600,000 unified credit, and thereafter a tax will be triggered.

As a result of these limitations, nonmarried couples should begin a gift program early. In addition, the techniques discussed in this book to discount gifts (lack of marketability discounts, limited partnerships, grantor retained annuity trusts, etc.) should be used.

HOW NONMARRIED COUPLES SHOULD OWN ASSETS

Joint Ownership of Property

There are many different ways to own property. You can own property solely in your own name. On death, the property is then transferred under your will to your designated beneficiary. Property can also be owned as joint tenants with the right of survivorship. This form of ownership provides that, on the death of the first joint owner (partner), ownership (title) automatically transfers by operation of law (i.e., without the need for probate) to the surviving joint owner. Joint ownership can provide a number of advantages. The property will assuredly pass to the surviving joint owner. There is no need for probate and the attendant publicity it brings to effect the transfer. This could be especially important for a nonmarried couple if family members are likely to challenge the inheritance of the surviving partner. Joint ownership is also an inexpensive and simple method of transferring ownership at death.

There are, however, a number of shortcomings to the joint ownership approach. For federal estate tax purposes, the full value of the property will be included in the estate of the first joint owner to die, unless the survivor can demonstrate that he or she has made a contribution to the acquisition or improvement of the property. Often this is not the case. Almost always proving contribution toward the purchase or improvement of the property is quite difficult. Where the estate of the first to die exceeds $600,000, there will be a federal estate tax. Joint ownership also has other limitations.

This rule is less favorable than the rule that applies when spouses own property jointly. For spouses, only one-half of the value of the property is included in the estate of the first spouse to die. If the partnership dissolves, joint ownership can be difficult to untangle. If one of the partners has greater liability exposure than the other (e.g., one is an artist and the other partner a physician), joint ownership may be undesirable from an asset protection perspective. In some instances, trusts can offer better options.

Trusts Are a Key Ownership Technique for Nonmarital Partners

The ownership of property can be vested in a trust instead of individual or joint ownership. Several different types of trust can own property and be used to the advantage of nonmarried couples. You don't generally need different planning techniques, you just have to apply the planning techniques and trusts described in this book to fit your personal circumstances.

Revocable Living Trusts

A flexible and advantageous ownership structure for nonmarried partners is the funded revocable living trust (see Chapter 10). The trust must be funded (i.e., property actually transferred to the trust) to obtain the benefits it offers. A revocable living trust has several advantages over other types of planning. The trust is far more flexible then joint ownership. Also, the partner owning the property retains control so that if partnership dissolves ownership does not become an issue. As contrasted with a will, having a revocable living trust own the property avoids the probate and publicity that could invite more scrutiny, problems, and even legal challenges from the family of the deceased partner.

TIP: Consider transferring only some portion, but not all, of your assets to the revocable living trust. Thus, your will would be subject to probate and some assets indicated. This may make it less likely that family or others seeking to create problems will know even to look for the trust. If all assets are transferred to the trust so that there are no probate assets, suspicions of other arrangements will exist.

A revocable living trust offers the partners the ability to address other issues such as management of assets in the event of disability better than either a durable power of attorney or joint ownership. A will, since it only becomes effective on death, offers no disability planning benefits.

Irrevocable Grantor Trust

The wealthier partner could transfer assets to a trust for the benefit of the less wealthy partner. If the trust is effective under state law, the transfer would be complete thus assuring that partner receipt of the assets involved on the death of the transferor partner. This could also help insulate the assets of the wealthier partner from creditors, potential malpractice claimants, and others. The irrevocable trust could be structured so that it intentionally is ineffective as a property transfer for federal gift and estate tax purposes. For example, the wealthy partner could retain a general power of appointment over the trust assets (e.g., the right to designate who should receive the assets) so that the transfer would not be complete for federal gift tax purposes. This would avoid any current gift tax cost for the transfer.

This approach, however, does nothing to reduce potential estate tax costs since the entire balance of the trust would be included in the estate of the partner who transfers the assets to the trust.

Special Needs Trust

If your partner is ill, a trust can be the ideal vehicle to protect him or her. Your partner could perhaps be a co-trustee with a friend, and you can name a list of friends or family members as successor trustees. This will assure trusted and caring people selected by the two of you to be available to help if your partner's illness should become incapacitating. In some situations, it may be advisable to consider planning such a trust to qualify as a special needs trust. This trust is designed to make funds available for services and needs that are not provided by state- or other government-sponsored programs. Since the programs and rules vary significantly from state to state, consult with a specialist in the state where you live. An elder law attorney may be the most familiar with these types of programs. See Chapter 15.

Insurance Trusts

If life insurance is to be purchased to fund an estate tax (or to provide an estate for the surviving partner), the insurance could be owned by an insurance trust. This will assure that it is not taxed in the estate of the insured partner. Further, it can protect insurance proceeds from creditors, provide a management structure for the insurance proceeds, and so forth. See Chapter 16.

CONCLUSION

Any nonmarried couple involved in trust and related planning must exercise additional care because of the substantial unfairness of the tax and property laws relating to nonmarried couples. The need for using trusts in planning can be even more important than for married couples because statutory law does not provide any of the protection given to married couples. Also, the need for privacy can be greater.

13 TRUSTS FOR CHILDREN

This chapter will explain the importance of trusts in providing for your children, grandchildren, and other minors. The discussions will apply whether the intended beneficiary is your child, grandchild, niece, nephew, or any other minor. With the exception of the generation-skipping transfer (GST) tax, which affects trusts for grandchildren and certain others (discussed in Chapter 8), the considerations for all these beneficiaries are quite similar. Thus, with that exception, when you read "child" in the discussions, you can generally substitute any beneficiary (other than a spouse) you are seeking to benefit. Trusts are commonly used with minor children and for years after they reach the legal status of adult. Even when this chapter discusses minors, consider the importance of using trusts to protect children or other heirs in later years when they are older.

TRUSTS ARE KEY FOR PLANNING FOR CHILDREN AND OTHER MINOR HEIRS

When people think of trusts, they often think first of trusts for children. This is natural since an essential characteristic of trusts is that they provide for the separation of ownership and management of an asset (in the trustee) and the beneficial enjoyment of that asset (the beneficiaries). For children, who have important financial needs for their education and care and the immaturity that requires another to manage their assets, trusts are often ideal. They answer the need to provide for management of assets and to protect children from themselves, a potential divorce, or creditors.

The desire to help your children, reinforced by the high gift, estate, and generation-skipping transfer tax rates, often provides a strong impetus to make gifts to take maximum advantage of the annual $10,000 exclusion. Where the gifts made can be significant, the next question is whether they will become large enough to use a trust. This is primarily a question of costs.

GIFT AND ESTATE TAXES ENCOURAGE CHILDREN'S TRUSTS

The gift and estate tax rates reach higher than 50 percent. With the generation-skipping transfer (GST) tax, the rate can exceed 75 percent. To avoid these costly taxes you should consider taking advantage of the various exclusions and special rules discussed in Chapters 7 and 8. One of the basic exclusions is your right to give away $10,000 per year to as many different people as you wish. This right is noncumulative. If you do not give a $10,000 gift in one year to a particular beneficiary, you cannot give more than $10,000 in the next year. Thus, a cornerstone of estate planning for many people is to make the maximum annual $10,000 gifts to as many family members as possible. When a gift program is pursued on a regular basis, year after year, and the funds are well invested, it does not take long for sizable amounts of money to be transferred to each beneficiary. When children are involved, a trust is a natural step to protect this large and growing nest egg.

EXAMPLE: In one of the most common trust arrangements, Grandfather establishes an "Education Trust" for Grandchild. Grandmother and Child (who is the parent of Grandchild) are co-trustees. Grandfather makes $10,000 annual gifts to the trust, which are invested and saved for Grandchild's college and graduate school education. Often the trust funds will not be needed for education if sufficient other assets are transferred or if the grandparents take advantage of the other common gift tax exclusion—paying any amounts to educational institutions directly for tuition. The trust will then typically distribute the principal amounts to Grandchild in approximately equal increments at ages 25, 30, and the balance at 35.

When setting up trust for a child or other heir, care must be taken to address the gift tax consequences of a gift to a trust since they are more complicated than the gift tax consequences of a gift made directly outside any trust. It is more difficult to avoid a current gift tax (or use of your unified credit) by qualifying for the $10,000 per year annual gift tax exclusion. To avoid gift tax, the gift must be a "gift of a present interest." This can be done with what is called a Crummey power (described in Chapter 7) or with a special trust known by the Internal Revenue Code Section that created it—a "2503(c) Trust," described later in this chapter.

In addition to the complexities caused by the gift tax annual exclusion rules, there are two potential income tax problems. If the trust's distribution and power provisions are not properly structured, there is a risk trust funds could be used to meet your legal obligation to support the child. Where trust income or assets are used for education, medical, or other obligations that the law requires you as a parent to provide for, the income earned by the trust may be taxed to you instead of the trust. The trust assets could be taxed in your estate. The second problem to consider is the compression of trust income tax rates. Once the trust realizes a modest level of income, its income is taxed at the maximum tax rates. Thus, investments have to be carefully planned. Often this will include growth-oriented stocks, mutual funds managed to minimize current taxable income, and tax-exempt bonds (see Chapter 8). So long as you are cautious to address these issues with your tax adviser, the use of trusts to hold assets of minors is an ideal planning device.

TIP: In some situations, you can use a family limited partnership or limited liability company to control assets for children. The advantage of these entities over a trust is that they are not irrevocable; agreements governing them can be modified in the future. More cautious taxpayers actually combine the two techniques. They will transfer assets to a family limited partnership or limited liability company, and then form trusts for the benefit of their children to own the limited partnership interests or the limited liability company membership interests. This approach, while more complex and expensive, affords even greater protection and tax-planning possibilities (by permitting lack of marketability discounts and other techniques).

"KIDDIE TAX" MUST BE CONSIDERED IN PLANNING GIFTS TO CHILDREN

When planning for gifts to children, or trusts for the benefit of a child, you must consider the Kiddie Tax. Any gifts to a custodial account will be subject to the Kiddie Tax. If instead, you use a trust for your child, the Kiddie Tax will apply to distributions from the trust. The trustee of a child's trust will have to weigh the benefits of retaining income in the trust and subjecting it to trust tax rates, versus distributing the income to the child so that the Kiddie Tax may apply. Also, you must determine what assets to keep outside of the trust (e.g., in a Uniform Gifts to Minor's Act account to take advantage of the modest income a child can earn before the Kiddie Tax applies).

Where a child who has not reached the age of 14 before year-end earns income, special tax rules, called the "Kiddie Tax," apply. The Kiddie Tax taxes the net unearned income of a child under 14 at the parents' tax rate. The unearned income of your child includes income earned on assets (stocks, bonds, etc.) in your child's name, income earned on certain bank accounts with the child's name and your name, income on Uniform Gifts to Minors Act accounts, and income distributed from a trust. This will occur to the extent that the trust income is taxable to the child. The child's income is divided into two components: (1) earned income (e.g., wages from a paper route); and (2) unearned income. The unearned income is reduced by the portion of the standard deduction that the child can claim, generally $600 (which is inflation adjusted). However, if the child has itemized deductions relating to unearned income (investment expenses) of more than $600, then they are applied to reduce the taxable unearned income. The result of this adjustment is called net unearned income and is the amount subject to the Kiddie Tax. The child's earned income is taxed under the regular rules. The child's unearned income is taxed as follows: The unearned income of all your children is added to your income and your income tax is recalculated. The difference between the tax you would have to pay after the recalculation, and the tax due on your return, is the additional tax attributable to your children's unearned income.

The Kiddie Tax rules can be summarized as follows:

- Wages your child earns working are not subject to the Kiddie Tax. They are taxed at the child's own tax rate.

- The first $600 of your child's income is offset by the child's standard deduction. The child is not permitted a personal exemption if claimed as a dependent on the parent's tax return.

- The next $600 of income is taxed to the child at the tax rate of 15 percent.

- Unearned income above this first $1,200 is taxed at the top tax rate of the parents, which could be 39.6 percent or even higher. Prior to the Clinton tax act, the highest rate for the Kiddie Tax applicable to the child's income was 31 percent.

EXAMPLE: Father gives Child $10,000 of stock which generates dividends of $975. The first $600 is offset by the child's $600 personal exemption. The next $375 is taxed at Child's tax rate of 15 percent. Child's tax can be calculated on Form 1040A.

EXAMPLE: Mother also gives Child $10,000 of stock, which generates an additional $952 in dividends. Child's income now totals $1,927 [$975 + $952]. Child must file Form 8615 "Computation of Tax for Children Under Age 14 Who Have Investment Income of More Than $1,200." The first $600 is not taxed as a result of Child's standard deduction. The next $600 is taxed at Child's tax rate, presumably 15 percent. The remaining income of $772 is taxed at the parents' marginal tax rate.

Where any parent's estate planning involves gifts to their child under age 14, the careful selection of an appropriate investment strategy can minimize the burden of the Kiddie Tax. Any assets are appropriate until the $1,200 income level is reached. After that point, invest in assets that will appreciate rather than generate current income. This can include growth stocks, raw land, tax exempt bonds, and Series EE United States bonds. After the child reaches age 14, the Kiddie Tax will no longer apply so these assets can be traded for income-producing assets.

There is an election that can save some of the cost and paperwork of preparing a separate tax return for the child. A parent may report the child's income on the parent's tax return. To qualify, the child's income must not be more than $5,000 and must consist only of interest and dividend income. A special form must be filed by the parent, Form 8814— "Parent's Election to Report Child's Interest and Dividends." The parent must also pay the lesser of an additional $75 or 15 percent of the child's income in excess of $600, in tax to make this election.

Although the Kiddie Tax can be a costly trap for children under age 14, the costly estate tax rates of up to 55 percent can make gifts to a child under 14 still advantageous if your net worth is large enough. When these gifts are made, the most common approach is to plan the gifts to comply with the requirements of the annual $10,000 exclusion from the gift tax, which will avoid any gift tax implications.

CUSTODIAL ACCOUNTS: UNIFORM GIFTS (TRANSFERS) TO MINORS ACT

Custodial Accounts Are the Most Common Arrangement

The most common arrangement for gifts to minor children is not a trust. Most parents, grandparents, and others simply make gifts to the child under the Uniform Gifts (or Transfers) to Minors Acts. These acts are a series of laws, somewhat different in each state, which provide that a designated person acts as custodian for the minor's assets in the account until the minor reaches a specified age. The Uniform Transfers to Minors Acts are similar to the Uniform Gifts to Minors Acts, but are often more recently enacted and broader in scope, permitting investments in real estate and other assets. These are often referred to by the acronyms UGMA or UTMA.

Advantages of Custodial Accounts

Making gifts to UGMA or UTMA accounts instead of to trusts has two merits: It costs nothing to use and it's easy. To give a gift to your children under your state's version of UGMA or UTMA, simply open a brokerage account or bank account and tell your broker or bank teller that you want the account name to reflect that the gift is being made under the Uniform Gifts (or Transfers) to Minors Act with your name as guardian. You can then administer the account, for the child's benefit. When the child reaches the age of majority (the age at which state law considers the child an adult in financial matters), the assets will belong to the child. The Uniform Gift to Minors Act in each state has a number of drawbacks, however, which is why a trust is always preferable if the cost is not excessive compared with the assets being saved.

Disadvantages of Custodial Accounts

The effect of a gift under a Uniform Gifts to Minors Act is to irrevocably transfer the property to the child and to indefeasibly vest legal title to the property in the child. The property is the child's and the custodian can only use the property as permitted by state law, for the benefit of the child. The powers that the custodian has over the account may include the power to collect, hold, manage, invest, and reinvest the custodial property; and to pay to your children, or expend for their benefit, the amount reasonably advisable for their support, maintenance, education, and benefit. When you compare this with the detailed and flexible arrangements that this book describes for trusts, it becomes clear that trusts have substantial advantages where the costs are justified.

If you give assets to a minor in a custodial account and serve as custodian, on your death all the assets in the account will be taxable in your estate. This is a major tax trap few parents are aware of.

A minor owning assets in an UGMA account can, after reaching age 14, petition the court to have an accounting of the money, stock, or other assets in the account. The minor, after reaching age 14, can petition the court to require the custodian to make payments for support, maintenance, or education. Where a trust is used, these rights are within the control of the grantor, in that the grantor can place almost any terms in trust when it is drafted. The rights you give the beneficiaries and trustees under your trust agreement are generally the rights that will control.

To designate a successor trustee under an UGMA account, a custodian must execute and date a written designation and have the document witnessed as required under your state laws. This is rarely done. Where a trust arrangement is used, one or more alternate trustees are almost always named in case the initial trustees can no longer serve.

When the assets you gift to the child will become large enough to justify the legal cost and formality of setting up a trust, and filing tax returns for the trust each year, a trust instead of a custodial account, is almost always the better choice.

TYPES OF TRUSTS FOR MINORS

Tax Considerations in Selecting a Minor's Trust

Almost any trust in this book can be used to benefit a minor child. Once the trust is formed, whether during your life or after your death, under your will, income tax planning for the trust is important. This was discussed in Chapter 19. When the trusts are formed under your will, the primary tax concern is how your estate tax will be allocated among the assets passing to the child's trust and the other assets in your estate. This is an issue to discuss with the attorney drafting your will.

When the trusts for minors are formed during your lifetime, the key tax concern is qualifying gifts to the trust for the annual $10,000 gift tax exclusion. The annual gift tax exclusion permits every taxpayer to give away up to $10,000 per year to any person without incurring a gift tax, and without using up any of their once-in-a-lifetime $600,000 annual exclusion. To qualify for this benefit, a gift must generally be a "gift of a present interest." A gift in trust will only qualify where your child, or the other beneficiary, is entitled to all the income currently, or to withdraw up to the $10,000 (or lesser amount) that was given to the trust, or the special rules of Code Section 2503(c) are met. The manner in which this goal is accomplished helps determine how the trust should be structured. Much of the discussion of this chapter is organized along the lines of the options available to meet this important goal. Each of the trusts described in the following sections will qualify, in a different way, for the annual gift tax exclusion.

Income Only Trust (Section 2503(b) Trust)

One type of trust for minor children that permits gifts to qualify for the annual gift tax exclusion is formed under the provisions of Internal Revenue Code Section 2503(b). It is often called by that section, or alternatively, an "income only" trust.

This trust must require that all of the trust's income be distributed annually to your child or other beneficiary. This will permit you to make a gift of up to $10,000 per year and qualify for the annual gift tax exclusion. The child will then be taxed on all of the income earned by the trust. Where the child is under 14, the Kiddie Tax described earlier will apply. The income can be distributed to a Uniform Gift to Minors Act trust without jeopardizing the benefits of the annual exclusion. The assets in the trust will have to be income-producing for the IRS to respect the arrangement (e.g., raw land that is not leased will not qualify). This type of trust offers additional flexibility over the 2503(c) special minor's trust, which will be described—the remainder beneficiary (the person who gets the trust property after the trust ends) does not have to be the same person who receives the trust income while the trust is in existence. Where different beneficiaries are named, great care must be taken in wording the trust agreement. If the child-beneficiary receiving certain income during the existence of the trust has an emergency, should the trustee be permitted to dip into trust principal for this child? If this is done, it will reduce the amount available to the person receiving the assets when the trust terminates. Clear rules advising what the trustee should do are important. A major problem with this approach is that it conflicts with investment strategies you may prefer (e.g., long term growth).

Right to Withdraw under Crummey Power

Perhaps the most common way to structure a minor's trust to qualify for the annual exclusion is to use a Crummey power arrangement.

If a trust can accumulate income, you will not qualify for the annual $10,000 gift tax exclusion on gifts to the trust (with the exception of a special trust for minor children that will be discussed). However, a gift to a trust will qualify as a gift of a present interest (i.e., you will qualify for the annual exclusion) up to the amount that the child can withdraw each year from the trust. This is called an "annual demand power," or a "Crummey power." This right gives the child-beneficiary the absolute right to presently enjoy the gift made by the parent. Even if not exercised by the child, so that the money remains in the trust, the existence of this right enables the parent to avoid any gift tax. There are a host of complications to this type of planning which you should review carefully with your attorney (see Chapter 7).

The Crummey power approach to a minor's trust is generally preferred, although it has perhaps the most burdensome tax rules to comply with, because most parents and grandparents want as much flexibility as possible to structure the trust to best serve the needs of the child-beneficiary, and to best protect that beneficiary. The typical child's trust—which accumulates income and makes distributions in the trustee's discretion until the principal is distributed in thirds at ages 25, 30, and 35—is a Crummey power trust.

Special Trust for Children under Age 21 (Section 2503(c) Trust)

There is yet another manner in which you can plan a trust so that gifts to the trust will qualify for the annual gift tax exclusion. If neither of the preceding trusts appeal to you in light of the child you are planning for, this third approach should be considered. The law provides for another special rule that permits you to transfer $10,000 per year to a trust, the trust can accumulate the income, and you can still qualify for the annual gift tax exclusion. To qualify, the trust must be set up to benefit a minor child. The trustee must have the ability to use the income for the benefit of the minor child without restriction. (This latter requirement is not all that different from the broad discretion usually given to a trustee under a Crummey power trust.) The trust assets must be invested in income-producing assets (stocks, bonds, and CDs, not raw land). If the child dies prior to age 21, the trust assets must be distributed to the child's estate, or in a manner that the child appoints. When the child reaches age 21, the trust must be distributed to the child. This latter requirement is why this trust is not commonly used. Most custodial accounts can hold assets to age 21. The primary reason many parents opt for trusts is to protect and manage the income until a later age. If all of the principal must be distributed at age 21, the primary benefit of using a trust is defeated.

All is not lost however. There is no requirement that the child actually take the assets at age 21, merely that the child have the right to do so. Thus, the child can be given the right to receive the assets of the trust at age 21, but voluntarily elect not to take the money. This option, however, does not compare favorably to the Crummey power arrangement. If a child who is beneficiary of a Crummey power trust exercises the right to take the money (something the parent will probably intend not be done), the most the child can take is often $10,000. Contrast this with a Code Section 2503(c) trust. At age 21, the child legally can demand the entire trust! Is this a risk worth taking?

For income tax purposes, the trust will pay income tax on income it does not distribute and the child will pay income tax on income distributed to it.

Trusts for Grandchildren

If you plan significant gifts to grandchildren, you should consider establishing trusts for their benefit. When forming grandchildren trusts, the issues and options discussed for children's trusts are identical. The same decisions must be made to qualify for the annual gift tax exclusion. When planning grandchildren's trusts, however, an additional layer of complexity must be addressed, the generation-skipping transfer (GST) tax.

Gifts that qualify for the annual $10,000 per year gift tax exclusion can also escape the clutches of the extremely expensive generation-skipping transfer tax. The requirements to qualify for the GST tax annual exclusion are somewhat more restrictive. Generally, the grandchild-beneficiary should be the only beneficiary. Further, if the grandchild-beneficiary should die before the trust ends, the assets must be included in the grandchild's estate. This can be done by actually distributing the trust assets to the grandchild's estate, or alternatively by giving the grandchild a general power of appointment to appoint the trust to anyone. Many grandparents are not comfortable with these options. They can instead elect to allocate a portion of their $1 million GST tax lifetime exclusion to the trust each year by filing a gift tax return (see Chapter 8).

Trusts for Special Children

Where a child has special needs as a result of a handicap or illness, trusts represent the most important tools to protect that child. This is because a trust arrangement can provide for care for many years into the future, even when you are no longer able to assist. These trusts, however, can raise several unique issues.

CAUTION: When planning for the special child, trusts are only one component. It is important to sign durable powers of attorney so that in the event of your disability monies can be applied for the benefit of your child. Your durable power of attorney can even include a provision authorizing expenditures on behalf of your special child, if such distributions can be made without jeopardizing the child's governmental benefits. These provisions can take the same form as the provisions to include in the trusts that will be described. Also, pay careful attention to the provisions of your will, and select guardians with the willingness and ability to assist your special child. Be certain that you select enough guardians and trustees to provide care for the life of your child, not merely through the age of majority. This long time horizon is an important difference in planning for the special child. Thus, several alternate trustees should be named as well as a corporate trust department as a final trustee to assure continuity. A guardianship designation with several alternates, including a state agency as a final selection, may be essential. Don't forget that the guardianship provisions of your will only become effective on your death. You must also address the needs of your special child in the event of your disability. Consider insurance as another means of assuring adequate financial assets to protect the special child.

A basic planning goal for many families is to preserve the family's wealth for later generations. Where a special child is involved, however, this can be more difficult because the child's medical and care needs may severely deplete the family's resources.

NOTE: One of the most difficult issues for many families is how to apply limited resources. One extreme would be to apply all of the family's resources to the special child, to the exclusion of the others. The other extreme would be to allocate no resources to the special child and let the various government programs provide for care. Where on this spectrum you decide to allocate resources will depend on several factors, including personal feelings, the extent of family resources available, the needs of all of your children and other family members, the nature and extent of government programs. These issues are best addressed with an estate or financial planner with experience in planning for special children.

EXAMPLE: If you are extremely wealthy, you may be able to plan for all of your children, including maximum care and attention for your special child. In this case, the loss of government resources that could otherwise be available to your child may not be a concern. You want the best and will pay for it. On the other hand, if your financial resources are extremely limited, you may almost be forced to disinherit your special child, not out of lack of love, but rather out of the financial necessity to rely on government programs. The disinheritance can also be intentional where another child can be fully trusted to fulfill a moral obligation to provide for the special child. The moderate estates between these extremes are where planning is most important, and the decisions the most difficult: Parents want to preserve some resources for the family unit, but also to provide for the special child.

A complex patchwork of government programs can provide benefits for a special child. Thus, the difficult goals for many families are to preserve wealth for the family unit, maximize the availability of public and other program resources for the special child, and assure that the special child's needs are met.

These are difficult goals and can often be contradictory. The laws and various entitlement programs not only are complex, but can change frequently. These trusts are also subject to all of the concerns and problems of avoiding creditors described in detail in Chapter 15.

One of the most effective and important tools for a family with a special child is the irrevocable life insurance trust discussed in Chapter 16. Where the resources are not adequate, and health conditions permit, life insurance can be an important safety net to assure a minimum level of support for the special child. The trust format permits you to provide for as many of the special contingencies necessary to assure proper care. By using an irrevocable trust arrangement, you can keep the proceeds out of your estate.

Trusts can also be set up to hold assets, in part for the benefit of the special child, and to provide for distributions to or for the benefit of the child. The trust can be set up during your lifetime, or created under your will after your death. The critical provisions of any trust will be those that determine when distributions can be made. Where a trust requires that all of the income (or any other mandatory amount) be distributed to or for benefit of the special child, these amounts will undoubtedly be considered as available to the child when any income tests are made to determine eligibility for government benefits. Where the trustee is given the discretion to apply trust income and principal for the support or maintenance of the special child, the income and assets of the trust will similarly be considered available to pay for shelter and medical care in lieu of many government benefits that might have otherwise been available.

Where the trustee has the discretion to apply income in any manner to several different beneficiaries, it will be more difficult for any state or government agency to argue that the income or assets of the trust should be considered as available. Where the trustee has total discretion, but the only beneficiary is the special child, the trust may still be effective in some instances for removing the trust income and assets from assets included in calculating qualification for government benefits, though the result may be somewhat less certain than where there are other beneficiaries as well.

When planning a trust for your special child, you should probably include a spendthrift provision.

Another technique used in most trusts for special children is to add a provision indicating that the trust's income and assets cannot be distributed to or for the benefit of the special child where the distributions or expenditures would jeopardize qualification for government benefits or distributions from charitable organizations. Your trust can clearly state that the trustee is not to make distributions that can be met from other government or charitable sources. Rather, only the gaps in those programs, and additional items for personal comfort, should be provided for.

Where the state or other government agency can reach the trust assets, a more extreme provision may be included that will terminate the trust and require the distribution of all of the assets in the trust to children other than the special child. The objective is to dissuade government agencies from suing the trust for reimbursements for medical care. The effectiveness of any of the provisions suggested previously, however, is not guaranteed.

You can state your personal preferences for the care of your child and instruct your trustees to apply trust assets to that end. There is no need to limit the trust to the formal language and provisions only. Your personal statements can also be included.

When planning any trust for a special child, each of the available government or charitable programs, and the requirements and qualifications of each, must be considered. Medicare and Social Security are two important federal programs. Social Security can provide benefits where the special child is totally disabled. Medicare provides for limited basic medical coverage. Supplemental Security Income (SSI), Medicaid, welfare, and other programs may be available as well. To qualify for these need-based programs, the income and assets of the child/recipient must be quite limited. Assuring qualification for these, and any other, need-based programs is a cornerstone of planning. The trust arrangement that you set up must not result in the child being considered to have more income or assets than permitted by the qualification requirements for these programs, or the benefits will be lost. Various states have additional programs, such as cost-of-care programs, which may also be available. These should all be reviewed with an experienced estate or financial planner.

Finally, when planning a trust for a special child, the Crummey power and other techniques described earlier for children's trusts generally are not likely to be appropriate. The child may not have the ability to exercise the withdrawal power, and therefore the IRS may not recognize the validity of that power and hence the qualification for the annual exclusion. Further, the right to withdraw $10,000, or the mandatory income distributions of the other types of trusts, may all defeat the "special needs" protective language typical of a trust for a child with special needs. Thus, special needs trusts are often not formed during your lifetime; they are funded instead under a will.

WHAT OTHER TRUSTS INCLUDE MINOR TRUSTS

Insurance Trust

Most insurance trusts used in traditional family planning are designed for the benefit of the surviving spouse (except for trusts holding second-to-die insurance) and thereafter for the children of the marriage. Thus, most insurance trusts will eventually provide that the trust assets (insurance proceeds and the investments made with them) are to be divided among the children and distributed to trusts for each child.

QPRTs, GRATs, GRUTs, CLTs

These tax-oriented trusts are designed to remove assets from your estate at discounted rates. A qualified personal residence trust (QPRT) is designed to gift your home or vacation home to designated heirs, such as your children, at some future date (see Chapter 19). Grantor retained annuity trusts (GRATs) and grantor retained unitrusts (GRUTs) are intended to remove securities or other assets from your estate at discounted rates (see Chapter 17). A charitable lead trust (CLT) is designed to make payments to a charity for a fixed number of years after which designated beneficiaries, typically children and sometimes grandchildren, receive the trust assets. If, for any of these trusts, the beneficiaries will be too young when the trust is planned to end, consider pouring the beneficiary's interest into a minor's trust.

Revocable Living Trust Can Include Minor Trusts

A revocable living trust can be used as a will substitute. When this is done, trusts for minor children should be included in the disposition provisions of your living trust.

CONSIDERATIONS WHEN DRAFTING TRUSTS FOR MINORS

Choosing Trustees

Carefully consider the choice of trustees and successor trustees (see Chapter 6). Should you name the same persons who are named the guardians of your children under your will? This provides complete control and avoids any conflict between the guardian's need for money for your children, and a trustee's opinion of what is appropriate to spend. Many parents prefer to separate these functions so that some checks and balances are built into the arrangement. Also, serving as a guardian requires personal skills. Serving as a trustee requires financial skills. Different people may have different attributes and should be picked accordingly. A common compromise approach is to have the guardian serve as co-trustee with another person who is not the guardian. This gives the guardian some input, but prevents the guardian from having complete control.

Investment Planning

Every trust should specify the investment considerations, goals, and limitations applicable to the trustees. For minors' trusts, the tax consequences of trust taxation, taxation of distributions to the minors, and the expected needs of the minor should all be considerations. For example, if the child will need help paying for private elementary school education, investment criteria will be different than in a trust where the monies won't be needed until graduate school. Trusts that require the distribution of income (Code Section 2503(b) income-only trust) will require a different approach from the trusts that do not (e.g., Crummey power trust).

Spendthrift Provision

A trust can contain a spendthrift provision to limit the rights creditors of your children may have to the assets of the trust. This is an extremely important protection for the child-beneficiary. However, including a spendthrift provision will make it very difficult to get a court to approve an early termination of the trust if it seems advisable.

Distribution Provisions

The trustee can be authorized to distribute income of the trust among your children and other beneficiaries based on their need or simply in the trustee's discretion (a sprinkling power). This approach can be advantageous since it is often impossible to determine what the needs of each child will be in the future and the sprinkle power provides the flexibility to make decisions when the circumstances are known. A right for the trustee to spend the principal (not just income) can be provided for in the event of emergencies.

You must decide at what ages your children should be given the assets from the trust. A common approach is one-third at ages 25, 30, and 35. The idea is to accustom the child to receiving money over time so that if the child is irresponsible at the first distribution, there will be two more opportunities to learn responsibility. For older children, older ages are often used.

TIP: Coordinate the ages for distributions of all your trusts. These may include a qualified personal residence trust (QPRT) that ends in 20 years (Chapter 19), an insurance trust (Chapter 16), trusts for your children under your will. You may also form trusts for each of your children and grandchildren while you are alive to hold annual gifts. The ages at which your children, grandchildren, or others will receive distributions under each of these trusts should be planned. You probably do not want your beneficiaries to receive all the assets from all of the trusts in the same year, or even in just a few years. Generally, it is preferable to spread distributions out over many years. Alternatively, you may prefer that several trusts provide for distributions at the same age so that the different trusts can be easily consolidated to minimize administrative burdens and costs.

You must determine whether you should have one trust for all of your children, or separate trusts for each child. If the beneficiary is a grandchild, you will need separate trusts for purposes of qualifying annual $10,000 gifts for the GST gift tax exclusion (see Chapter 8). If your assets are not that substantial, you may prefer a single trust to minimize cost. Similarly, if there are substantial differences in needs or age of the children, you may prefer a single "pot" trust to provide for all of the beneficiaries. For example, if three children are past college and the fourth child is in grade school, a pot trust may be appropriate. This can permit the trustees to use the money primarily for the youngest child who has had the least help, and has the greatest needs. In an emergency, however, the money will be available for any child in need. When the youngest child completes his or her education, perhaps the trust can then be divided equally between all four children. Generally, however, where resources are adequate, its usually best to have a separate trust for each child. This avoids problems of jealousy, funding different needs of different children, and so forth.

CONCLUSION

Planning for the welfare of your children, grandchildren, particularly minor children, or other heirs (nieces, nephews, or others) is often accomplished with trusts. A number of approaches can be used. They should all be considered carefully in light of the tax, financial, and emotional background of your family. In all cases, the long-expected time duration of the trust requires careful planning, selection of many alternate trustees, and building in flexibility in the trust terms to deal with future contingencies.

14 TRUSTS FOR CHARITIES

Charitable trusts are not only for the charitably inclined. Charitable trust planning can provide such substantial tax and other benefits that everyone considering estate, trust, and financial planning should consider the possible benefits of charitable trusts. Apart from tax benefits, leaving your heirs the legacy of being charitably inclined may be the most valuable bequest you can make. This chapter will explain two common types of charitable trusts: the charitable remainder trust and the charitable lead trust.

CHARITABLE GIFTS TO TRUSTS PROVIDE TAX BENEFITS

Large-value charitable gifts that are properly structured can significantly reduce potential estate and gift taxes. This can help address potential estate liquidity problems, thus increasing flexibility to retain relatively nonliquid business or real estate interests. The estate tax charitable deduction rules, except for the noticeable absence of percentage limitations, are generally similar to the rules applicable for income tax purposes with which most taxpayers have some familiarity.

A deduction for charitable contributions is permitted for gift tax purposes on qualifying gifts to charities. A contribution after your death, such as under the provisions of a living trust you established during your life, to a qualified charitable organization can provide an estate tax deduction. The amount of the charitable contribution deduction available is limited to the amount or value that actually becomes available to the charitable organization. Where the charitable bequest is limited as a result of an allocation of administrative expenses, or estate tax (as a possible result of an improperly drafted tax allocation clause in your will), the charitable contribution deduction will be reduced accordingly. Where such a problem occurs, each dollar of tax deduction could reduce the amount of the charitable bequest and thus increase the tax due. The result requires the solution to a simultaneous equation to calculate the net tax cost.

Where the estate includes closely held active business interests on which the estate tax is deferred for the approximately 14-year period under Code Section 6166, the IRS has held that the estimated amount of the interest expense to be paid on the deferred tax may have to be applied to reduce the amount of a charitable bequest made from the residuary.

GIFTS OF CHARITABLE REMAINDER INTERESTS

Tax Benefits of a CRT

If you use a Charitable Remainder Trust (CRT), you donate property (e.g., real property, stock, business interests) to a charity and receive a charitable contribution tax deduction in the year of the donation. The charity will only receive the full benefit of the property at some future time. For example, you can reserve an income interest in the charitable remainder trust for your life and the life of your spouse as the income beneficiaries. If this is done, the income generated from the donated property will be paid to you for your life and thereafter to your spouse for his or her life. After the death of the last of you and your spouse, the charity will obtain full use and benefit of the donated property.

The savings in income taxes, federal gift or estate tax, state inheritance tax, and probate and administrative costs, can enable you to transfer substantial benefit to a deserving charity at a very favorable cost.

Other Benefits of CRTs

A CRT can be a tremendous estate and financial planning vehicle.

EXAMPLE: Ira Investor purchased XYZ, Inc., stock in 1989 for $1.00 per share. The value per share is now $100.00 per share. The stock pays almost no dividends. Ira is retiring and needs more income to cover living expenses. He also wishes to diversify his XYZ, Inc., holdings because they have become such a substantial portion of his estate. However, to sell XYZ, Inc., stock would trigger a substantial capital gains tax. Ira could instead donate the stock to a CRT and receive back a monthly payment for life (and even for the life of his wife as well). The charity could sell the stock and invest in a diversified portfolio geared to generate income. The charity should not have to recognize any capital gains tax on sale. As a result, Ira can effectively have the entire investment, undiminished by capital gains tax, working to generate his monthly income. The financial benefits are potentially tremendous.

If you have some charitable intent, but don't wish to part entirely with the benefits of your property (e.g., the income it generates) presently, a CRT may be appropriate.

Types of Charitable Remainder Trusts

Where the gift of a remainder interest is made in trust, it must be in the form of a annuity trust or unitrust payment. These are the two types of CRTs available. With the exception of gifts of a remainder interest in a personal residence or farm property, you cannot qualify for an income, gift and estate tax deduction for a donation to a charitable remainder trust, unless the donation is in a trust that qualifies as either an annuity trust or a unitrust.

Charitable Remainder Annuity Trust (CRAT)

A charitable remainder annuity trust (CRAT) will provide a fixed annuity to yourself, or the people you designate in the trust agreement, as the income beneficiaries. The minimum rate of return to them cannot be less than 5 percent and it must be a fixed or determinable amount. The beneficiaries' income is calculated based on the fair market value of the property transferred to the trust. Once the trust is established, no further contributions can be made to it. Where the trust income is insufficient to meet the required annual return, principal must be invaded.

Charitable Remainder Unitrust

A charitable remainder unitrust (CRUT) provides a variable annuity benefit to its income beneficiaries. The minimum rate of return to the income beneficiaries must be 5 percent. This rate is calculated on the fair market value of the property determined on an annual basis. This requires an annual appraisal, which for any property that is difficult to value (e.g., closely held business interests and real estate), could be prohibitively expensive. For this reason, an annuity trust approach is likely to prove more appropriate when such assets are to be contributed. The trust may provide that if the annual income earned by the trust property is insufficient to meet the required distribution to the income beneficiaries, principal may be invaded. If principal is not required to be invaded, then the trust must provide that the deficit will be made up in later years. Once a unitrust is established, additional contributions may be made in later years under certain conditions.

The valuation of the remainder interest of the unitrust is determined under methods provided for in the Treasury regulations. The valuation considers the value of the property transferred to the trust, the age of the income beneficiary, and the payout rate from the trust (e.g., 5 percent or some greater figure).

Phases in the Use of a CRUT

When a charitable remainder trust is used for the donation to a charity, the donor transfers property (real property in this instance, although publicly traded securities, stock in a closely held business, and other assets may also be used) to the charity. The donor then receives a charitable contribution income tax deduction in the year of the donation.

The donor reserves for the income beneficiaries an income interest in the CRUT for the beneficiaries' lives. This means that a portion of the income generated from the donated property will be paid to the donor for life and concurrently to the donor's spouse (when the spouse is the second beneficiary) for life.

On the death of the donors, there will be no estate tax from the value of the life income interest retained by the donor since it is exactly offset by the estate tax charitable contribution deduction. If the only other beneficiary is the decedent's spouse, there will be no tax on the income interest passing to him or her as a result of the unlimited estate tax marital deduction.

The charitable remainder beneficiary only receives the full benefit of the property (i.e., the principal of the charitable remainder trust) on the death of the last of the designated income beneficiaries.

Tax Consequences of a CRT

Income Tax Deduction on Forming a CRT

The donor of property to a charitable remainder trust is entitled to a deduction for income and estate or gift tax purposes based on the present value of the charitable remainder interest. For income tax purposes, the gift of a remainder interest to a charity is treated as a gift "to" the remainderman. If the remainderman charity is a public charity, the maximum deduction is allowed up to either 30 percent or 50 percent of the donor's adjusted gross income. The amount of the charitable contribution deduction is equal to the fair market value of the property at the time of the donation to the CRT, less the present value of the income interest retained by you (or you and your spouse if she is named a beneficiary). This contribution deduction is calculated using IRS tables and some rather complex formulas. These methods consider the value of the property transferred, the age of the income beneficiaries, and the payout rate. The actual value of the tax deduction will depend on numerous factors, including the marginal tax bracket of the donor, the income interest reserved to the donor (and others), the income level of the donor relative to the tax deduction (which will affect the applicability of the charitable contribution percentage limitations), and other factors.

Gift and Estate Tax Consequences of a CRT

In addition to the current income tax deduction, you may receive a valuable estate tax benefit as well. If you are one of the income beneficiaries of the charitable trust, the value of the trust will be included in your gross estate when you die. Since the interest will pass to the charity, however, there will be an offsetting estate tax charitable contribution deduction. Thus, the value of the property donated will be effectively removed from your estate.

Assuming you, as the donor, predecease your spouse, the value of the CRT will be included in your gross estate when you die because you will have owned at your death an income interest for your life from the CRT. However, since the interest will pass to your spouse, there will be an offsetting estate tax marital deduction. Thus, the value of the property donated will be effectively removed from your estate.

Similarly, on the death of the surviving spouse, the value of the charitable remainder trust will be included in his or her gross estate. However, since the interest will pass to a qualified charity, there will be an offsetting estate tax charitable contribution deduction. Hence, the value of the donated property will effectively be removed from the spouse's estate as well.

HOW BENEFICIARIES ARE TAXED ON CRT INCOME

The amounts paid to a trust beneficiary under a charitable remainder trust retain the character they had in the trust. Regular trusts characterize payments based on the trust's income and other activities during the particular year. A charitable remainder trust characterizes payments based on the trust's income and other activities with reference to the entire history of the trust. Thus, you as the noncharitable income beneficiary of a charitable remainder unitrust or annuity trust, are taxed as receiving ordinary income to the extent of the trust's current and prior undistributed income.

After all ordinary income is exhausted, amounts will be taxed as follows:

- As short-term capital gain to the extent of current and past undistributed short-term capital gains.
- As long-term capital gain to the extent of current and past undistributed long-term capital gains.
- As other income, such as tax-exempt income, to the extent of the trust's current and past undistributed income of such character.
- As tax-free distributions of principal.

The trust will generally be exempt from tax. However, where the trust generates unrelated business taxable income (UBTI), it can be subject to tax. This can be an issue where trust assets are debt financed, stock in an active business is contributed, and so forth. These rules are extremely complex and require professional assistance.

Variations and Special Techniques Using CRTs

Combining Insurance with the Charitable Remainder Trust

The reason insurance planning is so frequently combined with charitable remainder trust planning is to replace the value of the property donated to the charity with insurance passing to your heirs. The concept is quite simple. You fund a CRT with appreciated assets and receive an income stream back. You then use some portion of the increased income stream to establish and fund an irrevocable life insurance trust for the benefit of your heirs (e.g., children). Where all works as hoped for, the following goals can be achieved:

- You can meet your desired charitable goals of providing for a favored cause or organization.
- The income tax savings from the charitable contribution deduction provide cash flow to make gifts to an irrevocable life insurance trust, or to your heirs directly.
- Your investment is diversified and you receive an increased and more certain income stream.
- The trustee of the irrevocable life insurance trust purchases life insurance on your life (or if you are married, second-to-die life insurance on the lives of both you and your spouse) in an amount that is sufficient to replace the value of the assets transferred to the charitable remainder trust. In many cases a larger amount of insurance is used under the presumption that the asset given to the charitable remainder trust would have grown prior to your death.
- On your death, the insurance proceeds are not taxable in your estate. Your heirs receive the insurance proceeds in an amount approximating the value of the assets that you had transferred to the charitable remainder trust.

EXAMPLE: Donor owns real estate worth $1 million with an adjusted cost basis of $200,000. Transferring the property to a charitable remainder trust could generate a $400,000 contribution deduction. This could provide an income tax savings of approximately $140,000. Further, the donor will avoid approximately a $220,000 capital gain on the sale of the property. The trustee may be able to pay the donor an annual income of $60,000. The donor can make an annual gift, with his spouse, to their son and daughter-in-law totaling $40,000 under the annual gift tax exclusion. This amount can be used to purchase life insurance on the donor's life of $1 million, sufficient to replace the $1 million worth of real estate transferred to the charitable remainder trust. The son will receive the same $1 million on the parent's death that he would have received had the planning not been undertaken. However, had no planning been undertaken, the $1 million real estate that the son would have received might have been reduced by a 55 percent marginal estate tax. Thus, the son may actually receive more then double by implementing this charitable/insurance plan.

Life insurance can be used in a somewhat different manner in planning for charitable remainder trusts as well. These trusts assume that an income stream will be paid to a life beneficiary for some period of time. Should the sole life beneficiary die prematurely, the family unit will lose the benefit of the expected income stream. In the appropriate circumstances, the charitable remainder technique can be combined with an insurance policy on the life of the income beneficiary. If the life beneficiary dies prematurely, the insurance proceeds can supplement the family's income stream. This could be done, for example, with a life insurance trust for the benefit of the children or spouse of the named life beneficiary. The life insurance trust should be structured to assure that the proceeds are not included in the estate of the life beneficiary. In some cases, an insurance arrangement providing for decreasing coverage (to approximate the decline in the loss of expected income as the life beneficiary lives through the intended term of the trust), can be used. Note, however, that insurance to address income lost does not address the replacement of the assets given to the CRT.

CRT as a Retirement Plan: The Income Only Unitrust Option of CRT

A modified form of charitable remainder unitrust (CRUT) can be used where the income beneficiary receives what is called an "income only arrangement." In this CRUT, the income beneficiary would only receive the actual trust income if it is less than the fixed percentage payment required (e.g., 5% of principal of the trust). This trust can also include a "make-up provision." In early years, actual income is less than the 5 percent required CRUT payment. In later years, when the net income of the trust exceeds the specified percentage of trust assets required to be paid (e.g., 5%), this excess can then be paid to the income beneficiary to make up for the shortfall in prior years. The shortfall is based on the difference between the amounts actually paid in prior years, and the amounts that were required to have been paid under the fixed percentage.

EXAMPLE: Donor has a substantial income, is getting on in years, and wishes to provide for his favorite charity. He expects to retire in five years; his income will then drop, and be taxed in a lower tax bracket. Donor establishes an income-only charitable remainder unitrust arrangement with a make-up provision and funds it with a $1 million initial contribution invested in low-dividend-paying growth stocks. The unitrust percentage is set at the lowest permissible 5 percent amount. The dividends on the stock portfolio produce a mere .75 percent return, or $7500, which is paid to the donor. After year five, the donor retires. The stock portfolio, which has appreciated to $1.5 million, is liquidated and invested in high-yielding bond instruments. These bonds produce a return of 8 percent, or $120,000. The donor would be entitled to 5 percent of the $1.5 million asset value based on the unitrust amount provided, or $75,000. However, as a result of the make-up provision, the donor can be paid additional amounts in each of the remaining years of the trust to make up for the shortfall in prior, preretirement years. If the shortfall has totaled $212,500 [(5 years × $50,000) – (5 years × $7,500)], the donor will be entitled to all of the income from the income-only unitrust for a number of years to come. The IRS has not viewed these arrangements favorably.

CAUTION: A fallacy of the income-only unitrust approach in the preceding example is the assumption of lower tax rates on retirement. The client who would engage in such a sophisticated transaction is likely to have a substantial income at present, and in the future, even if the future postretirement income is expected to be lower. For such a client, it is likely that the maximum tax rates may apply both pre- and postretirement. Further, many tax practitioners anticipate increases in future tax rates, not decreases.

Generation-Skipping Transfers and Charitable Remainder Trust Planning

While the generation-skipping transfer tax (GST tax) will not apply to charitable gifts, GST tax considerations are important where your grandchild (or another skip person) is made the life or income beneficiary of the charitable remainder trust (or the remainder beneficiary of a charitable lead trust, as will be described). Where such a situation occurs, you, the donor, must carefully plan the allocation of any of your remaining GST lifetime $1 million exemption to the trust.

EXAMPLE: Assume that the donor transferred $500,000 into a charitable remainder unitrust. The value of the remainder interest is $275,000. Assume further that the donor has $450,000 of his GST tax exemption still available. The donor could allocate $225,000 [$500,000 total value − $275,000 charitable remainder value] of his remaining GST tax exemption to the trust. The trust will thus have an inclusion ratio of zero, and no GST tax will be due.

The complex GST tax is discussed in Chapter 8.

Charitable Gifts and the Closely Held Corporation

Charitable remainder trusts can have special use when a key asset is stock in a closely held business. A charitable bailout of a closely held business's stock can address important planning problems for a closely held business owner. Stock in a closely held corporation can be difficult, or impossible, to sell because any outsider will generally be reluctant to own a minority interest in a close corporation. Another problem could relate to the type of corporation involved. Assume that the corporation is a C corporation (i.e., not an S corporation) and has available cash that you would like to donate to charity. However, it may not be practical to make a dividend distribution to provide the cash for such donation since a dividend distribution will result in double taxation (the corporation first pays tax on the earnings and then you pay tax again on the receipt of the net earnings in the form of a dividend). Another common problem scenario for a closely held business is when a parent owns stock in a close corporation and wishes to transfer control to a child without triggering income tax on a redemption. One possible solution for this latter scenario is called a "stock bailout." You can make a gift of any portion of the stock in your corporation to a charity. At some later date, the charity may in its sole discretion, sell some of the stock that it then owns back to the corporation. This provides you with a charitable contribution deduction for income tax purposes for the stock donated. The charity can eventually receive a cash amount for the contribution. When the corporation redeems the stock, the interest of the children owning stock will increase because the charitable bailout/redemption of your stock will increase their relative ownership interest.

The charitable bailout arrangement has several drawbacks and problems. The charity cannot be obligated to sell any portion of the stock back to the corporation. Where a prearranged plan for the resale of the stock exists, it can be difficult to draw the line as to whether or not the charity was so obligated. Where the charity is, in fact, under no legal obligation to resell the stock it receives, it could possibly sell the stock to another, vote the shares in a manner that is not consistent with the donor's desires, and so forth. The alternative minimum tax could reduce the value of the gift. This technique can be quite beneficial in the appropriate circumstances. It is quite complex and should be carefully planned for with specialized estate planning professionals.

Combining Charitable and Marital Trusts

Another twist on the use of a charitable remainder trust is to combine a CRT with the marital trusts discussed in Chapter 11. Special rules apply if you wish to transfer property to both your spouse and a charity. These rules can permit you to take advantage of both charitable contribution deductions and the marital deduction, and thus they can provide valuable planning benefits in the appropriate circumstances. For example, assume that you transfer property to a charitable remainder trust. You and your spouse are the sole income beneficiaries. The only other beneficiary is a charitable remainder beneficiary. On your death, your estate will qualify for both a charitable contribution deduction and an estate tax marital deduction. This assures no tax as a result of any interest you had in the CRT on death.

An alternative approach is simply to establish a qualified terminable interest property (Q-TIP) trust for your spouse, with the remainder interest on your spouse's death to go to a specified charity. Q-TIP trusts are explained in detail in Chapter 11. A Q-TIP trust generally permits your spouse to receive all of the income from the trust, and on her death, the trust assets go to the persons, or in this case the charity, that you designate. Although this approach is simpler, there can be no income tax deduction for a Q-TIP with a charitable remainder, as would be available for a charitable remainder trust naming you and your spouse as income beneficiaries.

Planning the payment of income under the charitable remainder trust approach has more flexibility than using a Q-TIP with a charitable remainder beneficiary. This is because the charitable remainder trust need not require the payment of income at least annually, as does the Q-TIP trust.

What Provisions to Include in Your CRT Agreement

Choice of Trustee

While you, as the grantor, may be named as trustee, you should not serve as sole trustee if the assets of the trust do not have a reasonably determinable market value (e.g., interests in a closely held business). At minimum, name a co-trustee to address all valuation issues.

Restrictions on Investments

A trust can be disqualified as being a charitable remainder trust where the trust document restricts the trustee from investing in a manner that could result in the realization of reasonable income or gain.

EXAMPLE: A trustee was required to retain certain antiques for the life of the noncharitable income beneficiary. Since the antiques obviously could not produce any income, it was impossible for the trust to pay the required annual amounts to the beneficiaries and was therefore disqualified.

While investments in real estate and growth securities may not necessarily jeopardize the trust status, caution should be exercised. Thus, within reason, and with proper drafting, the trustee of a charitable remainder trust can exercise control over the investment selection process to control the income where the private noncharitable income beneficiary is in a high tax bracket, or not in need of funds.

Properly structured, a charitable remainder trust can be funded with tax-exempt securities. The donor would receive a potentially substantial tax deduction, tax-free annual payments, and thus realize a potential advantageous economic return on the transaction.

Designating the Charitable Remainder Beneficiary

The remainder of the trust must be paid over to a charity that is described in the tax law provisions governing charitable contribution deductions. Multiple charities can be used so long as it is clear what the relative shares of each charity will be on termination of the trust. Consideration should be given to naming one or more fallback charities in the trust agreement in the event that the named charity is no longer in existence, or is no longer qualified for an unlimited estate tax charitable contribution deduction. A private foundation can be named as the charitable remainder beneficiary, but the possible effects of the 30 percent limitation rule described earlier should be considered. Where a private foundation is involved, a host of restrictions may apply.

CHARITABLE LEAD TRUSTS

There are two major types of charitable trust: Charitable remainder trusts discussed in the preceding section and charitable lead trusts discussed in this section.

Overview of Charitable Lead Trusts

A charitable lead trust (CLT) is also called a front trust, because the charitable beneficiary receives its income in "front" of the ultimate beneficiaries ("remaindermen" or "remainder beneficiaries") receiving their share. Typically, the remaindermen are your children, although other beneficiaries can be named. While there can be many reasons for setting up a CLT, the primary one is to make transfers to the remaindermen at a substantially reduced gift or estate tax cost. The reduction in tax cost is achieved because the remaindermen must wait to receive the property until the expiration of the charitable beneficiary's interest.

EXAMPLE: You give $100,000 to a charitable trust. A designated charity will receive annual payments (usually in the form of an annuity or unitrust amount) for each year of the trust. Following the end of the trust, which will occur after the number of years you determined when setting it up (usually 10 to 20 years, sometimes longer), your children will receive the trust assets (this may be $100,000 or something more or less depending on the investment results during the period the charity received payments). The benefit of this technique is that the value of the gift you are making to your children, for purposes of calculating the gift tax due on the transfer, is reduced by the value of the income interest paid for the specified term of years to the charity. Thus, if the term of the charitable interest is long enough, the value of the gift to your children can be reduced to nearly zero for purposes of the gift tax.

The CLT is basically the opposite of a charitable remainder trust (CRT) arrangement. In a CRT, you, your spouse, and possibly other persons, can receive an annuity for life; and following your death, one or more charities receive the remaining trust assets. A CRT is the opposite in that the noncharitable beneficiary precedes the charitable beneficiary. There are several important differences in the technical requirements for these two types of trusts.

Comparison of CLTs and CRTs

Type of Trust	Type of Payment to Initial Beneficiary	Remainder Beneficiary
Charitable Lead Unitrust (CLUT)	Charity receives unitrust payment based on percentage of value of assets in trust each year.	Noncharitable beneficiaries, usually your adult children.
Charitable Lead Annuity Trust (CLAT)	Charity receives an annuity payment based on a fixed percentage of the value of the assets when the trust was formed.	Noncharitable beneficiaries, usually your adult children.
Charitable Remainder Unitrust (CRUT)	You or other noncharitable beneficiaries receive unitrust payments based on percentage of value of assets in trust each year. A minimum 5% payout is required.	One or more charitable beneficiaries.
Charitable Remainder Annuity Trust (CRAT)	You or other noncharitable beneficiaries receive an annuity payment based on a fixed percentage of the value of the assets when the trust was formed. A minimum 5% payout is required.	One or more charitable beneficiaries.

Variations of CLTs

Inter Vivos or Testamentary

You can form a CLT while you are alive (inter vivos). This was illustrated in the previous example. A key purpose for an inter vivos CLT is to reduce the gift tax on the gift to children or other remainder beneficiaries. Before forming a CLT during your lifetime, you should be certain that neither you, nor your family or dependents, will have need for income during the term of the trust. A CLT can also be a testamentary trust formed under your will.

Grantor or Nongrantor Trust

A CLT is usually structured as a nongrantor trust. This means that the transfer of assets to the CLT is a completed transfer at the inception of the trust for purposes of calculating any income tax. Since the trust is not a grantor trust, you will not be taxable on the income earned by the trust during its term. Similarly, you will not receive an income tax deduction for any charitable payments made by the CLT during its term.

Where the CLT is structured instead as a grantor trust, you will be taxable on the income earned by the trust (unless the income is primarily tax-exempt bond income). This income should largely be offset by deductions for the charitable contributions made by the CLT.

When a CLT May Make Sense for You

The CLT can be a valuable, and appropriate, estate planning tool where you have:

- Charitable intent.
- Desire to increase the eventual (but not current) net worth of family members or other designated heirs.
- Reduction of gift and estate taxes.
- No immediate need for additional income.

Benefits of a CLT

A CLT can provide numerous benefits.

Remove Substantial Assets from Your Estate

Appreciation on the property transferred to the CLT will ultimately pass to your designated remainder beneficiaries if the property is able to produce the required return to the charity during the term of the CLT so that the principal does not have to be invaded. This appreciation in the property transferred to the CLT, following the date of the transfer, will pass free of any further gift or estate taxes.

TIP: A CLT will have the most tax advantage where an asset is expected to have unusually large appreciation compared with the interest rates assumed in the applicable Treasury tables used in making the calculations. Ideally, you should use property most likely to appreciate for a gift to a CLT.

EXAMPLE: You fund a CLT for a 20-year term with $100,000. The CLT instrument requires the payout of a 6 percent annuity amount (CLAT) to the charitable beneficiary in each year. The funds are invested in high-yield corporate bonds that return 7.4 percent per year. There is no default during the term of the trust, and the bonds mature at the termination of the trust. The trust corpus that will pass to the remainder beneficiaries will be more than the $100,000 invested since it has grown by 1.4 percent (7.4% – 6%) per annum, compounded (assuming the cash was invested elsewhere), less any income tax paid.

EXAMPLE: There is certainly no assurance that the beneficiary will receive an appreciated trust corpus. If in the preceding example, the funds were invested in a diversified mutual fund that had in the past returned a current yield of 7.4 percent, but over the 20-year term of the trust returned only 5.8 percent, the value of the trust corpus passing to the remainder beneficiary would actually decline. This is because the $100,000 principal would have to be invaded to make up for the 0.2 percent shortfall (6% – 5.8%). Depreciation in the value of the underlying securities could also cause the remaindermen to receive less than anticipated.

Thus, net income in excess of that required to make the requisite charitable contributions is also removed from your estate (e.g., the 1.4 percent excess in the prior example). When the long terms of most CLTs are considered, even modest annual growth in the principal above that needed to pay the charity, can compound to huge value being removed from your estate with no transfer tax cost.

Meet Charitable Goals

You can meet long-term charitable giving objectives. Establishing a CLT will assure annual distributions of a specified amount (where an annuity arrangement is used) to designated charities for a specified number of years.

CLTs Can Be Coordinated with Your Overall Estate Plans

The duration for which a CLT lasts can be coordinated with other estate and financial planning to assure your children or other heirs the availability of assets for a long-term time horizon.

EXAMPLE: Taxpayer establishes a trust under his will to pay income annually to his child. Principal is to be paid out of the trust fund in approximately one-third equal amounts when the child attains ages 30, 35, and 40. The child is presently age 22. If Taxpayer establishes a CLT for a duration of 23 years [(40 − 22) + 5] the child will receive the assets of the CLT at age 45. This is timed to continue the five-year payment sequence with the hopes of distributing assets in stages to both protect the remaining assets as well as to minimize the potentially adverse consequences of the child receiving too much wealth at one time.

EXAMPLE: Taxpayer has a child, age 22, who is presently single and in medical school. Taxpayer is concerned about the high rate of divorce and the risks of potential malpractice claims, and wishes to secure some portion of child's inheritance for future use. Taxpayer establishes a 25-year CLT with the hope that, in 25 years, the child's marital status will be stable and her career more secure.

Gift Tax Can Be Removed from Your Estate

Gift tax paid on the formation of the CLT can often be excluded from your estate.

Avoid Charitable Contribution Limits

If your charitable contributions are so large that you cannot qualify to deduct them currently as a result of the limitations on the portion of your income that can be given to charity, the use of a CLT may help avoid these restrictions. Charitable contribution deductions are limited to specified percentages of the donor's income. Gifts (excluding capital gain property) to charitable organizations characterized as 50 percent limit organizations (generally public charities) can't exceed 50 percent of adjusted gross income. This includes public charities; certain private operating foundations; private nonoperating foundations that make qualifying distributions of 100 percent of the contribution within 2 ½ months following the close of the tax year in which they receive the contribution; and certain private foundations whose contributions are pooled in a common fund and the earnings of which are then paid to public charities. Certain organizations that have over a four-year period received a substantial amount of their donations from public sources may also qualify.

The following contributions are subject to the 30 percent limit: (1) contributions to private charities and other qualified organizations that do not qualify as 50 percent limit organizations; (2) contributions for the use of a charity (a contribution of an income interest in property, whether or not in a trust format, is characterized as a contribution "for the use of" the charity); and (3) contributions of capital gain property (where the taxpayer claims a deduction for the fair market value of the property) to 50 percent limit organizations.

Where the contribution is to a 20 percent limit charitable organization, this lower limit will apply. Contributions of property capital gain property (most real estate except that owned by a dealer) to organizations that do not qualify as 50 percent limit organizations are limited to 20 percent of the donor's adjusted gross income. Where these limitations apply, you can effectively circumvent them with a CLT. The contributions made to charity by the CLT will apply to offset the CLT's income without regard to your personal limitations on deducting contributions.

Drawbacks to Using a CLT

Prior to committing to a CLT as part of your overall estate and financial planning strategy, you should consider several important negative factors.

Cost and Complexity

A CLT is a creature of statute. You can realize the many tax and other benefits only if the CLT meets all applicable tax law requirements, operations and activities conform with the trust instrument and applicable law, and the governing trust instrument complies with IRS and other requirements. These requirements can be burdensome, costly, and difficult for many taxpayers.

Private Foundation Restrictions Can Affect CLTs

CLTs can be subject to the rules concerning self-dealing, excess business holdings, jeopardy investments, and so forth, of private foundations.

CLT Taxable on Certain Property Sales

A special tax is imposed on a CLT that sells or exchanges property within two years after the property was transferred to the CLT. When this rule applies, the CLT is taxed at your (i.e., the grantor's) income tax rate on certain gains from the property that was sold within two years of its transfer to the CLT and before your death. The objective of this provision is to prevent you from gaining a tax advantage by transferring property intended for sale to a trust and then having the trust make the sale. The amount of gain that the CLT has to recognize is the lesser of the actual gain the CLT recognized on its sale of the property and the excess of the fair market value of the property over the CLT's tax basis immediately after the transfer of the property. This special rule treats the transaction as if you sold the property and then transferred the proceeds, net of the applicable tax cost, to the CLT. When the trust is formed on death, or is a charitable remainder trust, this special tax does not apply. Special rules apply in several circumstances, such as when there is an installment sale or there are net operating losses.

CLT Taxation Generally

Although many taxpayers assume that the CLT is a tax-exempt trust since it benefits one or more charities, this is not correct. The CLT is a taxable entity and can, depending on the outcome of property and other transactions, be liable for an income tax. A CLT only avoids taxation where the amounts paid to charity, and hence deductible by the CLT, are sufficient to offset any income tax otherwise due by the CLT.

Gifts to CLTs Do Not Qualify for the Annual Exclusion

You can give away up to $10,000, to any person, in any tax year, without incurring a gift tax. Gifts to CLTs do not qualify for the gift tax annual exclusion. Thus, except to the extent that the gift tax charitable contribution deduction can offset the value of the property transferred, a current gift tax (or use of your $600,000 unified credit) will be due.

CLTs Create Complications for GST Planning

A basic principle of using trusts to plan for the generation-skipping transfer (GST) is to plan a trust so that it has an inclusion ratio of zero. This means that none of the trust assets will be subject to the GST (see Chapter 8). This rule gets quite tricky to apply when planning for CLTs. Should the calculation be made when the trust is formed, or when the noncharitable beneficiaries receive their interests? This is critical because the gift tax value of the trust, which is reduced by the charity's interest, is always quite small when formed. When the noncharitable beneficiaries receive the trust assets, there is no reduction since no charity will have an interest in the assets.

The tax laws contain a special rule applicable to the determination of a GST tax inclusion ratio for a CLAT. The concept of an inclusion ratio was explained in Chapter 8. The determination of the GST inclusion ratio cannot be made until the charitable interest ends. Thus, if a 20-year CLAT is used, the determination will be made at the end of year 20. When this calculation is made, the fraction used is the "adjusted GST amount" divided by the value of the trust at such time. The "adjusted GST amount" is the GST exemption (up to the maximum $1 million) allocated to the trust, increased by the applicable Code Section 7520 rate for the period of the charitable term, compounded annually. If the principal initially contributed to the trust equals the GST allocation, then the fraction is one (i.e., one minus the applicable fraction would have been zero, so that the inclusion ratio would be zero). This would mean that if the value of the investments (corpus) of the CLAT grew at the same Code Section 7520 rate as the tax laws increase the GST exemption, the inclusion ratio would remain zero. If the assets grew at a faster rate (which is the hope), then the inclusion ratio would not be zero and a GST tax could be due at the end of the term.

Although many people have criticized this view, it is not certain that the IRS will change its position. If based on the size of the estate, a CLAT is used, it could still become a significant issue depending on the growth of the CLAT assets. If no other bequests to grandchildren occur, you could allocate your entire GST exemption amount to the CLAT even though less than $1 million is used to fund the CLAT. This overallocation could help avoid any GST on the termination of the CLAT's charitable interest.

Another option is to use a charitable lead unitrust (CLUT) since the allocation of the GST amount can occur on funding of the trust. When a CLUT is used, the applicable fraction is the amount of GST exemption allocated at that time divided by the fair market value of CLUT assets reduced by the estate tax charitable contribution deduction (if a long term is used as intended and the charitable beneficiaries have been limited to qualified charities, this deduction should be significant).

Grantor or Nongrantor Trust Status of CLT

Another planning twist for CLTs is determining how your CLT will be taxed for income (as distinguished from estate, gift, and GST tax purposes). The issue is whether your CLT should be characterized as a "grantor" trust. Where the CLT is structured as a grantor trust (you're taxable on trust income), which is not the usual situation, you can obtain current income tax deductions for the annual payments to the charity.

NOTE: Because most CLTs are structured as nongrantor trusts (i.e., you are not taxable on the income of the trust), there will not be a current income tax deduction based on the payments to be made to the charity (i.e., based on the present worth in today's dollars of the future contributions to be made). Thus, a current income tax deduction is rarely a factor to be considered in evaluating a CLT.

If your CLT has certain characteristics, it will be classified as a grantor trust. If it does not have these characteristics, it will not be a grantor trust.

TIP: The characteristics that cause a CLT to be treated as a grantor trust (or not) are within your control and that of the attorney drafting the document. Determine the desired tax status in advance, and proceed accordingly.

If you create a CLT where you have retained the right under the terms of the trust agreement to any of the following items, your CLT could be characterized as a grantor trust:

- If you retain the right to remove and replace the trustee with a trustee who is not an independent trustee, you will probably be treated as though you retained the powers that the trustee has over the trust, and hence the trust will be a grantor trust.
- If you retain the right to revoke, terminate, alter, or amend the trust, you may be taxable on the income from the trust (or worse).
- If you have any right to obtain the assets of the trust for less than their fair value, the trust will be treated as a grantor trust taxable to you.
- If the trust principal may revert back to you (i.e., you have a reversionary interest), and if the terms of the trust agreement (or applicable law) provide that capital gains on the sale of trust assets must be allocated to the principal of the trust (rather than being allocated to the

income of the trust and paid to the current charitable beneficiary), then you will personally be taxable on these capital gains.

- Any time you have a reversionary interest in the income or principal of a trust, with a value of more than 5 percent of the total value of the trust (determined when the assets are first transferred to the trust), you will be treated as the owner of the trust principal.

- Any rights that your spouse has will be attributed to you for purposes of this test. Even if you have to have the permission of another person to get benefit from the trust property, you may continue to be taxed on the trust assets. This will not occur, however, where the other person whose permission you need is considered to have interests in the trust that are "adverse" to your interests. Someone who shares trust powers with you will only be considered adverse to your interests where that person has a substantial beneficial interest in the trust and that beneficial interest would be adversely affected by a power to revoke the trust (see Chapter 4).

CONCLUSION

Charitable planning with trusts can present valuable planning opportunities even if you are not particularly charitably inclined. The benefits can sometimes be far greater than expected. However, always obtain competent legal, tax, and insurance advice since charitable trusts are some of the most complicated trusts to work with. Finally, always review the reasons for using a charitable trust. If you really just want to be generous, an outright gift to the charity is far simpler.

Part Four

TRUSTS FOR SPECIFIC TYPES OF ASSETS

15 ASSETS AT RISK: USING TRUSTS TO PROTECT YOUR ASSETS

PROTECTING ASSETS SHOULD BE AN INTEGRAL PART OF MOST ESTATE AND FINANCIAL PLANS

Asset Protection Planning Involves Many Techniques

Many people are anxious to set up a trust to insulate their assets from the reach of creditors. While foreign situs (i.e., based in a foreign country) asset protection trusts (APTs) are a common technique to address liability exposure, this is only one part of asset protection planning. Another type of trust, the Medicaid qualifying trust, to protect assets from nursing home costs are not discussed in this chapter. As with most areas of trust law, and estate planning generally, the technique that you hear most about is not always the only, or even the best approach for you. As this chapter will explain, you will generally find that you will need arrangements other than trusts to protect assets. The S corporation, the family limited partnership, and the limited liability company are all integral parts of the asset protection process. Further, many of the trusts discussed in this book can have asset protection benefits, not just foreign situs asset protection trusts. Only through comprehensive planning, undertaken in advance of actual claims, can you obtain significant protection. However, far too few people consider the importance of asset protection planning until it is too late. This chapter will illustrate some of the many techniques, including trusts, you should consider.

If you are a professional, you should be concerned about avoiding potential malpractice claims. If you own real estate, you must be concerned about environmental problems, tenant and visitor claims, and so forth. If you own a business, you should consider protecting assets with different risk profiles from other assets. For example, if your manufacturing plant uses a building, the ownership of the building should be separated from the manufacturing business that likely creates different and greater risks.

EXAMPLE: You are a professional (e.g., doctor, lawyer, engineer) personally liable for all professional services you render to your clients. If you are sued for malpractice and either your malpractice insurance is insufficient, or an exception to the policy denies coverage for a particular event, you will be personally liable. Insulating some of your assets to preserve them in the event of a successful malpractice challenge could be the most important estate and financial planning step you can take.

CAUTION: Operating as a professional corporation (PC) or a limited liability corporation (or limited liability partnership) is not a guarantee of insulation from liability. Even as a shareholder of a professional corporation, you will generally remain personally liable for acts of malpractice committed by you, or employees under your supervision. Thus, a PC can help limit, but cannot eliminate, liability. If you have organized as a limited liability partnership (LLP), you may be relieved of professional liability due to acts of other principals, but you remain responsible for your professional malpractice and those operating under your supervision. You may also, depending on state law, be liable personally for contractual claims (e.g., lease liability).

EXAMPLE: You own several real estate properties as investments. One property is owned individually by you. You own 50 percent. You have ownership interest in two other properties in a general partnership format. You are therefore personally liable for any liability from any of the properties. If a tenant is injured on one of the rental properties and successfully sues for more than the amount of your insurance, you will be personally liable. Transferring assets to separate trusts to avoid a domino effect in the event a claimant from one property sues can be helpful, but is not the most common approach to this dilemma. Consideration should be given instead to changing the structure of your real estate properties to limited liability companies, S corporations, or limited partnerships, each of which can provide you with limited liability (i.e., your liability is limited to the value of your equity in the particular property). It is then common to have the interests in these entities (which will then own the properties involved) in turn owned by trusts for children or other beneficiaries to whom you wish to transfer ownership.

Lawsuits are not the only risk you may wish to protect yourself from. If you are old, and perhaps becoming infirm, a major concern may be to avoid losing assets in payments for medical expenses. There may be a number of steps you can take, including transferring your assets to special trusts to obtain some protection for them.

Considerations When Planning for Asset Protection

The Process Is Complex

Asset protection planning is extremely complex because it is affected by so many different legal disciplines. Laws governing property ownership, taxation, estate planning, debtor/creditor laws, bankruptcy, corporate law and possibly several others may all have to be considered. Where the transactions cross international boundaries, the complexity increases because laws of at least two countries, and any treaties or other agreements be-tween them, must be addressed. When planning to protect assets from medical costs, state programs, federal laws, tax issues, private insurance, and other issues must be considered. Thus, competent legal assistance should always be obtained.

Transfers That Defraud Creditors Will Not Be Successful

Debtor-creditor laws can be important considerations. Your attorney will have to review any applicable state laws, as well as federal bankruptcy laws. Many states have adopted some version of the Uniform Fraudulent Transfers Act. If you transfer property with the intent to defraud your creditors, the transfers will not be successful. A transfer of assets to hin-der or delay your creditors from collecting can be voided. Further, should you find yourself in bankruptcy, your prior attempts to hinder creditors could have substantial adverse consequences. The bankruptcy judge may not permit you to discharge certain debts and you will end up making your situation worse than had you done nothing at all. Thus, any transactions that could move assets out of the reach of your creditors must receive care-ful attention.

The rules are applied very strictly to protect creditors. Almost any trans-fer for which you do not receive a fair price (consideration) could be sus-pect. Further, transfers, even for a fair price, that occur within certain time periods before a declaration of bankruptcy or insolvency (liabilities are greater than assets) could be subject to question. These transfers may be classified as "preferences" to be set aside by a court.

Several factors can indicate a possible intent to defraud creditors (called badges of fraud), thus increasing the likelihood of a court setting aside the transfers. These can include:

- Transferring assets immediately before or after incurring a signifi-cant debt.
- Transferring substantially all of your assets at the same time.
- Transfers of assets outside the United States.
- Transfer of assets when you are nearly insolvent.
- Transferring assets to a close relative or business associate.

Husband or Wife: Who Should Own Assets?

Many asset protection plans are founded on the transfer of assets to your spouse's control (whether outright or in a trust controlled by your spouse). While your creditors may generally not be able to reach assets of your spouse, there are several exceptions. For example, if your spouse is a co-owner of the business involved or cosigned a note that is being sued on, the creditors will also be able to reach your spouse's assets.

Where a husband and wife own assets as tenants-by-the-entirety, there are special privileges. This type of ownership can provide some measure of protection from creditors, depending on state law. If the creditor only has a claim against one of the spouses, assets co-owned by the other spouse cannot always be reached. Even this protection, however, is not foolproof. When the nonliable spouse dies, the creditors of the surviving spouse may be able to reach the entire asset. These matters should carefully be considered before transferring any assets to your spouse, whether in trust, or outright and free of trust.

What Approaches Can Be Used to Protect Assets from Creditors?

Many different steps can be taken to protect assets against claims.

Insurance Should Always Be Considered First

Never overlook the benefits of adequate insurance protection. First, make sure you have the appropriate insurance protection in place and that the limits on the policy are reasonable in light of the risks you face.

Many people anxious about estate planning and asset protection overlook one of the least expensive (and most important) planning steps—umbrella liability insurance. This won't provide protection against professional malpractice, but if you are in a car accident, or someone is injured at your home, an umbrella liability insurance policy can provide substantial coverage above the limits contained in your homeowner's and auto insurance policies. A policy for as much as $5 million in coverage may cost not much more than $500 to $750. Not much to pay for the additional protection.

Use Corporations or Other Entities

If the activity giving rise to the risk is incorporated, or structured as a limited partnership or limited liability company from inception, substantial protection from liabilities will be afforded the owners. These types of legal arrangements for each business or investment asset can help prevent a domino effect when one asset becomes subject to a lawsuit.

Give Away Assets

- *Benefits.* Give away an asset where you can afford to do so and the potential gift and estate tax consequences can be planned for. Barring the applicability of a fraudulent conveyance statute, giving away an asset is perhaps the best way to protect it from your creditors. To do so, however, you must not need the income and value of the asset. A gift with strings may be completely ineffective in removing assets from the reach of your creditors. The assets should be given before claims arise. Also, whenever possible, be able to demonstrate nonasset protection motives for any transfer.
- *Costs of Gifts.* Giving away assets is not without drawbacks.

EXAMPLE: Giving away all of your assets to your spouse can have significant tax drawbacks, even if it is successful from a creditor protection perspective. Each tax-payer is entitled to transfer, in aggregate, $600,000 of assets without incurring a gift or estate tax. If your spouse has all family assets, your estate will waste your unified credit and no assets will pass tax-free (see Chapter 7). If the assets to be transferred are real estate, will the mortgage be accelerated (become due immediately on transfer)? Will there be transfer costs?

The preceding example highlights an important limitation on planning for asset protection. It is not always consistent with tax, personal, and other goals. Also, there can be substantial transfer and other costs involved. If assets are transferred to children or grandchildren to remove them from the reach of your future creditors, gift, estate, and generation-skipping transfer taxes could all be due. This becomes particularly problematic if you try to make the transfers quickly. Over the long term, substantial assets can be transferred using the annual $10,000 gift tax exclusion.

- *Divorce Risk.* Transferring assets to your spouse to avoid creditors has a risk that is potentially much greater than lost estate tax benefits: divorce. Although many states have equitable distributions laws stating that the manner in which property is owned should not determine how it is divided, these laws cannot assure that no negative consequences will occur from the transfer. Equitable distribution laws seek to equitably (loosely translated as fairly) divide assets, without regard to whose name the assets are in. However, even if the end result will be the same whether you keep your assets or transfer them to your spouse to avoid your potential creditors, the transfer could still have an important effect on the dynamics of the divorce process. If your spouse has title to all of the family's assets, it may be far easier for your spouse to raise money for legal and other fees to fight the divorce.

How Trusts Can Be Used to Protect Assets

Many Different Trusts Can Protect Assets

Trusts can be an important tool in your asset protection planning. Many trusts that you might consider using to meet tax, financial, personal, or other goals can have important asset protection benefits as well. Using trusts to transfer assets beyond the reach of creditors may offer an advantage over the use of outright gifts. It may be possible to make a transfer of assets to a trust that is complete for local law purposes. However, the transferor could be granted a sufficient power of appointment over the assets so that for gift and estate tax purposes the transfer may be deemed incomplete. This is tricky since the power retained should not be so significant that it is construed as a general power of appointment giving you the right to appoint assets to your estate or your creditors. The ability to successfully accomplish such an arrangement is not clear, so professional advice must be obtained, and great caution exercised.

Any or all of the following trusts can insulate, to varying degrees, trust assets from creditors:

- *Child's Trust.* One of the most common types of trusts is a trust to provide for your child (or multiple trusts one for each of your children). These trusts have strong nonasset protection motives: saving for your child's college education and protecting valuable assets from the whims of a young child (see Chapter 13).

- *Inter Vivos Q-TIP Trust for Your Spouse.* You can form a trust for your spouse during your lifetime. The trust can qualify for the unlimited gift tax marital deduction if your spouse receives all of the income annually and certain other requirements discussed in Chapter 11 are met.

- *GRUTs and GRATs.* Grantor Retained Unitrusts and Grantor Retained Annuity Trusts are used primarily to achieve tax savings when making large gifts (see Chapter 17). These trusts, however, may also provide a measure of asset protection in that you as grantor do not have the unilateral right to transfer the asset from the trusts because the remainder beneficiary has a significant right. However, a court may permit a creditor to reach the annual payments you receive from the trust.

- *Charitable Remainder Trust.* You could transfer assets to a charitable remainder trust where your spouse receives income for life from the charity, and on her death, the charity will receive all of the assets remaining in the trust (see Chapter 14).

- *Life Insurance Trust.* One of the most common types of trusts is an insurance trust. You transfer cash or other assets to an irrevocable trust that names your family, friends, or others as heirs, and family members, friends, or others as trustees. The monies are used to buy insurance on your life, although the trustee is not required to do so. The monies so transferred and the insurance purchased could be difficult to reach by your creditors if the required criteria discussed previously are met. Also, a measure of protection is afforded to insurance as an asset as well under some states' laws (see Chapter 16).

Include a "Spendthrift" Provision in the Trust

When asset protection is one of the motives for establishing a trust, the trust should include, if appropriate, a spendthrift provision. This clause can be helpful when you set up a trust for your children or your parents, or another person sets up a trust for you. It is unlikely to be effective when included in a trust you set up yourself and for your own benefit. This type of trust is called a "self-funded" trust, and the courts are generally loath to permit you to use your own trust to protect assets, especially if you continue as a beneficiary. A spendthrift clause prevents the beneficiary from assigning any part of his or her interest in the trust to third parties before it is received. There are two important exceptions to the protection afforded by a spendthrift provision. Many state laws permit creditors who have provided necessities (e.g., food, shelter, medical care, etc.) to a beneficiary of the trust to reach assets of the trust for payment. Also, as you would expect, the courts have held that the IRS can reach the assets of a spendthrift trust to satisfy a federal tax lien. Be certain to consult a lawyer in the state involved since state laws concerning the effectiveness of a spendthrift provision can vary considerably. In some states, a spendthrift clause will protect only the principal of the trust; in other states, such a clause may protect principal and income.

Trustees' Rights and Powers

When planning the use of trusts to shield assets, carefully consider the persons named as trustees, and the powers and rights given to the trustees. Generally, if protecting assets is even of the slightest concern, you should not be the sole trustee of any trust for your benefit. At minimum, consider not serving (and preferably not having your spouse serve) as trustee. If you or your spouse must serve, have a co-trustee who is independent. Consider having any distributions to yourself made solely in the discretion of this independent trustee. This is a tricky area requiring professional guidance.

If you are the grantor setting up and transferring assets to the trust, and you seek to protect your assets from creditors, you should preferably not have any right to the trust's assets. If you can reach the trust assets for your own benefit, it is more likely that your creditors will be able to as well. Even where another person forms a trust for your benefit, the degree of discretion that the trustees have to distribute trust income or assets to you can be important in determining the level of protection the trust assets will receive from your creditors. It may be possible for a trust to minimize the impact of an attack by your creditors if the trustees can only distribute money to you for your health and maintenance in accordance with your standard of living (an "ascertainable standard"), and to do so must first obtain the approval of a beneficiary with adverse interests (e.g., a beneficiary is adverse to you if a distribution to you would reduce future distributions to that beneficiary). The more difficult it is for any monies to be distributed to you, the more likely that you will achieve some measure of protection from your creditors. Even if you cannot receive any money or assets from the trust, but trust assets can be used to discharge your legal obligation to support your children, a court might view this as a distribution for your benefit making the assets reachable by your creditors.

There are two trusts that can provide exceptions to these rules. Medicaid trusts may be able to permit you to transfer assets to a trust from which you receive certain limited benefits yet the trust assets may not be reached to pay for nursing home costs. This result can only be achieved if federal laws and your state laws permit this type of arrangement and the elder law specialist you consult is sufficiently skilled to prepare the trust accordingly. The second exception is for a foreign situs asset protection trust. These trusts can achieve what may not be possible under U.S. law because the trusts are intentionally based in countries whose laws are less favorable to creditors and thus permit this type of planning. Both of these trusts are discussed later in this chapter.

Tips to Consider When Planning to Protect Assets

While some asset protection success can be achieved by transferring assets to a trust to avoid future creditors and claimants, you should consider several precautions:

- *Transfer Assets Early.* The longer a transfer is made before an event gives rise to a malpractice or creditor's claim, the greater the likelihood that the transfer will be respected. A transfer made after creditors are hot on your trail and lawsuits pending is unlikely to provide any protection. In fact, it may destroy any credibility you had.

CAUTION: This rule is often construed in the manner most favorable to the creditors or malpractice claimants. Thus, if the event (cause of action) that gives rise to the lawsuit has occurred, even though the matter has not yet been brought to trial, it may be too late to make the transfer. Some courts have held that liabilities which were at best contingent at the date assets were transferred should be protected against the results of those transfers.

Your professional advisers will be cautious about the timing of any transactions they assist you with since they will not wish to risk being involved in any transaction that could be construed as a fraud on existing creditors. The difficulty with advance planning is the basic problem with all types of planning, procrastination. Until the risk is all too real, many people will simply be too busy or unconcerned to take the necessary precautions.

- *Documentation.* Carefully document as many reasons for the transactions involved, other than avoiding creditors or potential malpractice claimants. When any transaction has strong non-asset-protection motives, it is less likely to appear as a device to avoid creditors. Further, non-asset-protection motives give more substance to the transaction. Make the transfers while you have significant net worth, not when teetering on bankruptcy. If you are contemplating a transfer, have your accountant prepare a personal financial statement that demonstrates net worth. While you may be confident your net worth is substantial, at some future time, with the benefit of hindsight, a court may view your situation as being less rosy.
- *Give Up Control.* The less control you can exert over any trust to which you've transferred assets, the more likely that the creditor and

malpractice protection will be successful. The transfer of assets to a trust where you are the only current beneficiary is less likely to be successful in insulating assets than a trust where the only current beneficiaries are a class consisting of your spouse, your children, and your spouse's parents. If you cannot revoke or modify the trust, it is more likely to withstand an attack by creditors than if you have the right to revoke or modify the trust, or to change the beneficiaries. If you are a trustee or co-trustee, the trust agreement should preclude any distributions in your discretion to family members that would satisfy your support obligations under local law. You should have no control or influence over where trust assets or income can be distributed. It is best if all such decisions are within the absolute discretionary authority of independent trustees.

- *Involve Everyone in the Planning Process.* Plan with your family members. If your parents have listed you in their will for an outright bequest, perhaps they can revise their wills to leave the money to you in a trust, with a spendthrift provision and an independent trustee, or to a trust for the benefit of your spouse or children. This can achieve a level of protection which you cannot achieve if your first receive the bequest and then try to transfer the assets into a trust.

- *Use Independent Trustees.* The trustees should be as independent of you as possible. If possible, they should not be relatives, business associates, or anyone who could arguably be controlled by you.

- *Consult a Lawyer.* The methods involved, and the legal risks that can jeopardize your planning are substantial. Also, other techniques, such as the limited partnership or S corporation often may be useful. These will all require legal assistance for implementation and consultation with a specialist.

USING FOREIGN TRUSTS IN ASSET PROTECTION PLANNING

Foreign Trusts as Part of Your Asset Protection Plan

A foreign situs trust (FST) is also known by other names, including "asset protection trust" (APT), "international offshore estate planning trust" (IOEPT), or simply "foreign trust." Foreign trusts are often the first thing most people think of when the phrase "asset protection planning" is heard. Foreign trusts can provide asset protection planning benefits, but the limitations, costs, complexities, and risks of using these trusts should also be addressed before proceeding. Finally, foreign trusts are generally not the entire answer to your asset protection concerns. They should be used as only part of an overall program that includes any other appropriate asset protection techniques. The foreign trust can provide a means to protect the assets of high net worth people. For foreign trust planning to be effective, however, there should not be any existing judgments or claims currently pending. This is essential because any attempt to defraud creditors may result in the trust being set aside as a fraudulent transfer, which would defeat the very purpose of the trust.

Benefits of a Foreign Trust

Using a foreign situs trust offers investors several potential benefits.

Grantor's Lack of Control Insulates Assets

Where the foreign trust is established as an irrevocable trust, you (as grantor) may have no authority to terminate the trust or direct distribution of its assets. Thus, if a judgment creditor is successful in a U. S. court, the court may not succeed in ordering you to turn over trust assets to the creditor. Many foreign trusts are set up as revocable trusts, however, to avoid the U.S. excise and gift taxes that may otherwise be due on the transfer of assets.

More Favorable Statute of Limitations than under the Applicable United States Law

If you select the country for your foreign trust using proper criteria, the benefits of the laws of that foreign jurisdiction may be available. These laws may be more favorable to your protection than to creditor rights under United States law. For example, the statute of limitations for filing claims may be shorter. This statute sets forth the time period during which a creditor must file a claim. Once it has elapsed, creditors are prohibited from this recourse.

The United States Uniform Fraudulent Transfer Act (UFTA) provides that the statute of limitations will begin to run on actual discovery of the transfer of the assets. However, this discovery rule is not applicable in many countries which were former British colonies. Instead, the laws in these countries provide that the statute of limitations begins to run at the actual time of the transfer. Thus, in many instances, the statute of limitations will have already expired by the time the creditor obtains a judgment.

In some foreign countries, in addition to a shorter statute of limitations, the foreign law equivalent of a fraudulent conveyance law is more favorable for you than the applicable United States law. For example, foreign law may preclude a fraudulent conveyance challenge by a creditor who was not known to be a creditor at the time of your transferring assets to the foreign trust.

National Barriers to Claims and Actions

Assets held in foreign trusts can provide a measure of protection in that they may be more difficult to discover, identify, and seize than assets held in a domestic trust. Using a foreign trust to own assets may inhibit actions of creditors as a result of the actual or perceived costs, time delays, and difficulties of enforcing a United States judgment against foreign trust assets. Even if the foreign trust's assets can be reached, the creditor must first evaluate whether the process is worth the reward.

There is a barrier faced by an American claimant who will have to file a foreign legal action to pursue and obtain recovery from the assets located in the foreign country. The creditor may first attempt to seek an order from a United States court to have the assets of the trust turned over to the creditor. However, the beneficiary may not have the power to revoke the trust when an irrevocable trust is used. Even under some foreign trusts that are structured to be grantor trusts for United States tax purposes, you may not have the power to require the trustee to distribute the assets to the creditor. Therefore, the creditor's only remedy might be to fight you in the foreign country's courts.

Where a creditor seeks to pursue the claim in a foreign country, he must establish your personal liability again under the laws of that foreign country. For such a court action to be successful, the foreign jurisdiction where the trust is based must have jurisdiction over you (personal jurisdiction) and jurisdiction over the matter being contested (subject matter jurisdiction). If the action is successful the claimant—to reach the trust assets—must then prove that the transfer of assets by you to the trust was somehow a fraudulent transfer, under the laws of the foreign country.

Foreign Jurisdiction May Not Recognize United States Judgment

Some foreign jurisdictions will not recognize a judgment by a United States court. In legal parlance, there is no "comity." Therefore, a new case would have to be brought in the foreign country where the trust was organized. The cost and difficulties of such a trial could dissuade less than serious claimants in the United States from pursuing such claims. The creditor must retain an attorney in the foreign jurisdiction to seek execution of the judgment against the trust assets. The foreign court must have sufficient personal and subject matter jurisdiction, and the alleged violation must also be a violation of the laws of the foreign jurisdiction for the creditor to assert a proper cause of action.

Global Investment Opportunities Increased

The foreign trust can be a good vehicle for global investing since foreign jurisdictions often are subject to less stringent securities regulation than in the United States. As a result, investment products available to overseas investors are not always available to U.S-based investors. This can be a legitimate and important non-asset-protection motive for establishing a foreign situs trust.

Secrecy

The secrecy laws of foreign jurisdictions may provide more privacy than domestic trusts can offer. In many instances, however, the secrecy may be somewhat less than you anticipate because of U.S. tax-reporting requirements. For example, to avoid gift and excise tax on transferring assets to a foreign trust, the person seeking creditor protection may establish the trust as a form of grantor trust so that the assets and income of the trust may be ascertainable once a U.S. income tax return is obtained in discovery.

Options for Structuring the Foreign Trust

Nongrantor/Completed Gift versus Grantor/Noncompleted Gift

A threshold issue in planning the use of a foreign trust is to determine whether the foreign trust should be a grantor trust. If it is a grantor trust, the transfers of property to the trust should not be deemed completed gifts for gift tax purposes, trust income will be taxable annually to you, and the assets of the trust will be included in your estate on death. Grantor trust status is achieved by the grantor retaining sufficient powers under the provisions of the trust agreement to cause this result for federal tax purposes without retaining sufficient powers to taint the creditor protection aspects of the trust (see Chapter 4). Where this is not the desired result, the trust could be structured to be a nongrantor trust. In such a situation, the transfer of assets to the trust may be a completed gift for gift tax purposes and may trigger a 35 percent excise tax. Once these taxes are paid, however, the trust assets may be able to grow completely tax-free, and possibly be made available in perpetuity as a financial resource to your family without diminution by any taxes.

Foreign Trust Combined with Family Limited Partnership

The foreign trust may be structured with both a family limited partnership (FLP) and a trust created in a foreign jurisdiction. You could first create an S corporation to serve as general partner of the family limited partnership. You could retain substantial control by serving as general partner or through controlling the corporate general partner. A trust is then created in a foreign country and the limited partnership interests are transferred to the trustees of that foreign trust. Alternatively, you could sell the limited partnership interests to the foreign trust in exchange for installment notes, or a private annuity. The bulk of the value of the assets would then be owned by the limited partnership interests.

In some cases where this limited partnership structure is used, you do not have to transfer the limited partnership's assets offshore initially. Instead, the assets, such as a securities account, could remain in the United States and be transferred offshore by the trustee if and when a lawsuit is threatened. This approach, however, could increase the vulnerability of trust assets to a claim. What if the assets are not transferred quickly enough? How would a United States court view such a transfer just ahead of a claim?

Steps to Establish Your Foreign Trust

The following steps are commonly used to implement the family limited partnership/foreign situs trust structure:

STEP 1. Form a limited partnership by hiring a lawyer to file the appropriate certificate of limited partnership and naming yourself, and perhaps your spouse (to avoid any tax consequences from the transfer of ownership interests). You could "take back" (i.e., in exchange for the transfer of the initial assets transferred) all of the general partnership interests and 99 percent of the limited partnership interests. Your spouse could "take back" 1 percent of the limited partnership interests.

STEP 2. Have a lawyer prepare a family limited partnership agreement that includes restrictions on transfer of any partnership interests, language sufficient to address various limited partnership tax issues, and so forth.

STEP 3. Transfer stock (except in S corporations), bonds, real estate (except a personal residence), and cash to the family limited partnership.

STEP 4. Transfer the limited partnership interests to the foreign trust. The interests in the foreign trust are managed by the trustee (perhaps only foreign, or foreign and U.S. cotrustees) and the trust protector. A trust protector is a person given special limited powers in the foreign trust agreement. These could include the right to change the location and law governing the trust and to change trustees. However, since the assets of the limited partnership are managed by the general partner of the family limited partnership, you as the general partner (or perhaps you as president of the S corporation serving as general partner) control the underlying assets.

STEP 5. In an emergency, the foreign trustee can liquidate the limited partnership into the foreign trust and remove the U.S. trustees to sever any and all ties with the United States. The trust protector could change trustees or locations (i.e., transfer the trust to another foreign country), and take other actions if litigation is threatened.

Other Options for Structuring a Foreign Trust

In some instances, the investments are made through a corporation organized in a tax haven country, all of the stock of which is owned by the trust. The advantage of using a corporation is that it can be organized in a country with more favorable tax and creditor protection laws than in the country in which the trustee is based or in which the trust is organized. This may serve as yet another hurdle for a potential claimant.

Where to Locate the Foreign Trust

Review the following matters with your attorney in deciding which foreign country to use as the location of your foreign trust:

- The political, economic, and social stability of the jurisdiction.
- The jurisdiction's reputation in the world business community.
- Whether language barriers exist.
- Whether the jurisdiction has modern telecommunications facilities.
- Whether the jurisdiction offers adequate legal, accounting, and financial services.
- The lack of any significant income, gift or estate taxes in the jurisdiction. If taxes are enacted after the trust is formed, however, the trust protector (as described earlier) could exercise a provision in the trust agreement to change the location of trust assets to a more favorable host country.
- The standard of proof that a creditor must meet in attempting to show fraudulent intent on the part of the transferor.
- The extent to which a transferor may retain benefit in, and control over, a foreign trust without exposing the trust to the transferor's creditors.
- The importance of the grantor's solvency following transfers to the foreign trust.
- The point at which the statute of limitations begins to run on a particular action.
- Whether the particular jurisdiction recognizes the holdings of a United States court in a particular case.
- Whether the jurisdiction's trust law is favorable, well-defined, and protective.
- The recognition to be given to judgments and orders of foreign courts that affect a foreign trust, its trustees, and its assets.

What Assets to Transfer to Your Foreign Trust

The assets transferred to your foreign trust should generally not be tainted by legal or other risks. For example, a business with liability claims or real estate with hazardous waste problems should not be transferred. To transfer a tainted asset could jeopardize the integrity of the trust and its other nontainted assets.

Where a family limited partnership is combined with the foreign trust, a personal residence should not be transferred to the family limited partnership. If this were done, important tax benefits such as the rollover of gain on the sale of a principal residence could be lost. Similarly, the ability to exclude up to $125,000 of gain for taxpayers over age 55 could be lost. A personal residence, however, could be transferred directly to the foreign trust (i.e., bypassing the family limited partnership) if the trust is taxed for U.S. tax purposes as a grantor trust. This would not jeopardize the tax benefits. Where stock in an S corporation is to be transferred to a family limited partnership/foreign trust structure, the tax status of the S corporation election could be jeopardized. It may be feasible to transfer the stock in the S corporation directly to the foreign trust to avoid this risk.

Some assets should not generally be transferred to either the limited partnership or the foreign trust. For example, interests in a professional corporation must be owned by a licensed professional and cannot therefore be transferred. KEOGH, IRA, and pension assets should generally not be transferred.

CONCLUSION

Setting up a trust to protect assets, whether from creditors using a foreign trust, or from Medicaid using a Medicaid qualifying trust, can provide numerous advantages. Great care, however, must be exercised in preparing the trust document to meet your specific objectives, transferring assets to your trust, and then operating it with the proper formality. This is particularly important where you hope to obtain some protection from the claims of future creditors, malpractice claimants, or the state on account of Medicaid payments.

16 LIFE INSURANCE TRUSTS

WHY IS A LIFE INSURANCE TRUST SO IMPORTANT?

Insurance Is Not Tax Free without Use of an Insurance Trust

Life insurance trusts are one of the most important trusts. They are unfortunately too often not used by those needing them most. Why are they so often overlooked? Because most taxpayers erroneously assume that life insurance is tax-free. It is not. Life insurance is taxable in your estate if you owned the policy. Even if life insurance escapes taxation on your death because it is paid to your spouse, this is simply a result of the unlimited marital deduction, not an indication that insurance is tax-free. On the later death of your spouse, 55 percent of the proceeds remaining could be paid in estate tax. Because life insurance trusts can help you to avoid this estate tax bite, they are an extremely powerful planning tool. Even people of modest means could often benefit from an insurance trust.

EXAMPLE: The Youngcouples have negligible net worth. They have two children and own a fully mortgaged home. Because of their limited resources and great needs (i.e., the two children), Mr. and Mrs. Youngcouple each purchase a $1 million term life insurance policy. The premiums, based on their young ages, are very inexpensive. If both Mr. and Mrs. Youngcouple are killed in an automobile accident, their children may have to pay nearly $700,000 in estate taxes.

Although almost any trust can own insurance policies and receive insurance proceeds, what is generally thought of as a life insurance trust is formed with the thought of it owning only life insurance policies on your life, or even the life of another person, such as your spouse.

EXAMPLE: Your estate is worth $2 million. Assume that your estate taxes and expenses are estimated at $800,000. You purchase an $800,000 life insurance policy to cover the cost. The policy, however, is included in your estate since you own it at death. Thus your estate has been increased to $2.8 million, and your taxes and expenses increased to $1.2 million. Thus, one-half of the insurance proceeds could be lost to additional tax costs. As an alternative, you could set up an irrevocable life insurance trust to purchase the policy. Since the policy is owned by the trust, the proceeds will not be included in your estate. Your estate remains valued

---

at $2 million and your taxes and costs remain at $800,000. But in addition, your trustee now has a pool of $800,000 that can be used to purchase nonliquid assets from your estate thus providing your estate with cash to meet its tax and expense obligations. The value of the assets then held in the trust can be used to provide for the needs of your loved ones. This can be an advantage over having the beneficiaries own the policies: more control, protection from the creditors of the beneficiaries, protection from becoming a marital asset in the event of a beneficiary divorce, and so forth.

Benefits of an Insurance Trust

NOTE: If you buy second-to-die (also called survivors) insurance to pay estate tax, you need an insurance trust. But you don't have to be rich to need an insurance trust. A young family with children, and a modest estate, needs substantial insurance to protect against the death of a breadwinner. That insurance could trigger a huge estate tax and make the government your biggest beneficiary. An insurance trust is the answer.

Advantages of an irrevocable insurance trust can include:

- Insurance proceeds can be excluded from both your estate and your spouse's estate, thus completely escaping transfer taxes at your generation. Properly established, an irrevocable life insurance trust can enable both your estate and your spouse's or partner's estate, if any) to avoid tax on life insurance proceeds. Your surviving spouse can receive some or all of the annual income from the insurance trust, distributions of the principal in the trust, and even a right to demand up to $5,000, or 5 percent of the trust principal, in any year. This right, however, must be noncumulative—use it or lose it. Your surviving spouse, however, cannot hold a general power of appointment over the insurance proceeds if they are to be excluded from his or her estate.

- Trust assets are protected from claims by creditors (spendthrift provision; limiting beneficiary's rights; etc.). Thus, physicians and other professionals and businesspersons seeking to protect their assets should consider this technique as part of their overall asset protection strategy.

- Investments from insurance proceeds retained in the insurance trust are protected from claims by divorcing spouse (e.g., an insurance trust with your child as beneficiary could be protected from equitable distribution claims of your child's ex-spouse).

- There is some additional flexibility in selecting the choice of applicable law when a trust is used to own insurance.

- For those concerned about publicity, the insurance proceeds included in the trust are not included in your probate estate. So if there is no legal challenge to the trust, the insurance proceeds and how they are to be distributed should not be made available for public knowledge.

- When an insurance trust owns life insurance, the death benefit can be removed from the insured's estate. Since insurance is often one of the largest assets in an estate, this technique alone (or coupled with the maximum unified credit available to the decedent or the decedent and his or her spouse) can effectively eliminate federal estate taxes on the majority of estates.

- Assets can be managed to protect the insurance proceeds for the ultimate care and use of the beneficiary. You can assist a minor or disabled beneficiary by carefully selecting the trustees who will invest the ultimate insurance proceeds. To assure that the insurance proceeds are removed from your estate as the grantor of the trust, you as insured must not possess any significant powers.

Typical Use of a Second-to-Die Insurance Trust

Perhaps one of the most common uses of an irrevocable insurance trust is to hold second-to-die or survivor's insurance. In a typical estate plan, here is how this technique works. Assume that your estate is worth $2.2 million. The proper use of credit shelter trusts in the wills for you and your spouse (and retitling of assets to be certain those trusts are funded) can remove $1.2 million from your combined taxable estates. Ignoring expenses, that leaves a $1 million taxable estate. Anticipating a 50 percent estate tax bracket, a $500,000 second-to-die (survivor's) insurance policy is purchased by the irrevocable insurance trust you established. On the death of the last of you or your spouse, the $500,000 insurance proceeds are paid to the trust. The trustee can then invest the proceeds and use them to care for your heirs, to purchase assets from your estate, or loan your estate the money to pay the tax, thus assuring your estate of sufficient cash to pay any estate tax due.

PROVISIONS TO INCLUDE IN THE INSURANCE TRUST

Revocable versus Irrevocable Trusts

Most life insurance trusts are carefully structured to be irrevocable (you cannot change the trust once signed) to assure that the proceeds will not be included in your estate (or your spouse's estate if second-to-die insurance is involved).

In some instances, however, insurance will be placed in a revocable trust. Carefully review the consequences of using a revocable trust with your tax adviser before using this approach. With a revocable trust, there is no gift tax cost on the transfer of money or policies to the trust because the gift is considered incomplete for gift tax purposes. No tax cost can be triggered until you give up control over the trust assets. Why use a revocable trust? It can help you achieve any of the benefits that the living trust can provide: management, avoiding probate, confidentiality, and so forth. However, it cannot provide estate tax savings. If the insurance involved is insurance only on your life, and the proceeds will be payable to your spouse, there will be no estate tax cost on your death as a result of the unlimited marital deduction offsetting the insurance included in your estate. Further, if your spouse is young, or you have young children, the insurance proceeds may be spent before her death so that there will be no estate tax cost at that time either. Where you estate is less than the $600,000 lifetime exclusion, this will not create any additional cost. In fact, it can be an affirmative tax-planning technique to use your lifetime exclusion. The trust, however, should not qualify for the marital deduction for this result to be achieved. The important benefit of revocable insurance trust where tax costs are not a concern is that it can be changed when circumstances change. If you divorce, you can change beneficiaries. You cannot change an irrevocable life insurance trust.

Grantor versus Nongrantor Trust

Under the tax law grantor trust rules, an insurance trust will be deemed to be a grantor trust to the extent that the income of the trust is used to pay insurance premiums on the grantor's life, or where income is paid to or for the benefit of the grantor or the grantor's spouse, or is accumulated for later distribution to grantor or grantor's spouse. Because of this, most insurance trusts are not funded during the insured's lifetime with any significant assets other than the insurance policy.

Selecting a Trustee

It is preferable that you not be the sole trustee of an insurance trust if you are a beneficiary. It is better to serve as a co-trustee along with an independent person. Where a second-to-die policy is purchased, neither you or your spouse should be trustees. A statement should also be added to the trust document prohibiting either you or your spouse from being appointed to serve as a trustee. The grantor of the trust (whoever sets it up) and/or the beneficiaries, however, may be given limited rights to change the trustee. Often this right is limited to naming an institutional trustee. In some situations, however, it can be extended to naming any independent trustee.

Crummey Power

The annual demand or Crummey power discussed earlier often should be included to minimize the tax consequences of contributing money to the trust (see Chapter 7).

Distribution Provisions

The provisions that address how the insurance proceeds should be distributed are quite important since in most cases the trust will be irrevocable and the amounts involved quite large. Where minor children are involved, consider a broad range of issues. Since the proceeds may not be paid for many years into the future, and anticipating what circumstances your family or loved ones may face is so difficult, it is often best to give more, rather than less, flexibility to your trustee. This can be done by providing substantial discretion to the trustee to allocate income and principal of the trust to the beneficiaries most in need. Should a child have special needs, the ability that a well-drafted insurance trust can give the trustee to apply the money where it is most needed can be invaluable. If grandchildren (or other skip persons) could be beneficiaries, be certain, too, that your estate planner has carefully considered the generation-skipping transfer (GST) tax discussed in Chapter 8.

The proper mechanism for an insurance trust to fund the payment of an estate tax is for the trust to loan money to your estate, or purchase assets from your estate. Where assets are purchased, they will then be owned by the insurance trust and not your estate. If this occurs, the ultimate distribution of those assets must be addressed in the trust. If your estate includes business assets intended for particular heirs, will the dispositive provisions of the insurance trust result in the same distribution? While the trustees of the insurance trust may have the flexibility to allocate assets in a manner that conforms with the decedent/insured's wishes, this probably shouldn't be relied on. Consider using similar distribution provisions under your insurance trust as under your will.

Trustee Powers

The trustee can be provided authority to invest in any assets, including real estate, closely held business interests, and other assets your estate will own. The trustee should be authorized to purchase insurance and take any steps necessary to maintain the desired insurance in force. This could include the use of income or principal to pay for premiums (but see earlier comments concerning grantor trust status), the right to purchase additional policies, and so forth. However, the trustee should not be required to pay any debt or expense of your estate. It is generally preferable not to require the trustee to purchase or maintain any insurance policy.

Powers to Deal with Insured's Estate

This could enable your trustee to purchase assets from your estate to provide cash needed to pay estate taxes. If your estate includes valuable property, the trust could use insurance proceeds to purchase these nonliquid assets, thus providing your estate with the cash to meet expenses and estate taxes. When the trustee is granted this right, it may be advisable to have the trust document give the trustee broad powers for the management, lease, and improvement of the property.

Grantor's Rights with Respect to the Trust

To realize the estate tax benefits of removing life insurance proceeds from your estate, the trust must be irrevocable. Generally, you cannot reserve any rights to receive the assets transferred to the trust, or to change the provisions of the trust. It is common to include a clause to the trust stating that you specifically intend that the trust is irrevocable.

Savings Clauses

If you die within three years of transferring the insurance to your trust, the insurance proceeds will be included in your taxable estate. There is a backup approach that can salvage an estate tax benefit. If you are married, transfers to your spouse can qualify for the unlimited marital tax deduction. Thus, your life insurance trust can provide that if the insurance is to be included in your estate as a result of your dying within three years of making the transfer, the proceeds will be transferred into a trust that qualifies for the marital deduction. This will typically be a qualified terminal interest property trust, more commonly called a Q-TIP. To qualify, a number of requirements will have to be met, including that your spouse will be entitled to all of the income from the trust, at least annually, for her life (see Chapter 14).

WHAT STEPS ARE NECESSARY TO IMPLEMENT A LIFE INSURANCE TRUST?

STEP 1.   *Evaluate Your Needs.* Evaluate your insurance, estate tax, and living expense needs with your financial planner, accountant, and insurance agent. Make a determination of appropriate insurance type, payment structure, and so forth. Be sure to discuss all your concerns with the insurance agent. Carefully review, analyze and question the assumptions in the insurance projections you are considering. Also, be sure to investigate the quality and soundness of the insurance company. If you are buying several millions of dollars of coverage, consider splitting your policy between a few insurance companies to diversify the risk of company failure. Decide whom to appoint as your trustees and who should benefit from the insurance proceeds (how much, when, etc.).

STEP 2.   *Applications.* Have the trustees complete and sign (in their capacity as trustees) all applications and forms from your insurance agent. You should take any required medical examinations to qualify for the insurance desired. There is no point in incurring legal and other fees if your health or other reasons disqualify you for insurance. If you already have existing insurance policies that will be transferred to your insurance trust, skip this step.

Your lawyer should also provide your insurance agent with a copy of the insurance trust with the correct name of the trust and trustee for use in the insurance applications. It is always better to fill out everything properly in the beginning rather than to repair errors later.

STEP 3.   *Complete the Trust Document.* Have your lawyer prepare your insurance trust after you determine whether the trust should be revocable or irrevocable, and what provisions should be included. Make enough copies of the trust to open the bank account the trust will need and to purchase the insurance.

STEP 4.   *Obtain a Tax Identification Number.* Have your accountant obtain a federal tax identification number by filing Form SS-4 with the IRS. He or she should have a copy of the insurance trust to verify its name. The identification number can be obtained quite simply by calling the IRS.

STEP 5.   *Transfer Insurance to the Trust.* If you are planning to transfer existing insurance policies to your life insurance trust, contact your insurance agent and request a written estimate of the value of the insurance policies being transferred, the balance of any loans outstanding, the amount of the policy that can be borrowed against. Your insurance agent should be able to calculate the value of the insurance given, in accordance with prescribed IRS formulas. This is important because if it is too large (which can occur on large dollar whole life or similar policies), the transfer could incur a gift tax.

This does not mean that you should not transfer such a policy to your insurance trust, but it does mean that you should plan for the tax consequences. Since you will lose all rights to borrow against the policy, it is best to give policies with little or no cash value. This will also minimize any possible gift tax implications. Where loans are outstanding, there can be tax problems from the transfer.

There can be substantial advantage in transferring existing insurance policies in your name to another owner, perhaps a trust. To successfully accomplish this objective, the policy, and all incidence of ownership in the policy, must be given away. Further, this gift must be accomplished at least three years prior to your death. If not, the insurance proceeds will be included in your estate and will be subject to estate tax.

If you are able to transfer all incidence of ownership more than three years prior to your death, the estate tax can be avoided. Determining whether you have effectively transferred all incidence of ownership in a policy becomes quite difficult especially if you wind up as a trustee of the trust owning the policy. This concept will be explored in greater detail later in this chapter. Similar complications can arise where you are a partner or shareholder in a partnership or corporation that owns insurance policies on your life.

Estate tax will not be due on insurance proceeds paid to a beneficiary other than your estate, or the executor of the estate, if you (the insured) had no incidence of ownership in the insurance policy at the time of your death. This "incidence of ownership" test is vitally important, and unfortunately broad and complex.

To remove the death benefit of an insurance policy you own from your estate, you must effectively transfer all economic benefits of ownership of the policy.

EXAMPLE: You transfer an insurance policy to your spouse. However, you retain the right to borrow against the policy in the event of a business emergency. This single right could, if you die five years later, result in the inclusion of the entire policy proceeds in your estate because all incidence of ownership must be surrendered more than three years prior to death. If you make a commitment to pay the premium in the policy application, and then die in less than three years, the IRS may argue that the proceeds should be included in your estate. The courts, however, have held that the mere payment of premiums should not result in the inclusion of the policy proceeds in your estate.

"Incidence of ownership" includes the right to borrow the cash value, change the name of the beneficiary, assign the policy to another person, borrow against the policy, and so forth. To eliminate all incidence of ownership, and remove the proceeds of an insurance policy from your estate, you must assign the policy a new owner and surrender every power over the policy and all of the benefits the policy can provide. You must irrevocably give up all these rights. Where you transfer insurance to a trust, you should not have a reversionary interest equal to more than 5 percent of the value of the policy. That is, there cannot be more than a 5 percent possibility that the insurance policy or the proceeds of the policy may return to you.

STEP 6.   *Open a Bank Account.* Your trustee should take a signed copy of your trust agreement and your tax identification number to a bank and open a bank account. Deposit a nominal amount to get the account started, or a larger amount if your trustee will have to pay an insurance premium.

STEP 7.   *Gift Cash to the Trust.* You should gift sufficient cash to the trust to open and maintain an account and to cover the first insurance premium.

STEP 8.   *Follow Crummey Power Requirements.* Your insurance trust
will probably include an annual, noncumulative, demand or
Crummey power. This power will lapse at least annually. The
Crummey power gives the beneficiaries the right to demand
distribution of a certain amount of money each year. This
can permit you to qualify your gifts to the trust for the annual $10,000 exclusion amounts and thus avoid any gift tax.
The Crummey power should be drafted to avoid an IRS argument that the hanging power includes a condition subsequent which the IRS may ignore for gift tax purposes. Since
an audit of a trust may not occur for many years, it can be
difficult to keep track of all the Crummey notices you have
sent. You may wish to provide your accountant a copy to retain in the permanent tax file for your trust (where he or she
maintains a copy of the trust, tax election information, etc.).
This will also alert your accountant to any gift tax return filing requirements (see Chapter 7).

STEP 9.   *Pay for Premiums.* Your trustee can pay for the insurance
premium and accept the policy. If existing policies are being
transferred, the necessary steps discussed in the previous
section concerning Crummey powers should be addressed.
Considerable care should be taken in structuring the payment of premiums. It is preferable that the trust, and not
you, the insured, pay the premiums to the insurance company. Although the IRS has lost several cases concerning its
"beamed transfer" theory, it is still advisable to have the
donor gift cash to the trust, and for the trustees, after expiration of the Crummey power notice period, pay for any
premiums. Further, if money is transferred each year to the
insurance trust to pay for the insurance premiums, the
transfers should not be exactly equal to the insurance premiums. It is probably preferable that the trustee not pay for insurance premiums with the cash given until the 30-day
Crummey power notice expires. This requirement, however,
does not seem necessary based on some IRS precedents.

STEP 10.   *Tax Filings.* Your accountant will prepare the necessary annual tax returns, which will be signed and filed by your
trustee.

PROBLEMS IN IMPLEMENTING THE IRREVOCABLE LIFE INSURANCE TRUST

The "Here Today, Gone Tomorrow" Problem

Not so long ago, insurance companies were viewed by the public as pillars
of stability. This view is no longer realistic, and professionals must be

wary of recommending a specific product without having done the appropriate due diligence. Perhaps the best approach is for you and your financial planner or insurance consultant to make the final selection. Also consider buying two or three policies from different companies instead of one policy from a single company.

The Three-Year Rule

Where an existing insurance policy is transferred by the insured to an irrevocable life insurance trust (ILIT), the insured must survive for three years following the transfer or the death benefit of the policy will be included in your estate. Solutions to this problem include:

- Where feasible, have the trustees, on behalf of the trust, purchase a new policy. Where the insured's health has deteriorated or a significant cash value has accrued in the existing policy, this may not be feasible.
- A savings provision (which makes the insurance trust into a tax-deductible marital trust) can be included. This technique would avoid taxation of the insurance proceeds on the death of the first spouse.

CAUTION: Several matters should be addressed carefully to avoid the three-year rule. Where the insurance trust purchases the policy directly, the three-year rule should not apply. However, careless preparation and execution of the insurance application could taint the policy as subject to the three-year rule. Be certain that the trustees, on behalf of the trust, purchase the policy. Further, if the trust were not properly formed prior to the application, could the trustees possibly have purchased the insurance? It is therefore best that the trust be formed (the trust agreement fully executed) prior to submitting any application.

Where the insured pays insurance premiums on a policy within three years of death, but the policy itself is not otherwise tainted by the three-year rule (i.e., the policy wasn't transferred to the trust less than three years prior to death), this payment of premiums alone should not taint the policy proceeds as taxable in the insured's estate.

Value of Transferred Policy Exceeds Annual Exclusion

A potential problem when transferring an existing policy to an insurance trust is that the value of the policy may exceed the annual exclusion amounts (see previous discussion of Crummey powers and in Chapter 7). The value of a life insurance policy is determined under prescribed Treasury regulation guidelines. Where a permanent insurance product has cash surrender value, the interpolated terminal reserve value is used. For term insurance, the value is generally only the unexpired premium.

It may be feasible, insurance contract permitting, to address this problem by having the insured borrow some portion of the cash value of the policy to reduce the value of the policy for gift tax purposes on its transfer to the trust. However, this raises the issue of transferring a policy subject to a loan to a trust. In some instances, the tax costs could weigh against this approach. Be certain to review this with your tax advisor before proceeding.

Group Term Insurance Doesn't Avoid the Gift Tax Issue

For a group term insurance policy, the premiums are typically paid by your employer. This situation has caused many taxpayers to forget the gift tax implications of such arrangements. The IRS views the employer's payment of premiums as an indirect gift from the insured/employee to the beneficiaries of the ILIT.

"Incidents of Ownership" Problem

If proceeds of an insurance policy are receivable by or for the benefit of your estate, or if the proceeds are receivable by other beneficiaries and at your death you possessed any incidents of ownership in the policy (e.g., the unfettered power to change the beneficiary), the death benefit will be included in your estate. This will occur whether the powers of the policies can be exercised either alone or in conjunction with another person. Incidents of ownership can include any of the economic benefits flowing from the insurance policy.

The following rights could be deemed incidents of ownership that could taint the planning:

- The right to change or designate a beneficiary or contingent beneficiary of the policy.
- The power to prevent a change in beneficiary by withholding consent.
- The option to repurchase insurance from an assignee in some instances.
- Other reversionary interests with a value, immediately before the decedent's death, that exceeded 5 percent of the value of the policy.
- Incidents of ownership can flow indirectly such as through a controlled corporation.

The preceding rules can be violated in less than obvious situations. For example, if your insurance trust is legally obligated to pay taxes, debts, or other charges against your estate, the entire proceeds would be included in your estate. This is why, contrary to what most taxpayers believe (i.e., that the money in the insurance trust will directly pay their estate tax), the insurance trust can have no legal obligation to pay the tax on your estate, nor can it pay that tax. Instead, it can loan money at an arm's length rate to the decedent's estate and thereby infuse liquidity to pay the tax. Alternatively, the trust can purchase assets at an arm's length fair market value from your estate, again infusing cash to pay the tax.

Even if the ILIT is not obligated to pay estate tax on the deceased insured's estate, if it applied any of the proceeds from the policy to do so, the proceeds would be included in the taxable estate.

The Insured Should Not Serve as Trustee

Generally, the insured should not serve as a trustee or a co-trustee of an ILIT owning insurance on his or her life. However, there are exceptions. If the decedent obtains the power by being named a trustee of a testamentary trust that owns life insurance on his or her life and the powers cannot be exercised for his or her benefit, the proceeds may not be included in the insured's gross estate.

This must be carefully contrasted with the situation where you transferred an insurance policy into the ILIT and retained incidents of ownership. In this latter situation, the proceeds would be included in your estate. Similarly, the grantor (typically, the insured) should not have the power to appoint him- or herself as a trustee. It is preferable that you are not a trustee. This is true even though you can serve as a trustee in certain very limited circumstances, where your powers over the trust are solely as a fiduciary and cannot be exercised for your benefit, and your becoming a trustee was not part of a prearranged plan. Where a second-to-die policy is used, your spouse should also not be a trustee. A statement should also be added to the trust document prohibiting either you or your spouse from being a trustee. The grantor of the trust (whoever sets it up) should also not be given the right to change the trustee, except where such powers are limited to current rulings and other pronouncements.

Completing the Assignment

Too many taxpayers mistakenly believe that once an insurance trust is signed, their job is done. Even if the trust lists, on a Schedule A attached the specific policy and policy number that is to be transferred to the trust, this is probably inadequate. It is advisable that you follow up with the insurance agent and properly have all incidence of ownership, beneficiary, and designations of an existing insurance policy irrevocably transferred to the new insurance trust.

If a new policy is purchased, the policy should be taken out in the name of the insurance trust and the application signed by the trustee on behalf of the insurance trust.

TAX CONSIDERATIONS OF USING LIFE INSURANCE TRUSTS

Income Tax Considerations of Life Insurance

Where income of the trust can be used to purchase life insurance on the life of the grantor, some portion or all of the trust income will be taxable to the grantor under the grantor trust rules. There is also an argument that it is the beneficiary who should be taxable on trust income.

Gift Tax Considerations of Life Insurance

You will probably transfer cash to your insurance trust at least annually so the trustee can pay expenses, essentially the insurance premium. These transfers, and the transfer of any existing insurance policy (to the extent of its value), constitute gifts. Unless those gifts qualify for the gift tax annual exclusion, you will use up a portion of your unified credit. Once you have depleted your credit, a gift tax will be currently due. The gift tax annual exclusion for gifts to your insurance trust is generally determined by the availability of a Crummey power that converts what would otherwise be a gift of a future interest into a gift of a present interest (see Chapter 7).

Estate Tax Considerations of Life Insurance

The primary goal of most life insurance trust planning is to assure that the life insurance is removed from your estate. The general concept is that you must not retain any incidence of ownership in the policy. This includes ownership of the policy, but is much broader. The proceeds from a life insurance policy are included in your gross estate if the proceeds are receivable by your executor. Insurance proceeds are also included in your estate if you owned, at the date of your death, any incidence of ownership in the policy. This latter rule applies even though the incidence of ownership had to be exercised in conjunction with another person, and even if the insurance proceeds were payable to another person as beneficiary. Incidence of ownership includes:

- Power to change beneficiaries.
- Power to change contingent beneficiaries.
- Power to borrow against the cash value of the policy.
- Power to convert group term life insurance coverage into individual insurance where an employee terminates employment with the employer providing such coverage.
- Power to cancel or surrender the policy.

In determining whether these rules apply, consideration of the rights that you as insured have as a shareholder in a closely held corporation, or trustee of a trust, will be analyzed to determine if the rights of the corporation and trustee should be imputed to you.

GST Tax Considerations of Life Insurance

If your insurance trust is created for the benefit of your grandchildren, then you must be concerned about the generation-skipping transfer (GST) tax. With the proper and timely filing of gift tax returns, this tax can be minimized, thereby reducing your overall tax liability on the transfer of property to your grandchildren in trust. To the extent that the GST tax exemption is allocated on your annual gift tax return to cover gifts you made to an insurance trust for grandchildren, the trust fund could be permanently exempt from GST tax.

CONCLUSION

Irrevocable life insurance trusts are a key estate-planning document for many people, not just the very wealthy. The tremendous benefits of these trusts should not be overlooked.

17 TRUSTS FOR SECURITIES

USING TRUSTS TO HOLD SECURITIES

- *Trusts and Securities Generally.* Trust are a common method for holding or owning stocks, bonds, and other securities. Many of the trusts discussed elsewhere in this book can be used to hold securities and will be summarized here. The focus in this chapter, however, is on grantor retained annuity trusts and grantor retained unitrusts, which can be used to transfer securities, in trust, to family members or others at tremendous tax savings.

- *Foreign Situs Asset Protection Trust (APT).* Securities are frequently transferred to foreign situs asset protection trusts to protect the assets from creditors, malpractice claimants, and others. This type of trust is discussed at length in Chapter 15.

- *Charitable Remainder Trust (CRT).* A charitable remainder trust can provide a tax-advantaged method of diversifying highly appreciated securities, avoiding all capital gains tax cost, and receiving an annuity or unitrust payment for a specified period of years or for your life (or your life and your spouse's life). This technique is discussed at length in Chapter 14.

- *Voting Trusts.* Voting trusts can be used to control the voting rights of stock which you or others own. This technique is discussed in Chapter 18.

INTRODUCTION TO GRANTOR RETAINED ANNUITY TRUSTS AND UNITRUSTS

Grantor retained annuity trusts (GRATs) and grantor retained unitrusts (GRUTs) are trusts designed and intended to reduce the gift tax cost of large gift transfers. Although many types of assets can be held in a GRAT or GRUT, such as closely held business interests, or real estate, one of the most commonly used assets is securities.

A GRAT or GRUT can be illustrated as follows. If you, as the donor or the grantor, give property to a trust for the benefit of your children, you would pay a gift tax on the full value of the property given to the trust. If instead the gift is structured through a GRAT or a GRUT, the value of an interest in the trust that is retained by you (i.e., the monthly, quarterly or annual required payments) may be subtracted from the value of the property given to the trust to determine the amount of the taxable gift. This reduction in value is only allowed if your retained interest is in the form of a qualifying "annuity" interest or "unitrust" interest.

A qualifying interest must be calculated using one of two required methods, unless the transfer is exempt from these tax rules. It must be either a fixed sum of money, usually defined as a percentage of the initial value of the property given to the trust, or it must be a "unitrust" interest. This is a fixed percentage of the annual value of the trust. The former is called a grantor retained annuity trust, or GRAT, the latter, a grantor retained unitrust, or a GRUT. Each of these techniques will be discussed.

Qualification as a GRAT or GRUT is only required for transfers to certain family members. These rules do not apply if an uncle gives property to a trust and retains an interest, with the property passing to his niece. The requirements apply to transfers to children, or other lineal descendants, such as grandchildren.

GRANTOR RETAINED ANNUITY TRUST (GRAT)

GRATs and GRUTs are quite similar. The comments in the following discussion address GRATs. In the next section, the differences between GRATs and GRUTs are pointed out, and pointers on how to choose between the two trust options are presented.

GRAT Required Annuity Payment

Your GRAT is required to pay an annuity amount equal to a specified percentage (e.g., 6%) of the value of the GRAT's assets determined as of the date of the trust agreement. This payment must be made in each taxable year of the trust's term, which can be any period (e.g., five years). This payment amount is required to be made at least annually, regardless of the amount of income actually earned by the trust, to you as the donor for the specified term.

Determining the Value of the Gift for Gift Tax Purposes on Forming Your GRAT

A number of different factors affect the value of the gift you make to your children or other heirs through a GRAT:

- *Value of the Property.* When the property contributed to the GRAT comprises marketable securities, the answer is generally quite simple: The value is the fair market value of the securities given to the GRAT. If nonmarketable assets such as real estate or interests in a closely held business are used to fund the GRAT, an appraisal must be obtained to determine value.

TIP: Discuss with your estate planner the possibility of transferring securities to a family limited partnership first. Then, limited partnership interests in the family limited partnership owning the securities, instead of the securities themselves, are given to the GRAT. When an appraisal is made of the partnership interests, the value assigned will be less than the value of the underlying securities because minority noncontrolling, nonvoting limited partnership interests are generally sold at a discount to their underlying asset value. If a 20 percent discount is accepted by the IRS, for example, this would discount the value of the assets given to the GRAT by 24 percent.

- *The Annuity Percentage Selected.* The higher the percentage annuity payment to be made periodically to you during the GRAT term, the lower the gift tax value. However, the reduced gift tax value comes at a cost, leakage of additional payments from the GRAT to you and hence back into your taxable estate. Also, if the GRAT does not produce enough income to make the annual payments, principal used to fund the GRAT will be paid back to your estate. This is not necessarily a negative depending on the growth in the principal remaining in the GRAT.

NOTE: The earnings (total return, not current income) of the GRAT in excess of the required payments will inure to the benefit of the remainder beneficiaries without any additional gift or estate tax cost. This is the primary benefit to the GRAT planning concept.

- *The Annuity Term Selected.* The longer the period for which the annuity payments will be made by the GRAT to you, the lower the value of the gift to the remainder beneficiaries (e.g., your children) for gift tax purposes. The longer the term, the better the tax result. However, if you do not survive the specified GRAT term, the entire principal of the GRAT is pulled back into your estate.
- *Frequency of Payments.* Under the GRAT, payments may be made annually, quarterly, or monthly. The more frequent the payments, the greater the value of your retained interest and the lower the value of the gift for gift tax purposes. The frequency, however, must be weighed against the administrative burdens it creates.
- *Your Age When the GRAT Is Created.* The key to many of the tax-oriented trusts discussed in this book is for you to undertake planning earlier rather than later. The younger you are when you establish the GRAT, the longer the term of years for the GRAT you can wager that you will survive.
- *The "Applicable Federal Rate."* This is the interest rate determined under tax law guidelines in effect for the month in which the GRAT is created.

The combination of these factors will determine the value of the gift upon creation of the GRAT (and hence the amount of gift tax that may be due).

Who Receives the Assets When the GRAT Ends?

At the end of the specified period (e.g., five years), the GRAT terminates and the assets are distributed to the named beneficiaries, typically your children. The persons receiving the GRAT assets after the trust term ends are called "Remainder Beneficiaries."

Provisions to Include in Your GRAT

A number of different provisions should be reviewed with your estate planner when discussing the trust document to be prepared to implement your GRAT:

- An annuity equal to a fixed amount must be paid to you periodically, equal to a specified percentage of the net fair market value of the GRAT assets on the date that the GRAT is created. The annuity percentage must be set at the time that the GRAT document is signed. This is generally a fixed percentage, say 6 percent.
- The periodic annuity can be paid either monthly, quarterly, or annually. The frequency must be decided at the time that the GRAT document is signed.
- The annuity payment for each tax year must be paid to you no later than by April 15 of the following year.
- The number of years (the fixed term) for which you will receive the annuity from the GRAT must be specified.
- If you do not survive the fixed term of the GRAT, the GRAT document should provide that the trust assets will be paid back to (and hence taxable in) your estate. An alternative with the same tax consequences is to provide that if you do not survive the fixed term of the GRAT, you will have a general power of appointment to state in your will to whom the GRAT assets will be distributed.
- The GRAT must explicitly prohibit additional contributions to the GRAT. The rules for a GRUT (to be discussed) are different.
- The GRAT must prohibit "commutation." Commutation is a prepayment made to you by the trust to terminate the trust at an earlier date than the fixed term established initially for the GRAT.
- The GRAT must prohibit payments to anyone other than you during the fixed term of the GRAT.
- The GRAT should state that your intention is to create a "qualified annuity interest" under applicable tax laws.
- The GRAT should explicitly state that it is irrevocable (cannot be changed once formed).

- The GRAT document must designate the persons who will receive the GRAT property after the fixed term of the trust. GRATs commonly provide for the property to be distributed to your children in equal shares, outright, and free of any trust (or to the children's descendants in the event that a child predeceases). In the latter situation, since minors could become involved, the trust document, as a precautionary measure, should provide that property would continue to be held in trust for your descendants, rather than passing outright where such descendants are less than a certain age (e.g., 35).

- The trust document must specify which state law will govern the GRAT.

- You should select several persons (and alternates in the event that the named persons cannot act) to act as trustees of the GRAT. Although you could serve as a co-trustee of your own GRAT, it is preferable not to do this. The co-trustees of the GRAT are responsible for managing the GRAT property (e.g., the securities portfolio) including the investment of the GRAT property.

Tax Consequences of a GRAT

Since a GRAT is an independent entity for tax purposes, you will have to obtain a tax identification number for the trust. Also, discuss any income tax filing requirements with your accountant. A gift tax return will be required.

Gift Tax in a GRAT

The gift you make to your children or other heirs through a GRAT cannot be protected by the $10,000 gift tax annual exclusion, which does not apply to a gift in a trust, such as a GRAT. The Crummey power technique discussed in several prior chapters, including Chapter 8, cannot be used since it would conflict with the required annuity payment that must be made from the GRAT. Your gifts to a GRAT, however, can avoid current gift tax by the use of your unified credit (presently sufficient to exempt asset transfers of $600,000). In fact, many GRAT arrangements are structured intentionally to avoid exceeding your (and perhaps your spouse's) remaining unified credits. There is, however, nothing inherently wrong with establishing a GRAT with sufficient assets to trigger a gift tax. The funds to pay the gift tax are removed from your estate, thus providing a savings when current lifetime taxable gifts are made compared with taxable transfers by your estate following your death.

CAUTION: You could manipulate the various options in structuring your GRAT so that your retained interest constitutes 100 percent of the value of the GRAT. This would mean that the remainder interest to the beneficiaries would have a zero value. This is called a "zeroed-out GRAT." The IRS has not looked favorably on this technique so that it is preferable to have some value to the remainder interest. If you have previously used up your entire unified credit, this value will result in a current gift tax cost.

Estate Tax Consequences of Creating a GRAT

If you survive the fixed term selected for the GRAT, the GRAT property should pass to the persons designated by you in the GRAT document without further gift or estate tax consequences. However, if you do not survive the fixed term of the GRAT, a portion or all of the GRAT property will be included in your estate for estate tax purposes. In general, it appears that the portion of the GRAT property that would be included in the estate in the event you died during the fixed term of the GRAT would be that portion of the GRAT principal required to generate the annuity based on the applicable federal rate in effect at the time of your death. Thus, depending on the facts, it is possible that only a portion of the GRAT property will be included in your estate. The IRS, however, may not accept this position. Because of this, discuss with your estate planner whether your GRAT document should include language providing that only the "includable portion" of the GRAT property will be paid over to your estate if you die before the GRAT term ends. If the IRS accepts this argument, it could prevent the inclusion of more of the GRAT property than absolutely required in your estate.

If the GRAT is included in your taxable estate, it will increase your estate tax. However, the GRAT document may not require that the assets actually be paid to your estate. Thus, your probate assets passing under your will could have to bear the tax cost created by the GRAT assets passing to the beneficiaries specified under the GRAT. This could create significant problems. Be certain to have your will reviewed, and in particular the tax allocation clause of the will (which addresses who pays the estate tax).

Generation-Skipping Transfer (GST) Tax and Your GRAT

If GRAT property is transferred to grandchildren (or more remote descendants), a generation-skipping transfer (GST) tax may also be payable. This tax is confiscatory in nature once the exclusions provided for are exhausted. Because the generation-skipping transfer tax is extremely costly, a GRAT is generally used for transfers intended for children rather than grandchildren (see Chapter 8).

Income Tax Consequences of a GRAT

A GRAT is planned to be a grantor trust based on terms included in the trust document. If you, as the donor, retained the power to reacquire the trust assets (corpus) by substituting assets of an equivalent value, all of the trust's income would be taxed directly to the donor. The advantages of having the trust taxed as a grantor trust are several. First, all income earned by the GRAT, even amounts in excess of the annuity payout, will be taxed to you as the donor. This is advantageous because by paying the income tax due, especially on income in excess of what you received, you as the donor are reducing your estate and enhancing the wealth of the remainder beneficiaries.

> **CAUTION:** The IRS has not been pleased with the preceding result. The IRS position appears to be that the payment of income tax on income retained in the trust for the remainder beneficiaries will constitute an additional gift for gift tax purposes. Be certain to discuss developments in this area with your tax adviser.

Second, if the income of the GRAT were not sufficient to meet the required payout to the donor, GRAT assets could be distributed in kind without realization of taxable gain. Lastly, to the extent the GRAT has low basis assets, the donor, prior to the expiration of the five-year term, can repurchase these assets at their fair market value. Because the donor is the income tax owner of the GRAT, the sale by the GRAT to the donor should not be deemed to be a taxable event. As a result there will be no capital gain to the GRAT or to the donor. The remainder beneficiaries, on expiration of the five-year term, will receive the then principal of the GRAT unencumbered by the low basis property.

GRANTOR RETAINED UNITRUST (GRUT)

Most of the rules governing the use of a grantor retained unitrust (GRUT) are the same as those governing a GRAT. This section will discuss the few differences between these closely related trusts, and how to decide which of these trusts is best for you.

Differences between a GRAT and a GRUT

In a GRUT, the periodic payment is determined by multiplying a set percentage by the annual value of the trust's assets. This contrasts with a GRAT where the percentage is applied to the value of the assets once, on formation.

The trustee of a GRUT can accept the contribution of additional assets to the trust after it is formed. The trustee of a GRAT is specifically prohibited from accepting additional contributions.

Choosing between a GRAT and a GRUT

The following pointers will help you discuss with your tax adviser which of the two trusts, GRAT or GRUT, will be preferable in your particular situation. You must select one approach exclusively for any trust. The different approaches cannot be combined in a single trust:

- If the assets in the trust are readily valued, such as marketable securities, a GRUT is relatively simple to use. However, because a GRUT (unlike a GRAT) requires annual valuation of trust assets, if the assets are difficult to value (e.g., a closely held business interest), then using a GRUT could be quite burdensome.

- If the interest rate for the periodic payment is greater than the applicable federal rate that you must use in determining the value of the gift, a GRAT will result in a lower gift value. The calculations under a GRAT assume that each year a piece of the GRAT principal will have to be distributed back to you to meet the payment. In contrast, a GRUT will result in a greater current gift tax cost because the annual percentage is applied to each year's principal balance of the trust. If the trust principal is reduced by payments back to you as grantor in excess of the assumed earnings, each year's payments to you will decline. Hence, in a GRUT less principal will be repaid.

- If the periodic payment is set at a rate less than the applicable federal rate required by the tax laws to be used in determining the value of the gift, then the GRUT will result in a lower current gift tax cost by applying the same analysis as in the previous paragraph.

CONCLUSION

A host of different trusts can be used to plan for securities you own. This chapter has listed many of these types of trusts, and explored in more detail, the use of grantor retained annuity trusts and grantor retained unitrusts.

18 TRUSTS FOR BUSINESS ASSETS

TRUSTS AND BUSINESS ASSETS GENERALLY

Trusts have long been used with business assets. A common planning technique for many family businesses is to have trusts for children own passive business assets (e.g., costly equipment, real estate, intangible property rights such as a trade name), which are then licensed or leased to the business. This approach has frequently been used to assure some economic benefits for children not active in the business. It also serves to separate, for liability and creditor protection, passive business assets from the active operation of the business itself. More recently, tax-oriented trusts have been used to remove, in a tax-advantaged manner, closely held business interests from the estates of parents or grandparents in efforts to transfer the business to later generations.

When planning for any trusts to hold business assets, review with your tax adviser the consequences of the trust planning with your estate's ability to qualify for the estate tax deferral provisions under Code Section 6166. These provisions can enable an estate, which consists of at least 35 percent closely held business interests, to defer paying estate taxes for about 14 years. If gifts to trusts reduce your ownership of closely held business below this 35 percent threshold, this valuable tax benefit could be lost.

This chapter will discuss many different types of trusts that can be used in planning for closely held businesses. In particular, qualified subchapter S (QSST) trusts used to own stock in S corporations, and voting trusts, used to control voting interests in businesses, will be discussed in detail. Several other trusts that can be useful in planning for business interests will be noted briefly, with references to the chapters where they are discussed in greater depth.

Grantor Retained Annuity Trusts

A grantor retained annuity trust (GRAT) is often used to make gifts to your children or other heirs at a discounted gift tax cost (see Chapter 17). For closely held business interests, the GRAT is often simpler and less burdensome to use than a grantor retained unitrust (GRUT). This is because an appraisal will have to be completed each year of the business to determine the required payments to be made by a GRUT. For a GRAT, on the other hand, an appraisal is only required once when the assets are initially transferred to the trust.

Charitable Remainder Trusts for Business Assets

Charitable remainder trusts (CRTs) can be a tremendous vehicle for removing highly appreciated business assets from your estate. Properly planned, a CRT can be used to "bail out" business interests. These planning concepts have been discussed in detail in Chapter 14.

QUALIFIED SUBCHAPTER S CORPORATION TRUSTS (QSST)

Why Planning for S Corporations Remains Important

S corporations are one of the most common forms for owning small and closely held businesses. The primary reasons for this popularity are that S corporations offer the protection of limited liability associated with any properly formed and run corporation and they generally can avoid any tax at the corporate level. All of the income (and loss) of an S corporation is taxed to its shareholders. Although limited liability companies (LLCs) have probably become the business entity of choice for new business ventures, millions of businesses remain organized as S corporations. Because of the tax costs of liquidating existing S corporations, they will continue to be the most common business entity for many decades. Thus, integrating the planning for your business and estate goals remains vital.

Owners of such businesses must undertake personal planning for family members' welfare, minimization of estate taxes, protection from creditors, succession planning to pass interests to the next generation, and management of assets. This planning will often affect the stock in the business. When this occurs, and the business is an S corporation, careful consideration must be given to the special rules that apply to trusts owning such stock.

Requirements to Qualify as an S Corporation

For a corporation to qualify for these valuable benefits, it must meet a number of requirements: It cannot have more than 75 shareholders (it had been 35), it must file the required election statement with the IRS (and possibly with state tax authorities), and it can have only one class of stock. In addition, the persons who can be shareholders are quite limited. Corporations and nonresident aliens (non-United States citizens) cannot be shareholders. Only trusts which meet very specific requirements can qualify to own stock in an S corporation, although these have been broadened by recent tax changes.

Trusts That Can Own S Corporation Stock

Several types of trusts can qualify to own S corporation stock. The most commonly used has been the qualified subchapter S trust (QSST). Recent tax legislation added a new type of qualifying trust called "electing small business trust." It is likely that the QSST will remain the most commonly used trust.

New S Corporation Trusts: Electing Small Business Trusts

Electing small business trusts (ESBTs) can be shareholders of S corporations after 1996. For a trust to qualify, all of its beneficiaries must be individuals or estates (i.e., partnerships, corporations, etc., cannot be beneficiaries). Certain charities can be contingent remaindermen (i.e., the beneficiaries who receive trust income or assets if all prior beneficiaries die or cease to qualify as beneficiaries). ESBTs can provide greater flexibility than QSSTs (to be described) in that they can have many current income beneficiaries. This means several people can receive income each year from the trust. QSSTs require a separate trust for each beneficiary.

QSSTs Can Qualify to Own S Corporation Stock

Special rules can permit several types of trust to qualify to own stock in an S corporation. Trusts that meet these requirements are called qualified subchapter S trusts, or QSSTs. When properly used, trusts meeting the QSST requirements can be a very useful income, estate, and creditor protection planning technique.

EXAMPLE: Father owns 55 percent of a mortgage servicing corporation that is organized as an S corporation. He decides to start transferring stock to his children to reduce his potential federal estate taxes. He sets up a qualified S corporation trust for each of his minor children. He joins with his spouse to jointly gift $20,000 in value (based on an appraisal of the corporation) of stock to each child's trust. This approach enables him to control the use of the assets for the benefit of each child, and the stock could be insulated from both his creditors and the child's creditors.

To obtain the benefits illustrated in the example, the trust owning the stock must meet some strict requirements. The trust will generally cease being a QSST on the date any requirement is no longer met.

Many of the trusts created to qualify for the marital deduction for federal gift and estate tax purposes can also meet the requirements of a

QSST. For example, the Qualified Terminable Interest Property (Q-TIP) trust discussed in Chapter 11 can be a QSST.

Many of the typical trusts established for minor children will not qualify for QSST treatment without modification because these trusts frequently give the trustee the authority to accumulate income rather than pay it currently to the minor child. The minor child's trusts discussed in Chapter 13 are an example. The provisions of such trusts can be drafted to meet the QSST requirements, but this must be done at inception since most children's trusts are irrevocable.

A charitable remainder trust may qualify as a QSST prior to the death of the individual income beneficiary. It cannot qualify after the death of the income beneficiary since a charitable organization cannot qualify as an S corporation shareholder. For example, the unitrust and annuity trust amounts required to be distributed to comply with charitable trust laws may be less than the actual income that would have to be distributed to comply with QSST rules (see Chapter 14).

Requirements for a Trust to Qualify as a QSST

- *Election.* The income beneficiary (such as your child) must elect to be taxed as the owner of the S corporation stock for income tax purposes. This is because the income beneficiary will be taxed on his or her share of the income from the S corporation. The election must be made within 2½ months of the trust becoming a shareholder, or within 2½ months of the beginning of the first tax year of the S corporation. Where this election is not properly made, the IRS may determine that the S corporation's election is not valid. The IRS has, in some situations, reinstated the S corporation's election where it deemed the failure to comply to be inadvertent.

- *Tax Reporting.* The concept of an S corporation is that all income and tax consequences generally flow through to the individual shareholder. A trust is permitted to be a shareholder where this result is not fundamentally changed. Thus the single beneficiary of the QSST trust will be treated as if he owns the portion of the trust that consists of stock in the S corporation. The effect of the election is to treat the beneficiary as the deemed owner of the S corporation stock. This means that the S corporation's income allocable to the shares of stock owned by the QSST flow directly to the beneficiary as if he were the shareholder. The trustee can simply attach a copy of the tax form it receives from the S corporation (Form 1120-S, Schedule K-1) to the tax form which the trustee issues to the beneficiary reporting his income (Form 1041, Schedule K-1).

- *Required Income Distributions.* During the life of the current income beneficiary (a child in the preceding example) the trust's income must be required by the terms of the trust agreement to be distributed to the beneficiary. This beneficiary must be a person who is qualified to be a shareholder of an S corporation (a nonresident alien cannot qualify). This means the trustee cannot have the power to sprinkle trust income to different beneficiaries. Where a trust holds assets other than stock in an S corporation, this requirement need only be applied to the income generated by the S corporation stock owned by the trust.

EXAMPLE: Father sets up a trust for the benefit of his minor child, Junior. Father makes gifts of two assets to the trust: (1) 10 shares of stock in XYZ Company, Inc., an S corporation, and (2) a certificate of deposit. The S corporation pays a dividend of $245 per share. The certificate of deposit pays $530 of interest. The trust agreement should require the distribution of the $2,450 S corporation dividend. However, the trust agreement could provide for a different treatment of the $530 of interest.

To determine the income that must be distributed, the fiduciary accounting income as calculated under the provisions of the trust agreement is used.

EXAMPLE: Assume a trust earns $100,000 of income from an S corporation, realizes a $25,000 capital gain on the sale of stock, and pays a $6,000 fee for the trustee's commission. The trust agreement requires that ordinary income be treated as income, but capital gains from the sale of assets be treated as principal (called "corpus"). If local law or the trust agreement requires that the trust commission be charged against principal, the accounting income for the trust will be $100,000 (the $25,000 capital gain, less the $6,000 commission is added to the principal of the trust). For tax purposes, the trust's income is $94,000 ($100,000 – $6,000) since the trustee commission may be deductible. Accounting income of $100,000 would have to be distributed, or required by the trust agreement to be distributed. The beneficiary, however, would be treated as taxed on the capital gains if they related to the S corporation stock. This could be capital gains realized by the S corporation and passed through to its shareholders as well as capital gains realized by the trust on the sale of some of its S corporation stock.

If the trust agreement contradicts state law, then the terms of the trust agreement may be overlooked in certain circumstances when making the calculation, but consult with an attorney specializing in trust and state law.

NOTE: Where the trust agreement requires that ordinary dividends (rather than extraordinary stock dividends) be charged to principal (rather than income) or capital gains be charged to income (rather than principal), the calculation of income may be completed assuming the opposite.

Where an S corporation doesn't distribute all of its income, the trust will not be required to distribute more than the income that it received.

EXAMPLE: XYZ Company, Inc., earned $450 per share but only distributed $245 per share. The Joe Junior Qualified S Corporation Trust, which owns 10 shares, will have to report $4,500 in income. However, it will not be required to distribute to the beneficiary more than $2,450. The trust's share of the $2,050 of undistributed XYZ Company, Inc., S corporation income [$4,500 – $2,450] need not be distributed.

This distribution requirement will not necessarily destroy the trust's status as a QSST where the trust requires that all income be distributed, but the trustee simply fails to do so. Where the trust agreement does not require that all income be distributed, it is sufficient that local law requires it.

- *Beneficiaries.* There can only be one beneficiary. Any distributions of trust assets (corpus) during the life of the current income beneficiary can only be made to that one beneficiary. This requirement, however, does not imply that any amount of the trust's assets must actually be distributed. Where distributions of trust assets occur, they can be made in the discretion of the trustee, so long as the distributions can only be to the income beneficiary. If you set up a trust for the benefit of your spouse, you could give the trustee the right, in the trustee's sole discretion, to distribute trust assets where necessary to maintain the health of your spouse. A trust will meet this requirement even if the trust agreement requires that all of the assets be distributed when a certain event occurs (e.g., the child beneficiary reaches age 35).

- *End of Required Distributions.* The current income beneficiary's income interest in the trust must end at the earlier of his or her death, or the termination of the trust. The trust can, however, end at an earlier date (e.g., when your child who is the beneficiary reaches age 30).

- *Distribution on Termination of QSST.* If the trust ends during the current income beneficiary's life, the trust assets must all be distributed to the current income beneficiary.

If the trust was not properly formed, it may be possible for the trust agreement to be corrected (reformed) by a court or by the consent of the beneficiaries, to meet this requirement.

Grantor Trusts Owning S Corporation Stock

Grantor trusts may qualify to own stock in an S corporation. If you set up a trust and retain certain reversionary rights, the trust income is taxable fully to you. An example is the living trust described in Chapter 10. For a discussion of other types of grantor trust, see Chapter 4. All grantor trusts will not qualify to hold S corporation stock. Therefore, have your estate planner carefully review any trust agreement before transferring S corporation stock to that trust.

Trusts That Cannot Own S Corporation Stock

Many common trusts cannot own stock in an S corporation. If stock in an S corporation is transferred to a nonqualifying trust, the S corporation could lose its favorable tax status as an S corporation. This means it could be taxed as a C corporation with income subject to corporate taxes and then individual taxes—a double tax bite that an S corporation generally avoids. The typical bypass trust used in many estate plans (Chapter 7) can create serious problems if the decedent owned shares in an S corporation. A trust to which S corporation stock is transferred pursuant to the terms of a will can only be an S corporation shareholder for two years (60 days under old law), or the S corporation status will be lost.

S corporations will remain a common business entity for decades. Planning trusts to avoid adverse tax consequences for your S corporation stock is a vital part of any estate, business, and financial plan.

VOTING TRUSTS

What Is a Voting Trust?

A voting trust is a legal arrangement, in the form of a trust, where shareholders join together to have their stock voted by a designated person who is the trustee of the voting trust. A voting trust provides the trustee an irrevocable right to vote stock in a corporation for a designated period, 10 years being common. A trust that gives the trustee the right to sell stock, or receive dividends paid on the stock is not a voting trust. Instead, such a trust would be one of the other types of trust discussed in this book because the purpose of a voting trust is merely to vote stock—it is not intended to do more. In fact, depending on the laws in your state, it may be illegal for it to do more.

When Should You Consider Using a Voting Trust?

There are many reasons you may benefit from using a voting trust as varied as the relationships in a family or other closely held business. Voting trusts are not restricted to closely held businesses; they can be used with corporations of any size. Large and even publicly traded corporations use voting trust arrangements for holding stock of subsidiary or parent corporations, and in certain joint venture transactions. However, the focus of this chapter is how small and closely held businesses can benefit from voting trust arrangements.

Certain shareholders may prefer not to be actively involved in business matters and thus appreciate the opportunity to relieve themselves of voting and related burdens. Certain shareholders may band together and vote their shares as a block to exert more influence. The voting trust can provide greater certainty for a longer period. Perhaps several shareholders in a closely held business are geographically distant from the corporate head-quarters. They may view a voting trust arrangement as an efficient method to address this problem. A promoter may structure an investment transaction and could use a voting trust arrangement to control the votes of the investors. Where a developer enters into a joint venture, organized as a corporation, with a group of investors, the investors may wish to pool their votes in a voting trust arrangement to protect their interests vis-à-vis the developer.

If a parent is considering a voting trust arrangement for making gifts of stock to children and grandchildren, a careful review of the estate tax rules is essential. A parent's retaining voting control through a voting trust arrangement could cause the inclusion of the stock in the parent's estate for estate tax purposes.

Another common situation that could benefit from a voting trust arrangement is divorce. Voting trusts are an ideal method to permit the ex-spouse who is active in a business to continue to control it, while the other ex-spouse can protect his or her interest in the divorce settlement agreement by actually owning stock in the business.

EXAMPLE: Ex-wife owns 60 percent of a design business. Ex-husband is awarded 25 percent of the value of the business as part of the equitable distribution divorce settlement negotiations. Ex-wife has resigned herself to transfer to the ex-husband the amount necessary to resolve the divorce; if she actually transferred 25 percent of the stock to ex-husband, however, she would lose control of the business. Worse yet, she would have put a sizable portion of the stock into the hands of someone who may be adverse to the business and other shareholders. The solution could be to give the ex-husband the 25 percent of the stock, but require that his shares be transferred to a voting trust controlled by the ex-wife. To fully protect the ex-husband's interests, however, he should also negotiate a shareholders' agreement that has reasonable restrictions on how much the ex-wife and other shareholders can withdraw as salary or benefits. Without this additional protection, there may be no money left in the corporation for distribution as dividends on the stock.

In one case, a court refused to permit an ex-spouse to revoke a voting trust agreement. The court reasoned that since the voting trust arrangement for a closely held business was bargained for at arm's length and was an integral part of the divorce settlement agreement, the ex-spouse should not be able to change it.

Other approaches may be used instead of a voting trust. For example, shareholders could sign a proxy giving a designated person a right to vote their shares. Alternatively, a shareholders' agreement among all of the shareholders of the corporation could provide rules for governing the corporation's operations. It could contain requirements that certain decisions be made by more than a 50 percent or more than a 75 percent vote of the shareholders. The voting trust, however, can be a more flexible and fluid arrangement giving the trustees greater latitude to respond to unforeseen situations.

How Does a Voting Trust Work?

Where a voting trust is going to be used, several steps are necessary:

STEP 1. The shareholders who will participate in the voting trust arrangement must retain a lawyer to review the estate tax inclusion issues and if they are acceptable, to then prepare a voting trust agreement.

STEP 2. The corporation must approve the voting trust agreement. This could require an action of the shareholders or board of directors, depending on the terms in the other legal documentation of a corporation. The simplest approach for a closely held business, which may be acceptable under your state's laws, is to use a single document called a "Unanimous Written Consent of All Shareholders and All Directors." Where there is only a handful of shareholders and directors, having them all sign, even if not required by law, is a simple process and assures that everyone is in agreement. Be certain to attach a copy of the voting trust agreement to the minutes and place it in the corporate kit (typically a ring binder embossed with the corporate name and containing all official corporate documents such as a certified copy of the certificate of incorporation used to form the corporation, minutes, banking resolutions, unissued stock certificates, and the stock transfer ledger, which is the record of all past and current shareholders).

Some courts have held that a voting trust agreement is not valid unless a copy is filed with the corporation. So don't overlook this step. Be certain that this is done in the exact manner required by state law.

STEP 3. When all of the participants agree on the terms of the agreement, and a trustee is selected, the agreement should be signed by each shareholder who will participate, the trustee, and an officer of the corporation. You should even consider having the successor trustees sign the agreement now (although they could sign at a later date, if and when, they are needed to replace the initial trustee). The corporate minutes described in Step 2 are a prerequisite to an officer of the corporation being able to sign the trust.

STEP 4. Each shareholder who has joined in the voting trust arrangement then transfers his or her stock certificates to the corporation, which then transfers the stock to the trustee of the voting trust.

CAUTION: If the stock certificates are merely handed to the trustee and not transferred officially on the corporation's books, the shareholders may not be prevented from voting their shares of stock.

Your rights as a holder of a voting trust certificate are governed by the provisions of the voting trust agreement and any applicable local laws. You will generally be required to follow any actions taken by the voting trustee.

STEP 5.   The trustee issues voting trust certificates (see the sample in the "For Your Notebook" section of this chapter) to each shareholder.

What Should Be Included in Your Voting Trust Agreement?

The agreement, as illustrated in the "For Your Notebook" section of this chapter, is quite simple and straightforward. It should indicate the name of the trustee and the shareholders who are participating. Be sure to have your lawyer review applicable state law and the corporation's shareholders' agreement for any additional requirements, or restrictions, that could affect the voting trust agreement. The length of time the voting trust will last should be specified. Be certain that your lawyer checks the state law that specifies how long a voting trust may last. You can have yours last any time period permitted by law.

The fact that all income will be distributed by the corporation directly to the shareholders, and not retained by the trustee, should be clarified.

The responsibilities, duties, powers, and rights of the trustee must be specified in the trust agreement.

Be certain that the voting trust agreement gives you the right, at any reasonable time, to obtain a copy of the names and addresses of all shareholders participating in the voting trust (i.e., the voting trust certificate holders) and to inspect the record and books of the corporation.

If the participating shareholders are supposed to have the right to change or revoke the voting trust, the agreement should say so. For example, it might say that if 75 percent or more of the participating shareholders vote to terminate the voting trust arrangement, they can. In other cases, such as where a parent is giving stock to a child, the voting trust agreement will probably be made irrevocable.

If the trustee is to be compensated, the exact arrangements should be spelled out in the agreement.

How a Voting Trust Affects Other Trust Planning

You should be able to have your will, or perhaps even a revocable living trust, transfer your voting trust certificates and the stock to a testamentary trust on your death.

Voting trusts are a flexible and useful technique for controlling the voting interests in a closely held business without affecting the economics of the transactions. They can be used in estate planning, financial planning (e.g., where someone unable to manage his business turns control over to another person), and in divorce planning.

CONCLUSION

There are many different types of trusts that can be used, depending on the circumstances and your objectives, in planning for business interests. This chapter has analyzed several of these trusts, and provided references to trusts in other chapters that can also be used in business planning. In addition to investigating tax concerns with your tax planner, be certain that the business's attorney, and other owners, have approved to the extent required, any transaction you are contemplating.

For Your Notebook

SAMPLE VOTING TRUST AGREEMENT

[DO NOT USE THIS AS A TRUST AGREEMENT. FOR DISCUSSION WITH YOUR LAWYER ONLY.]

XYZ CORPORATION VOTING TRUST AGREEMENT

VOTING TRUST AGREEMENT dated the 1st day of January, 1999, between and among XYZ CORPORATION, INC., a STATE NAME corporation doing business at CORPORATION'S AD-DRESS (the "Corporation"); FATHER'S NAME, who resides at 123 West Street, CITY NAME, STATE NAME ("Father"); CHILD-1 NAME, who resides at CHILD-1 ADDRESS, ("CHILD-1 NAME"); and CHILD-2 NAME, who resides at CHILD-2 ADDRESS ("CHILD-2 NAME") (collec-tively CHILD-1 NAME and CHILD-2 NAME are referred to as the "Shareholders"); and TRUSTEE NAME, who resides at TRUSTEE ADDRESS, and his successors in the trust (the "Trustees").

WHEREAS, in order to secure continuity and stability of policy and management of the Cor-poration, the certain Shareholders deem it advisable to deposit all of their shares of the Corpora-tion's capital stock ("Shares") with the Trustee; and

WHEREAS, the Trustee has consented to act under this Agreement for the purposes herein provided;

IT IS, THEREFORE, AGREED:

Agreement

Copies of this Agreement shall be filed in the office of the Corporation and shall be open to the inspection of the Shareholders during business hours. All Voting Trust Certificates issued as hereinafter provided shall be issued and held subject to the terms of this Agreement. Every Share-holder entitled to receive Voting Trust Certificates representing shares of capital stock, their transferees and assigns, upon accepting the Voting Trust Certificates issued hereunder, shall be bound by the provisions of this Agreement for a period of Ten (10) years from the date of this Agreement.

NOTE: While 10 years is a common length for a voting trust arrangement, shorter periods can be used. Be certain to inquire of the lawyer drafting the document as to whether your state has any restrictions on the term of a voting trust (or any fil-ing requirements which should be complied with).

Transfer of Stock

The Shareholders, simultaneously with the execution of this Agreement, shall assign and de-liver all of their Shares of capital stock to the Trustees, to be held by the Trustees subject to the terms of this Agreement. At the execution of this Agreement, the following Shares shall be so transferred:

Shareholder	Number of Shares	Outstanding Stock
CHILD-1 NAME	125.0	10%
CHILD-2 NAME	125.0	10%

NOTE: The more children and other recipients of a gift of stock the more useful a voting trust will become as a method of securely controlling the voting interests in a corporation.

The Trustee shall immediately cause the stock to be transferred to himself, as Trustee, on the books of the Corporation, and shall endorse all certificates held by them hereunder with the following legend:

> "This certificate is held subject to a Voting Trust Agreement dated the 1st day of January, 1999, a copy of which is in the possession of TRUSTEE NAME, as Trustee, and in the office of the Corporation."

NOTE: A "legend" is simply an inscription which is typed or stamped on the face of a stock certificate. The purpose is to alert any potential buyer of the stock as to the restrictions involved. This is similar to the step which is almost always taken in a closely held business of stamping a legend on each stock certificate issued stating that the transfer of the shares is subject to restriction under a particular shareholders' agreement.

Voting Trust Certificates

Upon receipt by the Trustee of the certificates for shares of capital stock and the transfer of the same into the names of the Trustee, the Trustee shall issue and deliver to the Shareholders Voting Trust Certificates for the shares so deposited. The Voting Trust Certificates shall be in the following form:

NO._____   _____ Shares

XYZ CORPORATION, INC.
a STATE NAME Corporation

VOTING TRUST CERTIFICATE FOR S CORPORATION STOCK

This certifies that _____ is entitled to all the benefits arising from the deposit with the Trustee under the Voting Trust Agreement dated January 1, 1999, of certificates for _____ (_____) shares of the capital stock of **XYZ CORPORATION INC.**, a STATE NAME corporation, in such Trust Agreement and subject to the terms thereof.

Stock certificates for the number of shares of capital stock represented by this certificate, or the net proceeds in cash or property of such shares, shall be due and deliverable hereunder upon the termination of such Trust Agreement as provided therein.

This certificate shall not be valid for any purpose until duly signed by the Trustee.

IN WITNESS WHEREOF, the Trustee has signed this certificate on January 1, 1999.

By: _____
     TRUSTEE NAME, Trustee

Dividends; Distributions; Tax Attributes

A. Each Shareholder shall be entitled to receive, and shall receive, payments from the Trustee of all cash dividends or other distributions made by the Corporation with respect to the stock of the Corporation held by the Trustee hereunder.

B. Any and all tax benefits each Shareholder shall recognize shall be the same benefits which would be recognized had that Shareholder held said Shares directly.

NOTE: These requirements must be met to protect the tax status of the corporation as an S corporation. Where the stock is of a C corporation (i.e., a non-S corporation), these requirements would not have to be adhered to unless some requirement existed under state law.

Voting

At all meetings of Shareholders of the Corporation, and in all proceedings affecting the Corporation, the Trustee shall vote the shares transferred to him hereunder in such manner as he may determine, in his sole and absolute discretion.

Liability of the Trustee

The Trustee shall not be liable for the consequence of any vote cast in good faith by him.

Dissolution of the Corporation

In the event of the dissolution or total or partial liquidation of the Corporation, whether voluntary or involuntary, the Trustee shall receive the monies, securities, rights or property to which the holders of the capital stock of the Corporation deposited hereunder are entitled, and shall distribute the same among the registered holders of Voting Trust Certificates in proportion to their interests, as shown by the books of the Trustee, or the Trustee may, in his discretion, deposit such monies, securities, rights or property with any bank or title and trust company doing business in the state of STATE NAME, with the authority and instructions to distribute the same as provided above, and upon such deposit all further obligations and liabilities of the Trustee in respect to such monies, securities, rights or property so deposited shall cease.

Trustee

A. The Trustee shall have the right at any time hereafter to designate a successor Trustee to act upon the death or resignation of a Trustee. Such designated successor Trustee shall not be required at the time of his succession to be a Shareholder of the corporation, and no such succession shall give any such successor Trustee any rights to require shares in the Corporation. Such designation may be made by filing in the principal office of the Corporation, an appointment in writing of such successor Trustee duly executed and acknowledged. Any such designation of a successor Trustee may be revoked in whole or in part by the Trustee at any time, without notice to any person, by filing a notice of revocation in the same form as the appointment hereinabove provided for and in the same place. Upon the death or resignation of the Trustee, the designated successor Trustee shall become successor Trustee hereunder; and upon the death or resignation of a Trustee without having appointed a successor Trustee, a successor Trustee shall be designated by a majority of the Shareholders party to this Agreement at a meeting called for that purpose. The rights, powers and privileges of the Trustee named hereunder shall be possessed by the successor Trustee with the same effect as though such successor had originally been a party to this Agreement. The word "Trustee" as used in this Agreement means the Trustee or any successor Trustee acting hereunder.

B. In the event of the unwillingness or inability of TRUSTEE NAME to serve as Trustee, then SUCCESSOR TRUSTEE NO. 1 shall serve as successor Trustee ("Successor Trustee").

C. In the event of the death, disability, inability or unwillingness of both the Trustee and Successor Trustee to act hereunder, without the Trustee or Successor Trustee having appointed a further successor Trustee, then SUCCESSOR TRUSTEE NO. 2, shall serve as Trustee.

Term

A. This Agreement shall continue in full force and effect until the earlier of the following events:

1. The 10th anniversary date of this Agreement.

2. The execution and acknowledgment by the Trustee hereunder of a document of termination duly filed in the office of the Corporation.

3. 90 days following the final distribution from the Corporation of its remaining assets in dissolution or complete liquidation of the Corporation.

4. As required under the laws of the State of STATE NAME.

B. Upon termination of this Agreement, the title and possession of each Share of stock of the Corporation which was delivered to this Trust shall be delivered back to its beneficial owners.

Compensation of Trustees

Where TRUSTEE NAME shall serve as Trustee hereunder he shall serve as Trustee without compensation for such services. Any successor Trustee shall be permitted to charge the customary fees for hourly services, or for similar services, in the State of STATE NAME for rendering the services hereunder as Trustee. Any Trustee shall have the right to incur and pay reasonable expenses and charges as may be necessary for carrying this Agreement into effect. Any such fees, charges or expenses shall be reimbursed to the Trustee by the Shareholders who are party hereto shall be jointly and severally liable to reimburse same. In no event may any expense be charged against this Trust.

Notice

Any notice to or communication with any party to this Agreement shall be deemed sufficiently given or made if mailed by registered or certified mail addressed to the holder of Voting Trust Certificate, or to the Trustee, at the address appearing above, unless Notice in accordance with this Section is given of a new address. For any Notice to be effective, a copy of such Notice must also be given to the Corporation, and to: CORPORATION'S LAWYER'S NAME, who does business at CORPORATION'S LAWYER'S ADDRESS.

Modification

The Trustee is authorized, and is hereby granted by each Shareholder and the Corporation an irrevocable power of attorney, to make any modification to this Agreement necessary to assure the continued compliance of this Agreement with any requirements necessary to maintain the Corporation's status as an S Corporation and to assure that all requirements of Internal Revenue Code of 1986 Section 1361(c)(2)(A)(iv), as amended, and Treasury Regulation Section 1.1361-1A(h)(3)(ii), as amended, shall be complied with.

NOTE: These references are to various laws governing those permissible to be shareholders of an S corporation. The purpose is to prevent an inadvertent violation of the tax requirements for proper characterization as an S corporation.

Benefit

This Agreement shall insure to the benefit of and be binding upon the Corporation, the Shareholders, their successors and assigns, and upon the Trustees and their successors.

Counterparts

This Agreement may be executed in counterparts.

IN WITNESS WHEREOF, the parties have hereto duly executed the Agreement as of the date set forth herein.

XYZ CORPORATION, INC.

By: _____
       NAME OF PRESIDENT, President

SHAREHOLDERS JOINING VOTING TRUST:

_____

CHILD-1 NAME

_____

CHILD-2 NAME

TRUSTEE:

_____

TRUSTEE NAME

[Notary forms and witness lines omitted.]

19 TRUSTS FOR REAL ESTATE

TRUSTS FOR REAL ESTATE GENERALLY

One of the most common assets is real estate. A host of trusts can be used to hold real estate assets. The trusts and the benefits they can provide are quite varied. To be certain that you are making the right choices, you should obtain professional guidance.

Charitable Remainder Trusts

A charitable remainder trust (CRT) can be used to diversify a large investment in a real estate property while avoiding capital gains. It can generate a monthly annuity and eliminate the need for ongoing management. As you age, daily management of a residential rental property could grow increasingly difficult. If you give the property to a charitable remainder trust, the charity could sell the property without incurring capital gains, reinvest the proceeds, and pay you an annuity for life (see Chapter 14).

Grantor Retained Annuity Trusts

Grantor Retained Annuity Trusts (GRATs) can provide a method of transferring commercial real estate (or partnerships or limited liability companies owning commercial real estate) to your children or other heirs at substantially discounted gift tax costs (see Chapter 17).

Revocable Living Trusts

If you own real estate in a state other than where you reside, your heirs will probably have to go through probate in that state to transfer real estate located there. If you transfer the real estate to a revocable living trust, your heirs should be able to avoid this additional probate proceeding (see Chapter 10).

Life Insurance Trust

Since real estate is not always easily salable, many real estate owners purchase additional life insurance to assure liquidity and to avoid a forced sale (see Chapter 16).

QUALIFIED PERSONAL RESIDENCE TRUSTS (QPRTs)

What Is a QPRT and How Does It Work?

A Qualified Personal Residence Trust (QPRT) provides a mechanism to remove the value of your home or vacation home from your estate at a substantially discounted rate. With a QPRT, you, as grantor, transfer your residence to a trust, retaining a term interest (the right to live in the house for a specified number of years) and naming family members as remainder beneficiaries. QPRTs, like GRATs, GRUTs, and other estate planning techniques previously discussed, take advantage of the time value of money to dramatically reduce federal estate and gift taxation.

You transfer your residence (a principal residence, other qualifying residence or a vacation home) to a trust and reserve the sole and exclusive right to use the residence for a specified term of years. On the expiration of that term, the residence is then distributed to other family members, typically your children. The residence can be retained in a further trust for those family members at such time.

The key benefits of the QPRT technique thus include the ability to leverage your unified credit (by using the time value of money discount feature of the QPRT calculation) and remove future appreciation from the grantor's estate.

EXAMPLE: If a residence is worth $800,000, a gift of the residence could trigger an immediate gift tax (since the $800,000 gift would have used up the taxpayer's $600,000 unified credit and the $200,000 excess would trigger a current gift tax cost). Where the transfer is to a QPRT, none of this gift can qualify for the annual $10,000 gift tax exclusions. However, the discounting effect of the QPRT calculation can reduce the current value (for gift tax purposes) of the residence to $600,000 or less, thus protecting the transfer from any current tax cost.

EXAMPLE: If the residence in the preceding example appreciates to $1,400,000 at the end of the 10-year QPRT term, the entire appreciation of $600,000 ($1,400,000 – $800,000) is removed from the grantor's estate.

EXAMPLE: If the discounted QPRT value of the residence at the date of the gift (which will depend on the term of the QPRT and the applicable interest rate for the month of the transaction, and the age of the grantor) is $600,000, then assuming the grantor lives the 10-year term of the QPRT, he would have removed from his estate an asset valued at $1,400,000 at a cost of using up only his

$600,000 unified credit. Thus, $800,000 has been removed from his estate without any tax cost. Assuming a 50 percent estate tax bracket, the federal estate tax savings is $400,000. The only risk taken in this transaction is that if the grantor doesn't survive the term of the QPRT, the residence is bought back into the grantor's estate. However, since any portion of the unified credit used by the grantor is restored, the whole transaction (but for professional fees) is a wash. The downside should be negligible compared with the potential benefits—unless the grantor gets thrown out of his house at the end of the QPRT term by a disaffected remainder beneficiary!

For many taxpayers, yet a further advantage of the QPRT makes it even a more desirable planning tool. A QPRT can enable taxpayers to reduce the size of their taxable estate without the expenditure of investment assets they may need to support their retirement years.

EXAMPLE: Sam and Selma Senior have an estate consisting of $1,000,000 of securities and a principal residence, without a mortgage, valued at $750,000. Thus, their combined estate of $1,750,000 exceeds their combined unified credits by $550,000. This could result in a tax cost of $275,000. If their estate appreciates, the cost would be worse. This problem, however, could be solved in at most one year and one day with annual gifts. They have four children (each of whom is married and has three children of his or her own = 20 potential beneficiaries). Thus, the Seniors could gift $10,000 each to every child, spouse of child, and grandchild, without triggering any gift tax cost or use of their unified credits. This could total $400,000 ($20,000 × 20). In one year and one day, they could gift away $800,000, thus eliminating any potential estate tax cost. Few elderly taxpayers would be comfortable doing this. As the age of the taxpayers declines, the expected discomfort with such large gifts would grow dramatically. The QPRT offers a better option. If the residence is given to a QPRT, the value of the house could be removed from their estate at a discounted rate. Also, all future appreciation (which could only compound their tax problem) would also be removed. The key benefit—the Seniors may achieve their goals while retaining their investment portfolio (the earnings of which they live on) intact.

Personal Residence Trust (PRT)

The PRT, although similar to a QPRT, is subject to several additional restrictions. As noted, it cannot hold any asset other than the residence. A limited exception is provided if the residence is condemned or destroyed: The PRT then can hold qualified proceeds pending reinvestment if the PRT trust agreement requires reinvestment. The PRT agreement must proscribe the sale of the residence. For these reasons, a QPRT is used.

Requirements to Qualify as QPRT

The QPRT must meet a host of requirements to obtain the desired tax benefits.

Assets Excluding Cash

The only assets that the QPRT can hold are a residence (to be defined) and home insurance policies (and payments under such policies) and a modest amount of cash for upkeep. The personal residence trust (PRT) by contrast is only permitted to hold a residence (i.e., no cash).

Restrictions on Cash Held

A QPRT can hold cash only for the following:

- Funds to pay the QPRT's expenses. This can include any trust expenses, including but not limited to mortgage payments. Qualified expenses are those that have already been incurred, or that are reasonably expected to be incurred in the six months following.
- Funds to pay for improvements to the residence held by the QPRT over the next six months.
- Condemnation proceeds or proceeds from insurance paid for the damage or destruction of the residence (and any earnings on those proceeds) may be held for two years from the date of the event (condemnation or destruction) if the trustee intends to reinvest the proceeds.
- Upon formation, the QPRT can also hold funds to purchase a new residence in the next three months. However, the QPRT agreement must prohibit the gift of additional funds to the trust until a contract to purchase a residence exists. Cash funds in excess of those permitted by the regulations must be distributed quarterly to the grantor, and on the termination of the QPRT.

Residence

The property contributed to the QPRT must be a qualified residence. These include a principal residence, vacation home, or even a fractional interest in a principal residence. A key concept is that the property must be available for the grantor's use as a residence. Interests in a cooperative apartment can also qualify. The IRS has permitted interests in a cooperative apartment to qualify even where the cooperative board of directors refused to give permission to the grantor to make the transfer. The definition of vacation home provides that if the personal use of the property exceeds the greater of 14 days or 10 percent of the days the property is rented, it is classified as a residence. Any particular QPRT can only hold a single residence, used by the grantor, for the entire term of the QPRT. If the qualifying residence held by the QPRT is sold, another qualifying replacement residence must be acquired within two years. If the qualifying residence held by the QPRT is damaged or destroyed, it must be repaired or replaced within two years.

Number of QPRTs

A grantor may not have interests in more than two QPRTs.

Grantor Must Survive Trust Term

Another important characteristic of the QPRT is that the grantor must survive the retained term of years for the residence not to be taxed in the grantor's estate. If the grantor does not survive, then the residence is taxed in the grantor's estate at its then fair market value, thereby rendering this estate-planning technique unsuccessful. As a result, it is generally recommended that the trust contain a provision that if the grantor dies during the term of his or her retained interest that the property revert to the grantor's estate. Having such a provision in the trust permits a further discount on the value of the gift ultimately going to the grantor's family members (i.e., the remainder interest). The rationale for the discount is that there is a possibility that the remaindermen will never receive the property. The value of this reversion is based on the age of the grantor and the use of actuarial tables to determine the likelihood of the grantor's death during the retained term of years.

QPRT Distribution Requirements

During the term of the QPRT, the trust agreement must prohibit the trustees from making income or principal distributions to any person other than the grantor. The only exception is that on trust termination, distributions can be made to the remainder beneficiaries instead of to the grantor. Income earned by the QPRT must be distributed to the grantor not less frequently than annually. This distribution must be made mandatory by the QPRT agreement.

Qualified Annuity Trust (QAT) in Event of Trust Failure

The trust agreement must also require that if the trust fails to qualify as a QPRT, the corpus (assets of the trust) will be distributed in one of two prescribed manners. This requirement further highlights the underlying purpose of a QPRT—to hold a residence. One of the options available in this instance is for the QPRT to be converted into a trust in which the grantor has a "qualified annuity interest," or a qualified annuity trust (QAT).

Tax Planning and QPRTs

A primary benefit of making a gift of real estate is that any appreciation on the gift following the date of transfer will avoid gift and estate taxation. In most QPRT planning situations, the gift consummated to the QPRT is structured (e.g., through structuring of the term of the trust) so that no current gift taxation on the transfer should occur. This is accomplished by making a gift that would be covered by the grantor's remaining unified credit (presently $600,000). When the unified credit of the grantor (and the grantor's spouse, if applicable) is reduced to zero, the grantor will have to pay gift taxes from 37 percent to more than 55 percent to establish a QPRT.

From a gift tax perspective, by setting up a QPRT, the grantor has still transferred the ultimate ownership of his or her residence to the children (or other family members), even if the children (or other heirs) must wait to actually obtain possession. Thus, the grantor has made a gift that is currently subject to gift tax. However, because the children do not benefit from the transfer for 10 years (or any other period of years until the trust terminates), the value of the gift cannot be measured by the current value of the house.

Where a house is transferred to a QPRT, the tax basis of the house in the hands of the trust and the remainder beneficiaries is the carryover basis of the property in the hands of the grantor (subject to adjustments for various items, such as possible improvements, etc.). Thus, by transferring a house to a QPRT, the donor's ability to step up his or her tax basis in the property on death is lost. However, a possible exception to this exists where the grantor repurchases the house from the QPRT before the termination of the trust and replaces it with high basis (i.e., basis approximating fair value) property (cash is the simplest) property. The IRS, however, has stated that it will not accept a QPRT with this provision. Therefore, if your house has appreciated substantially, you must use the estate tax benefits against the house.

MASSACHUSETTS REALTY TRUSTS

Throughout this book, great effort has been made to illustrate how diverse and flexible a planning tool trusts can be. Although Massachusetts realty trusts have limited applicability, they further demonstrate the tremendous variety of trusts and why it is wise to consult with a lawyer to learn the many options that may be available to you. The simple trusts most often discussed in trade books and financial literature do little justice to this complex and valuable topic.

What Is a Massachusetts Land Trust?

When structuring the ownership of real estate purchased in Massachusetts, a common approach is to use a Massachusetts land or realty trust as the named owner. In a Massachusetts realty trust, the trust holds nominal title (in name only) to the real estate for the beneficial owners (you and other investors). Secrecy is an important benefit. These trusts are frequently used to keep confidential the names of the actual owners of property. If you purchase real estate in your name (i.e., as the direct owner), your name will appear in the public records. However, with a Massachusetts realty trust, your name won't appear on the deed, and you don't have to file a schedule of the trust beneficiaries with the county registry of deeds. Any third-party buyer, lender, or other person, can rely on a certificate of the trustees that they have the requisite authority to act for the trust and its beneficiaries (i.e., the real property owners).

Using a Massachusetts realty trust has economic advantages as well. With this trust, you can avoid the payment of deed stamps on transferring the property by merely transferring beneficial interests in the trust to the new owners. This can provide a substantial savings.

Finally, where the owners anticipate frequent transfers of property, the Massachusetts realty trust can be a convenient mechanism since it is much easier to assign trust interests than to change the property deed. If a partnership with a non-Massachusetts corporate general partner desired to transfer Massachusetts real property, it would have to prove that it had authority to conduct business in Massachusetts and that the necessary corporate actions (a vote of directors etc., depending on the legal documents for the trust) were completed.

Problems Presented by Massachusetts Land Trust

There are several problems to watch for when setting up and operating a Massachusetts realty trust. The land trust offers no liability protection for the beneficiaries. They direct the trustees of the trust, so they can be held personally liable for any damages. This is critical because some investors mistakenly believe that the use of the trust, or its anonymity limits their liability. It doesn't. The trust is merely a nominee trust, so the beneficiary, and not the trustee is likely to be liable.

There is another important shortcoming that can surprise real estate investors reviewing their estate plans. First, a little background. You will usually be taxed and subject to probate in the state where you live when you die (in legal jargon, your domicile). In addition, many states will subject you to tax and probate if you own real estate within their borders. This is one reason many of the trusts described in this book are used—to avoid probate in states other than the state in which you live (called ancillary probate). Where you own an interest in a trust (corporation or partnership) that owns the property, you will own intangible property (trust interest, partnership interest, or stock in the corporation), not real estate. This is thus an effective planning technique to avoid tax and probate in a particular state.

While many investors may initially expect that transferring their interests in Massachusetts real estate to a Massachusetts realty trust will prevent taxation and probate, this benefit is not clear. The estates of non-Massachusetts domiciliary will probably be taxable on their interests in Massachusetts real estate owned through a Massachusetts realty trust. However, they would not be taxed on interests in a partnership owning Massachusetts realty because the partnership interest is personal property, not subject to tax.

Another potential problem relates to the income tax status of the Massachusetts realty trust. It is not certain that the trust will avoid being taxed. Several steps, however, may help the trust avoid tax problems. The trustees should not have any powers other than those specifically granted to them by the beneficiaries. It is permissible for a trustee to also be a beneficiary.

Don't open bank accounts in the trust's name. The trust agreement should not give the trustee power to use the funds from the property. Disbursements and receipts should not be handled by the trustees. The trust should not engage in any activity other than the holding of legal title to the property. The trust agreement should include this limitation. If any activity is conducted to manage the real estate, consider having an independent management company do it. Finally, the financial and tax records should be maintained in the name of the beneficiaries and not in the name of either the trust or the trustees.

Required Documents

The trust agreement is recorded with the registry of deeds for the county where the property is located. It should include the names of the trustees, but should not include the schedule of beneficiaries. If it did, the benefit of keeping the identity of the beneficiaries confidential would be lost. The trustees should maintain a signed schedule of beneficiaries that is updated to reflect changes. To protect anonymity, the trust agreement should explicitly authorize third parties (e.g., banks, management companies, insurance companies) to deal directly with the trustee. It is best to have at least two trustees. When one trustee wants to resign and a replacement needs to be appointed, the remaining trustee can authorize the necessary acts and thus avoid disclosing the names of the beneficiaries. The trustees should also be certain that the schedule of beneficial interests executed by the beneficiaries contains a "hold harmless" clause to protect them from claims.

Ancillary Tax Considerations

Many advisers file "inactive" Massachusetts and federal trust tax returns. Since a land trust is a mere nominee, providing no insulation from liability, it is common for the ultimate owners to organize as a limited partnership or occasionally as an S corporation (but that creates its own unique tax problems for real estate) which in turn owns the trust interests. This decision can best be reached with your tax and legal advisers who assist you in setting up the trust.

A Massachusetts realty trust has limited applicability, but where it can be used it can provide important financial, confidentiality, and other benefits that make it a valuable tool.

CONCLUSION

Numerous trusts can be useful in planning for your real estate. Proper trust planning can save taxes, minimize liability risks, provide for succession of management, and help meet other important objectives.

20 TRUSTS FOR PENSIONS AND EMPLOYEE BENEFITS

TRUSTS AND PENSION ASSETS GENERALLY

Pension assets, which represent a major asset for millions of taxpayers, involve unique considerations for trust planning. This chapter highlights some of the many ways you can use trust planning in conjunction with planning for your pension assets. Because of complexity of these assets, be certain to review income tax issues with your accountant, and pension issues with your pension or employee benefit adviser. A host of pension (profit sharing, money purchase, etc.) and employee benefit trusts (Voluntary Employee Benefit Associations (VEBAs) and other employee benefit trusts) are not discussed in this book.

RABBI TRUSTS

Many closely held and other businesses provide pension or other retirement benefits. These qualified plans, however, must generally benefit a substantial portion of the employees. To benefit selected employees, non-qualified plans are often used. When funds are set aside for such a plan, they must still remain nothing more than an unsecured promise of the employer to pay. If the money is protected for the employee, the employee could risk facing current income tax on the money. The trade-off is the risk that the employer will not remain financially sound until the non-qualified benefits are paid, or face current income tax cost to secure those benefits. Even if the employer appears financially secure, future creditor claims, a takeover by another entity, and other developments could all jeopardize these benefits.

There is a compromise. A special trust can provide some greater measure of comfort to the employee than a mere promise of the employer to pay the benefit, but a level of protection that is not so excessive as to cause the employee to be taxed currently. This special trust is called a "rabbi trust" because the first case in which the IRS approved it was for a synagogue seeking to provide benefits for its rabbi.

A rabbi trust is a trust to which the employer makes contributions on account of the deferred, but nonqualified, compensation arrangement with the employee. Because the trust is a grantor trust, creditors of the employer can reach trust assets. This risk is sufficient that the IRS will not tax the employee on the money contributed. However, the terms of the trust also prohibit the employer from making use of the money contributed to the trust. This restriction gives the employee greater security and protection than simply having the employer's promise to pay.

Since a rabbi trust is planned to qualify as a grantor trust, the employer, as grantor, is taxable on any income earned by the trust. Also, because it is a grantor trust, when payments are made to the employee from the trust at some future date, the employer is deemed to have made the payments and thus could be entitled to a tax deduction for the compensation so paid.

Rabbi trusts have become so common that the IRS has issued a model form.

PENSION SUBTRUST

Need for Subtrust Concept

Pension plans are a common asset as well as a major portion of many people's estates. As a result of the large balances in pension plans, many insurance agents have promoted the purchase of life insurance by qualified retirement plans. The intended purpose of this technique is to use pretax dollars for the purchase of insurance. This can be a substantial tax advantage. However, there is a cost to this type of arrangement. If improperly handled, this can result in the inclusion of the insurance proceeds in the insured's estate. A pension subtrust to prevent the inclusion of insurance proceeds in your estate is a possible option to address this problem.

The pension subtrust is similar to the insurance trust discussed in Chapter 16 but is adapted for use inside a pension plan to own insurance. It can be used to avoid inclusion in your estate of any insurance owned by your pension plan. The technique is called a "sub" trust because the trust used is subsidiary to, and incorporated under, the primary pension trust to hold the life insurance. Since a special trustee of the insurance subtrust under the pension plan, and not you as the insured (nor the trustees of the pension plan itself where you control the corporation and hence the trustees of the pension plan), control the insurance policies, and where the subtrust is properly structured so that no incidence of ownership is attributable to you, the insurance in the pension can arguably avoid estate tax inclusion.

Requirements for Subtrust

The subtrust should meet the following criteria:

- An independent trustee, and successors, are named.

- It is irrevocable.

- Powers of the subtrust special trustee are structured with consideration to the plan requirements.

- Powers are structured in a manner to assure the special trustees control over the insurance policies held in the subtrust.

- It proscribes any control by the special trustee of plan assets in the plan but outside the subtrust (generally anything other than the insurance).

- It permits the special trustee to designate the beneficiaries under the insurance plan.

- It permits the sale of the insurance policy to the insured for its fair market value if, for any reason, it cannot continue to be held in the subtrust.

- It prohibits any distribution, as part of the participant/insured's plan benefits or otherwise, of the insurance policy, an annuity, and so forth, to the insured.

- The insurance policy cannot be converted to an annuity for the benefit of the participant/insured.

- On the death of the insured, it pays the policy proceeds to the beneficiary designated.

Problems, Risks, and Considerations

Provision for a safety-valve Q-TIP or marital trust can be provided for in the subtrust plan documentation. If the subtrust concept is not approved by the IRS (which would mean that the entire subtrust insurance proceeds would be taxable on your death), or if the policies are transferred into the subtrust less than three years prior to your death, a tax could be due. Where a marital trust default provision is provided, similar to the savings provision included in many first-to-die trusts, then the argument would be made that the insurance would pass to the surviving spouse in a qualified marital deduction trust and no tax would be due on the first death. This approach raises two issues. First, it is unclear whether a decision by the special trustee of the pension subtrust would meet the requirements necessary to qualify for a marital deduction—do the proceeds pass from the deceased to the spouse?

The manner in which the subtrust language/agreement is added to the pension plan warrants consideration and verification of conformity with any plan or ERISA requirements.

If the plan (exclusive of the subtrust) has inadequate assets to pay the required retirement benefit to the participant/insured, the cash value of the insurance plan may have to be utilized.

USING PENSION ASSETS TO FUND MARITAL (Q-TIP) AND CREDIT SHELTER TRUSTS

Why Have Pension Assets Paid to Credit Shelter or Marital (Q-TIP) Trusts?

Individual Retirement Accounts (IRAs) and qualified pension and other plans often need to be used to fund a credit shelter trust (to protect the unified credit of the first spouse to die) because there are inadequate other assets. You may wish to have pension assets paid into a marital Q-TIP trust on death to protect the assets for children from a prior marriage, or for other reasons (see Chapter 11). When you are planning to achieve either of these goals, the complex tax rules discussed in Chapters 7 and 11 are compounded by the even more complex tax rules that apply to IRAs, pension plans, and other qualified plans. This section will alert you to some of these issues. The key point is that with proper planning and professional guidance, you can use pension assets with many of the trusts discussed in this book to best achieve your personal goals and minimize estate taxes.

Pension Concepts That Affect Use of Trusts for Pension Assets

To properly plan for the use of credit shelter and Q-TIP trusts with pension assets, some basic pension tax and distribution concepts must be considered. You should review these complex rules with your accountant, estate planner, and pension adviser before proceeding.

Required Beginning Date

Distributions from qualified plans and IRAs must begin by the required beginning date (RBD). The RBD is April 1 of the year following the year in which you reach age 70½. This rule, however, is modified for participants who are working at age 70½ so that distributions are postponed until you retire. IRAs are subject to the qualified plan distribution rules.

When you reach the required beginning date, you must either (1) take a lump-sum distribution of the pension plan balance on that date; (2) or start to receive yearly installments of at least the plan's account balance (as of December 31 of the prior year) divided by your life expectancy. If you had a designated beneficiary on your plan on the required beginning date, you can then use a joint life expectancy (the life expectancy for both you and the designated beneficiary) in the calculation (instead of your life expectancy). This will tend to lengthen the period over which withdrawals have to be made, thus maximizing the amount of the plan balance that can continue to grow on an income-tax-deferred basis.

Minimum Distribution Requirements after Death of Participant

If you die prior to required beginning date, the following steps must be taken. Your plan balance must be distributed within five years of death.

There are two exceptions to this rule. First, if you had named a designated beneficiary for the plan other than your spouse, and distributions begin within one year of your death, distributions may be made over the life expectancy of the designated beneficiary instead of the five-year default period.

Second, if your spouse is the designated beneficiary of your plan, then any estate tax is deferred. Income tax on distributions will be due when your spouse receives distributions. Any pension excise tax can be deferred until your spouse's later death. Your spouse has the following options for receiving distributions:

- If payments begin by the later of December 31 of the year following the year in which you died, or December 31 of the year you would have reached age 70½, then payment of your plan balance may be made over the life expectancy of your spouse.

- Your spouse can roll your plan balance into a rollover IRA account set up by your spouse. Distributions from that rollover IRA would have to begin when your spouse reaches age 70½. Your spouse could also designate beneficiaries for that rollover IRA account.

- Your spouse can treat your IRA as if it was his or her own IRA. Thus, your spouse can elect any distribution options that you had.

What happens if your spouse dies after your death? If your spouse dies before distributions of your plan balance begin, then payments of your plan balance are made over the life expectancy of the designated beneficiary. If instead your spouse dies after payments to your spouse of your plan balance had begun, the distribution options will depend on whether your spouse had elected to have his or her life expectancy recalculated annually to determine payments. If your spouse's life expectancy was recalculated annually, distributions of your plan balance must be completed within five years of your spouse's death. If your spouse's life expectancy was not recalculated, distributions may continue for the duration of the spouse's life expectancy. The fact that your spouse is no longer alive does not affect this latter distribution plan.

What happens if you die after the required beginning date? The distribution of your plan balance to the beneficiaries must be made over a period as least as short as a lifetime distribution. If the life expectancy of you and your spouse was recalculated every year, the entire balance must be distributed by December 31 of the year following the death of the last to die of you and your spouse.

Designated Beneficiaries

Designated beneficiaries are determined as of the required beginning date. Generally, only individuals can be designated beneficiaries. If your estate is the designated beneficiary (e.g., your IRA application indicates that on your death the plan balance should be paid to your estate), then the plan balance will be subject to income tax within five years of your death. No rollover of your plan balance will be permitted. The tax allocation clause in your will (the provision that says which beneficiaries and which assets should bear the estate tax burden) should identify which assets will bear any excise tax due.

When you name a trust as the designated beneficiary, it is the actual people (i.e., the beneficiaries of the trust, not the trust itself), who may be the designated beneficiaries. To qualify for this treatment, however, several requirements must be met at the later of the required beginning date or the date the trust is named beneficiary. These requirements are an important part of the steps that will be discussed for using qualified plan assets to fund credit shelter and Q-TIP trusts. The trust must be valid under state law except for not having current assets (corpus). The trust beneficiaries must be identifiable and must be individuals. The trust must be irrevocable on the later of the date it is designated as the beneficiary of the plan, or the required beginning date.

The requirement that the trust must be irrevocable by the required beginning date may not have any practical significance because you can change the designated beneficiary of your plan after the required beginning date. If you do change the designated beneficiary and the life expectancy of the new beneficiary is shorter than the life expectancy of the old designated beneficiary (i.e., the beneficiary you replaced), then the period over which your plan balance will have to be distributed will be shortened. If the life expectancy of the new designated beneficiary is longer than the old designated beneficiary, there will not be any change in the distribution period. Although you would have expected that the period over which the distributions of your plan balance would have to be made would lengthen, this obviously could not be permitted since the IRS would have to wait for their tax. Why should the rules be consistent? There is one exception: If the first designated beneficiary died and the life expectancy of the new designated beneficiary is longer, you can lengthen the payment period. Death, however, is not a great tax-planning opportunity.

If the trust is irrevocable at the earlier of either the date of your death or the required beginning date, postdeath distributions can then be made over the life expectancy of the designated beneficiary.

You must provide a copy of trust document to the plan administrator.

Q-TIP Trust Is Designated Beneficiary

If you wish to name a marital Q-TIP trust as the designated beneficiary (so that there will be no estate tax on your death, but on the later death of your spouse the plan assets will be assured to be distributed to your children) complicated rules will apply. The marital deduction will be allowed for the Q-TIP trust. However, your surviving spouse will not be permitted any rollover. If you die prior to required beginning date, the rule that would require distributing your plan balance over a five-year period will not apply. If instead, you die after the required beginning date, your spouse's life expectancy may be used to calculate the period of time over which your plan balance must be distributed.

Each of the requirements for treating the beneficiaries of a trust as the designated beneficiaries (instead of the trust itself) must also be met for the Q-TIP marital trust to be treated as designated beneficiary. The plan balance payable after the death of your spouse is to be paid to the Q-TIP remainder beneficiaries (e.g., your children) over the remaining balance of your spouse's life expectancy.

Where a Q-TIP marital trust is named as designated beneficiary, any pension excise tax cannot be deferred. In contrast, if your spouse is named directly as the designated beneficiary, she could roll over the entire plan balance into an IRA and defer the excise tax.

If you form a Q-TIP marital trust as the designated beneficiary of your plan assets, be certain that your estate planner considers this in drafting the tax allocation clause in your will. This clause could clarify the source of payments of excise tax.

Several additional requirements or matters should be considered:

- Income earned by the qualified plan or IRA must be treated as income for purposes of Q-TIP trust payments to your spouse who is the income beneficiary of the Q-TIP trust.
- The Q-TIP trust should be paid the greater of: (1) the income earned by the qualified plan or IRA, or (2) the required minimum distribution.
- The trustees should be given the right to require the administrator or trustee of the qualified plan or IRA to convert non-income-producing, or low-income-producing assets into assets producing reasonable income. The trustees should be given the right to withdraw a portion of the accrued benefit under the qualified plan, or a portion of the IRA balance equal to the income that the plan/balance should have produced.
- The trustees must be directed to withdraw the minimum required distributions.
- If a Q-TIP trust holds qualified plan or IRA assets with no account set aside and accrued benefit, the trustee should have the right to define as income an amount of value of the accrued benefits, based on the state's Income and Principal Act.
- Any distribution that is income must be paid to your spouse.
- No expenses chargeable against principal of the Q-TIP trust can be paid from the income portion of the trust.
- Your spouse should be given the right to require the plan administrator or qualified plan or IRA trustee to convert any plan assets into income-producing assets.
- The Q-TIP (marital) election must be made for the trust.

Credit Shelter Trust Is Designated Beneficiary

For some taxpayers, the maximum $600,000 of assets that can avoid estate taxation under the unified credit are not available to fund a credit shelter trust. When this occurs, the first option is to consider changing the ownership (title) of assets to facilitate funding the maximum credit shelter trust in each estate (see Chapter 7). If this does not suffice, then consider purchasing insurance to fund the tax (see Chapter 6). Finally, you can plan to use retirement plan assets to fund the credit shelter trust. With this latter approach, the qualified plan or IRA must meet the minimum distribution rules. The minimum amounts required to be distributed are measured by the life expectancy of your spouse, if your spouse is the oldest eligible designated beneficiary. The trust could include a requirement that the trustee withdraw from the qualified plan or IRA the required minimum distribution amounts. Once these amounts are received by the credit shelter trust, the terms of the distributions from the trust to the beneficiaries are based on the provisions contained in the credit shelter trust document.

The trust could divide plan proceeds into two shares: (1) One share would pass to a Q-TIP (marital) trust or outright to your spouse; (2) the second share could be planned to use up any remaining unified credit available to your estate. Your spouse should be the sole income beneficiary of both shares, so that the beneficiaries are ascertainable.

There are two ways a credit shelter trust can be the recipient of IRA and qualified plan assets. First, you can use the direct approach and name the trust as the designated beneficiary. The second alternative is to name your spouse as the primary beneficiary of the IRA plan and have your will provide that if your spouse disclaims (renounces; files papers in court stating that she does not wish the inheritance provided) the interests in your IRA or qualified plan assets, these funds are then to be distributed into the marital deduction trust or into a credit shelter trust under your will. These trusts, which would be included under your will, would be drafted to receive the IRA or qualified plan assets as a result of a disclaimer. They should meet the minimum distribution requirements necessary.

Additional rules may apply:

- Your spouse cannot roll over your plan assets into an IRA account.
- The measuring life for determining the period over which payments must be made is your spouse's life expectancy, if your spouse is the oldest designated beneficiary.
- The balance payable after the death of your spouse is paid to the remainder beneficiaries over the remaining balance of your spouse's life expectancy.
- Any pension excise tax cannot be deferred; it must be paid on your death. This should be addressed in the tax allocation clause in your will.
- Estate tax can be deferred and avoided through the application of your unified credit against the plan assets transferred to this trust.

Documents

If a trust is the designated beneficiary, your estate planner should prepare forms (or in some cases the plan administrator may have forms you can use) and file them with the plan administrator. These forms should include the following provisions:

- *Identify Payment Schedule.* If payments are to be made in the discretion of the designated beneficiary, the form should include limitations required by the tax laws. The plan must permit all distributions.
- *Amount of Payout for Q-TIP Trust.* If you are planning to have IRA or other qualified plan assets distributed to a Q-TIP (marital) trust, the forms should direct the plan administrator to pay out the greater of the following amounts: (1) the minimum distribution requirement; (2) income on the amounts held in qualified plan or IRA; (3) amount requested by trustees. The forms can indicate that the trustees have the right to require that the plan administrator convert nonincome-producing (or low-income-producing) assets into assets that generate reasonable income. The trustees can also be given the right to withdraw a portion of the accrued benefit of the qualified plan, or a portion of the IRA balance, equal to the income that the qualified plan or IRA balance should have produced.
- *Amount of Payout for Credit Shelter Trust.* If you are planning to have IRA or other qualified plan assets distributed to a credit shelter trust, the forms should direct the plan administrator to pay out the greater of (1) minimum distribution requirements, or (2) the amount requested by trustees. The forms should also identify the designated beneficiaries. A copy of the trust agreement must be provided to the plan administrator with the forms. The forms must identify the beneficiary class so that a measuring life may be determined. The oldest beneficiary's age is used.

CONCLUSION

Pensions and employee benefits are a major asset for many people and therefore cannot be ignored in trust planning. If your employer has a human resources department, begin your investigation and inquiries there. They may have dealt with the same issues you face many times and thus be in a position to offer guidance. After that initial inquiry, coordinate pension and employee benefit planning with your estate planner, accountant, and pension consultant.

INDEX